MYSTICISM EXAMINED

PHILOSOPHICAL INQUIRIES INTO MYSTICISM

RICHARD H. JONES

STATE UNIVERSITY OF NEW YORK PRESS

Published by
State University of New York Press, Albany

Printed in the United States of America

For information, address State University of New York
Press, State University Plaza, Albany, N.Y., 12246

Production by Diane Ganeles
Marketing by Dana E. Yanulavich

Library of Congress Cataloging-in-Publication Data

Jones, Richard H., 1951-
Mysticism examined : philosophical inquiries into mysticism / Richard H. Jones.
p. cm.—(SUNY series in western esoteric traditions)
Includes bibliographical references and index.
ISBN 0-7914-1435-3 (hard : alk. paper). — ISBN 0-7914-1436-1 (pbk. : alk. paper)
1. Mysticism. 2. Mysticism—Moral and ethical aspects.
3. Knowledge, Theory of (Religion) 4. Philosophy and religion.
I. Title.
BL625.J64 1993
291.4′22′01—dc20 92-16480
CIP

10 9 8 7 6 5 4 3 2 1

Mysticism Examined

SUNY Series in Western Esoteric Traditions
David Appelbaum, Editor

Contents

Part VI. Mysticism and Psychology

Part VII. Mysticism and Ethics

Acknowledgments

The chapters are revised versions of articles that originally appeared under the following names in the following journals:

1. "Experience and Conceptualization in Mystical Knowledge," *Zygon: A Journal of Religion and Science* 18 (1983): 139–165.
2. "*Vidyā* and *Avidyā* in the *Īśa Upaniṣad*," *Philosophy East and West* 31 (1981): 79–87.
3. "Rationality and Mysticism," *International Philosophical Quarterly* 27 (1987): 263–279.
4. "The Nature and Function of Nāgārjuna's Arguments," *Philosophy East and West* 28 (1978): 485–502.
5. "A Philosophical Analysis of Mystical Utterances," *Philosophy East and West* 29 (1979): 255–274.
6. "Mysticism and Science: Against Needham on Taoism," *Journal of Chinese Philosophy* 8 (1981): 245–266.
7. "The Religious Irrelevance of the Ontological Argument," *Essays in Honor of James A. Martin, Jr., Union Seminary Quarterly Review* 37 (1981–1982): 143–157.
8. "Jung and Eastern Religious Traditions," *Religion* 9 (1979): 141–156.
9. "Must Enlightened Mystics Be Moral?" *Philosophy East and West* 34 (1984): 273–293.
10. "Theravāda Buddhism and Morality," *Journal of the American Academy of Religion* 47 (1979): 371–387.

All articles are published and revised with the permission of the copyright owners.

Introduction

In discussing mysticism, the first thing one must do is specify exactly what phenomenon is being talked about. The term "mysticism" has been used to refer to any religious experience, mythology, miracles, schizophrenia, hallucinations, trances, any altered state of consciousness, alleged psychic powers such as levitation, visions, parapsychology, and in general anything considered irrational, unintelligible, or occult. But the term "mysticism" for purposes of this book will refer only to two types of experiences, knowledge-claims centered upon such experiences, and ways of life in which these experiences figure centrally. Mystical experiences result from a process of turning one's attention inward and stilling all normal cognitive and emotional activities. It is a process of "forgetting," to use the medieval Christian term, or "fasting of the mind," to use a phrase from many mystical traditions. Meister Eckhart speaks of "unknowing"—the withdrawal of all powers of the mind from all objects. The *Yoga Sūtras* describe the process as the removal by concentration (*samādhi*) of all obscuring and distorting memory traces (*saṃskāras*) accumulated over this and previous lives until the mind is completely clear and discriminating.

Two types of experiences allegedly result from this process. The first type occurs when sensory or other awarenesses remain present but the filters that our minds normally provide for ordering the content of awareness are significantly weakened or totally absent. Perception becomes free from what mystics consider distortions, including conceptual frameworks, emotional attachments, and even a sense of self. In the terms of the *Yoga Sūtras,* the mind becomes clear as a crystal and then shapes itself to the object. This type of mystical experience will be termed "nature-mystical experience." A sense of unity overcomes our normal sense of a duality of subject and object. This sense of oneness may encompass all that is experienced, although a sense of differentiations within the whole may remain. A range of experiences qualifies as nature-mystical, since awareness with a weakening of the grasp of normal conceptual apparatus can produce many different such experiences. This means that the boundary between ordinary sensory experiences and nature-mystical experiences is not well-defined.

The second type of mystical experience occurs when the mind is completely stilled. According to mystics, this state is not unconscious, but is in fact an intensely conscious state. There is no awareness of any object or of any content of any kind and yet there is still a realization of an ultimate reality. Unlike in sensory perception, the experiencer has no sense of differentiation from the reality experienced. But while the experience is occurring, no mental categorizing is present consciously or subconsciously, and so the mind seems free of content. Thus, the nature-mystical experience has a sense of unity, but this experience is free of all content. This type of mystical experience will be referred to as the "depth-mystical experience."[1] Only after the experience is over does its nature seem clear to the mystic and only then does its signifance have an impact, often profound, on the mystic's life.

For either of these experiences to occur, the grip our conceptual frameworks normally hold over our minds must be broken. But nothing can *force* a mystical experience to occur. However, many mystics practice meditative techniques. Depth-mystical experiences are connected with "concentrative" techniques which focus attention, with the objective of ultimately stilling all mental activity. Nature-mystical experiences are more usually connected with "pure awareness" techniques in which the content of our mind during sense-experience and thought is observed; this increases our "mindfulness" of the flux of our mental activity and loosens the hold our concepts normally produce. The distinction drawn in Theravāda Buddhism between *samatha* and *vipassanā* cultivation brings out the differences in these techniques and experiences.

Nature-mystical and depth-mystical experiences are what is particular to mysticism. It is their role in mystical knowledge and mystical ways of life that separates mysticism from other enterprises. Mystics may share values and beliefs with nonmystics but these experiences uniquely contribute to the mystics' beliefs and ways of life. The experiences may be called "religious" since they involve the realization of the reality providing the ultimate meaning of the experiencer's life. But there are also other types of experiences taken to be religious (e. g., worship or repenting or thinking about the universe as the creation of God) that are not taken to be a direct realization of ultimate reality. Mysticism differs from asceticism in that mystical paths and techniques are not ends in themselves (showing one's piety or obedience to God), but merely means to a further enlightenment. Similarly, other experiences taken to be cognitive do not involve the sense of unity or identity involved with mysticism. Other altered states of consciousness also do not share this sense of unity or identity that is central to mysticism.

Since the term "experience" suggests a subject distinct from other objects which experiences an object, when in fact no such duality is present, mystics often resist referring to the culmination of the path to a depth-mystical experience as an experience at all. Similarly, mystics assert that, since the reality realized in the depth-mystical experience is not available in our normal subject-object awareness, it is not "experiencable" at all. Also, the event seems outside the control of the mystic—it cannot be produced by the experiencer at will, but occurs spontaneously or involuntarily. Hence, it occurs by the "grace of God," according to theistic mystics, and is "unconstructed," according to Buddhists. However, the occurrence of the depth-mystical experience, unlike any state of the experiencer resulting from the event, can be usefully referred to as an experience. Other traditional terms—enlightenment, illumination, intuition, disclosure, realization, unitive consciousness, and so forth—all denote a subject experiencing an object or have other misleading connotations. In addition, none capture the transient nature of the depth-mystical event. Robert Forman refers to the depth-mystical experience as a "pure consciousness event" in an attempt to circumvent the problem of whether consciousness is possible without consciousness of some object.[2] But the term "experience" does indicate that the event is transient, that there is no event occurring distinct from what is occurring to the experiencer, and that the event is not the product of thinking. Thus, the term "experience" is appropriate.

Mystics in both devotional and non-devotional traditions claim that the process of forgetting produces in the depth-mystical experience a state of inward quietness that, while contentless, is, in fact, *cognitive*.[3] There is an implosion of reality at the end of the path—the "noetic quality" to which William James referred—usually accompanied by a sense of certainty and finality. Indeed, this reality is usually judged to be the ultimate reality. What is experienced in the depth-mystical experience when the mind is free of all conceptual thinking is often termed "ineffable" by mystics and the role of silence is stressed.[4] In this regard, it is important to note the mystics' emphasis that this reality is directly experienced; it is not a theoretical entity posited by speculative thought.

The purpose of the mystical paths to enlightenment is to depict and illustrate the way to overcome the nescience blocking the enlightening knowledge (as defined by the particular mystic's tradition). Mystics often arrange ways of knowing in a hierarchy. To modify the arrangement advanced by Chuang tzu, there are four stages: (1) the depth-mystical experience (in which there is no content to the awareness); (2) nature-mystical experiences (in which there is a sense of an indistinguishable unity of the subject with an object); (3) awareness of distinct objects denoted by names; and (4) awareness of objects as merely the instantiation of our concepts, names, and distinctions. William James describes the process by which the concepts we invent to cut the fluid continuum of perceptions and experiences into a useful order become substituted unconsciously for that continuum. The conceptual order becomes ossified and takes on a life of its own that blinds us to the fact that it is our own construction. Concepts become a barrier between us and the dynamic, continuous reality we confront in perceiving. According to mystics, this process of ossification can be overcome in nature-mystical experiences.

While some ordering of mystical experiences is inevitable, there is nothing inherent in the experiences themselves that requires a particular order. Mystical ways of life contain values that determine the significance assigned to each type of experience. For example, theistic traditions may devalue the depth-mystical experience as spiritual self-indulgence in favor of a continuing sense of the presence of God involved in a nature-mystical experience. Similarly, other mystical traditions may value the permanent transformation resulting in a state of enlightenment—a nature-mystical state—over any transient experience, including the depth-mystical experience. In each case, the various beliefs and values of the mystic's way of life as a whole, not the experiences in isolation, determine the value given each type of experience.

Determining whether a given text is mystical in nature is sometimes difficult to do. Traditions that have survived with recorded texts usually advance a complex belief-system. The texts themselves also develop over time. Furthermore, beliefs and values accepted for nonmystical reasons can be very similar to those centered upon mystical experiences.[5] In addition, despite the impression given by many commentators, mystics do not often discuss their own experiences or enlightenment in the abstract. Instead mystics discuss such topics as enlightening wisdom, types of experiences, meditative techniques, paths to enlightenment, goals, and the nature of reality. Indeed, mystics are not concerned with "mysticism."[6] However, whether mystical experiences do indeed inform the way of life encapsulated in a text usually becomes clear if one examines the text as a whole or the role the text plays in the mystical tradition.

The analytical philosophical approach to the study of mysticism involves one particular abstraction from total mystical ways of life: belief-claims (i. e., those claims about reality, persons, and so forth), and value-claims (i. e., goals and what is considered valuable or meaningful and why) either explicitly advanced by mystics or presupposed by the way of life. This aspect of a way of life is not the essence of a way of life or even its most important aspect, but this abstraction is central for our understanding and appreciation of a way of life.

Mystical knowledge is not "dualistic" knowledge of objects or events by a subject; it is not knowledge of facts. Instead, it is a form of *wisdom* (i. e., a matter of how we understand the significance or meaning of facts and how we apply facts to our lives). That is, mystical wisdom is not mere intellectual assent to propositions concerning states of affairs in the world, but is a way of looking at the world tied to how we live and, in the case of mysticism, to a path to a mystical enlightenment that transforms the experiencer in a radical way. Similarly, faith—religious or otherwise—is a way of life and is not reducible to belief-claims and value-claims. Such belief is more a disposition to act than an intellectual act of accepting abstract propositions. Thus, use of the word "belief" should not be taken to mean the opposite of "knowledge." Belief is a component of what is taken to be certain, not tentative or hypothetical; mystics speak of what they *know,* not what they *believe*. In short, the term "belief" is used merely to denote the intellectual content of a way of life.

Mystics do not advance disinterested claims about the nature of a person or the world. But adopting any way of life, including mystical ones, involves a commitment to certain values and ways of acting. And to make these values and ways of acting intelligible, one must acknowledge certain claims about the nature of reality once they are made explicit. For example, one cannot hold that enlightenment ends the cycle of rebirths without accepting the belief-claim that there is such a cycle for the unenlightened. In this sense, mystical wisdom and any way of life entails belief-claims and value-claims that are open to examination by persons outside the commitment to that way of life.

Philosophy in this context is the critical examination of the interconnection and reasonableness of such value-claims and belief-claims constituting the intellectual content of a way of life. It does not involve the "intellect" of perennial philosophy (i. e., an alleged power to know the absolute reflected in the mind in a direct and unquestionable intuition), but instead involves reason divorced from any such power. The analytical approach studies the alleged sacred wisdom from below, asking, for example, how can mystics be certain of their claims. A philosopher does not take the confessional stance of a committed believer but instead looks upon no mystical tradition as uniquely privileged.

The subject matter of the philosophical analysis of mysticism is supplied by the historical and comparative studies of mysticism. It is not disembodied philosophical reflection on the essence of mysticism but is empirically grounded. Its concerns are conditioned by modern Western culture. However, this does not eliminate the possibility that philosophical analysis may offer insights helping our understanding of mysticism that are not available from a merely historical approach.

The analytical philosophical approach begins with attempting to understand the meaning of mystics' claims within the original context of the mystics' particular way of life. This also involves an attempt to clarify the concepts used by the mystics and may require articulating the background belief-claims and value-claims. This step also brackets any issues of the existence of the mystical reality or the validity of mystics' claims. Such an approach is the only way to understand what the mystics are saying and in itself is not controversial.[7] However, unlike some socio-scientific approaches to mysticism, philosophers initially accept an irreducibly mystical component to the mystics' belief-claims. Mystical ideas are not reduced to mere effects of socio-scientific factors; instead, for a complete picture of mysticism under this approach, mystical ideas are taken to be one factor shaping mystics' actions. This is not to say that any phenomenon is exclusively mystical—all human phenomena have historical, social, and psychological components and are open to explanation as such. But philosophers do not replace the alleged mystical reality by means of a socio-scientific explanation.

However, this does not mean that philosophers must agree with the mystic's own assessment of his or her experience or accept the mystic's claim to knowledge. After the initial phase devoted to understanding the mystics' claims, analytical philosophers proceed with an examination of the reasonableness of the mystics' value-claims and belief-claims. And any conceptual relativism that might be needed as a premise for understanding mystics or anyone from another culture does not necessarily commit one to accepting a cognitive relativism in which all claims are equal. The philosophical approaches espoused by some followers of Ludwig Wittgenstein might end with establishing the role or usefulness of claims within their way of life. Nevertheless, the more usual analytical philosophical approach need not rule out a further appraisal, since such an approach does not rule out the possibility of cross-cultural standards by which to judge belief-claims. This may lead to the rejection of a particular mystic's assessment of the nature and value of the mystical experiences, or to the rejection of all mystical knowledge claims. That mystical claims often operate at the level of a metaphysical depiction of reality as a whole may make assessments more difficult. Whether there are any cross-cultural standards of comparison by which we may resolve at least some conflicts of belief-claims is an issue for chapter 3.

Examining the intellectual foundation of a way of life does not require denying the fullness of the way of life or devaluing what is important to the practitioners. However, philosophy does shift attention away from the total way of life. Thomas Aquinas had an experience late in his life from which he concluded that all his writings were as straw. But the philosophy of mysticism can have a more positive, if still limited, role in the lives of mystics: It is an unmystical enterprise, but, as will be discussed in chapters 1 and 3, it can contribute to the mystics' own understanding of their commitments. Philosophical examination can be especially crucial to the mystics who are aware of alternative ways of life. And even if mystics were unaware of alternative ways of life, there is still no guarantee that mystics are experts on the nature of their claims. Being a great mystic does not necessarily qualify one to see the various issues involved in these claims to knowledge, any more than being a great scientist makes one an expert on the nature of scientific claims. Indeed, the overwhelming significance mystics attach to mystical experiences may make it harder for them to examine their experiences critically and to avoid an unwarranted transfer of a sense of certainty in their experiences to their particular interpretative scheme. Therefore, philosophical examination should be especially important in this area.

It is the claim that mystical experiences are knowledge-giving that is central to the philosophical examination of mysticism. If mysticism were merely a matter of subjective phenomena (such as emotion, as Bertrand Russell argued), mystics' claims would not be of great interest to philosophers. But mystics claim to experience reality, indeed the ultimate reality. How are such claims to be assessed? How is it possible to claim that reality is experienced when there is allegedly no experiencing subject and no object experienced? Mystics' difficulty with language is challenging to philosophers also because of the claim that ultimate reality is involved in these experiences. Why do mystics have trouble expressing the reality experienced? Why is it that this reality is ineffable, but other experienced realities are not? Mystics' claims to justify moral or other values by the reality experienced and by goals connected to the mystical reality also constitute what is unique about mysticism in the area of values. In each case, mysticism introduces issues not found in considering nonmystical experiences and ways of life by themselves.

This role of philosophy in the examination of mysticism can be illustrated by the current debate over whether concepts are present in the depth-mystical experience. For nature-mystical experiences, most philosophers agree that the mystic's conceptual framework shapes his or her experiences themselves (as our beliefs are thought to shape visions). In a Gestalt-like switch, sensory input is reconfigured in nature-mystical experiences, for example, in terms of the presence of God or the impermanent constituents of all that we experience (the *dhammā* of Buddhism), without dissecting the flux of experience into discrete units. This is also true of the mystical enlightened state in which the mystic has completely internalized the prescribed way of looking at the world. However, two schools of thought have emerged concerning the depth-mystical experience. Steven Katz has edited two volumes presenting the view of the constructivists—that beliefs, concepts, and expectations shape or even constitute the depth-experience itself.[8] According to this theory, all experience has a conceptual element. In the words of the philosopher Wilfrid Sellars, "all awareness is a linguistic affair." In its strongest form, constructivism, in the words of philosopher of science Mary Hesse, attempts to assimilate knowledge totally to the nonempirical and the social.[9] Robert Forman has more recently edited a volume disputing this theory in the case of mysticism, arguing instead that the depth-mystical experience is a contentless consciousness and hence nothing is present in the mind to shape the awareness.[10] Nonconstructivists permit the possibility that the depth-mystical experience may figure in the justification of mystical belief-claims; constructivists must deny the possibility that the experience can be an independent source of evidence at all. Nonconstructivists also leave open the possibility of a realism grounded in an awareness unshaped by our concepts.

In defending their thesis with regard to the depth-mystical experience, constructivists cannot employ the usual distinction between external events and a witness's perception of those events. That distinction would apply to a nature-mystical perception of events. But there is no such distinction between a depth-mystical experience and a mystic's experience of that experience—the mystic's experience *is* the event. The only justification for constructivism is that it reflects the position most commonly accepted by philosophers concerning consciousness in nonmystical experiences: all such consciousness, including self-consciousness, is structured and hence there can be no "pure" consciousness. From this, constructivists infer that consciousness per se is intentional: to be conscious is to be conscious *of* something. However, constructivism was developed from nonmystical experiences without serious consideration of mystical experiences, and constructivists advance no independent arguments for why their theory must apply to all experiences, including depth-mystical experiences. In such circumstances, constructivism is merely advanced as an assumption required for all experiences, thereby dogmatically ruling out the possibility that the depth-experience might be an awareness free from all structure. Thus, on what is in effect exclusively *a priori* epistemological grounds, constructivists rule out the possibility that depth-mystical experience involves a valid form of knowing.

Both constructivists and nonconstructivists claim that they are not making *a priori* assumptions about mystical experiences but are only presenting empirical evidence for their conclusions from a careful study of mystical texts. It is true that mystics typically discuss the reality allegedly experienced rather than the experiences themselves. But constructivists cannot argue that there are no reports of an awareness free of all content, since there are instances in which this is precisely what mystics claim about some of their experiences. For example, Saint Teresa of Avila stated that she experienced union with God but that she, in fact, knew this to be the case only *after* the experience was over and when she had returned to a subject-object consciousness; during the experience itself, she was aware of nothing.[11] It would, of course, be circular for constructivists to argue that these reports must be false on the ground that no experience in principle can be free of content. Such a ploy would be an admission that the constructivist proposal is merely an *a priori* assumption and not a conclusion from empirical research at all. In light of such evidence, constructivists are left with applying a very forced interpretation of such mystical passages as Saint Teresa's in order to fit the passages into their theory and then claiming that their resulting interpretation is evidence for the constructivist theory.

Nonconstructivists operate with this premise: mystics are in a privileged position with respect to the depth-mystical experience, and so nonmystics should accept mystics at their word on the issue of there being experiences free from all conceptual and other elements. Under this approach, since there is nothing present in the depth-mystical experiences to differentiate them, the depth-mystical experiences must be identical for all experiencers regardless of their cultural and historical setting (at least to the extent that all humans' awareness is alike). In such circumstances, the depth-mystical experience would then merely be *interpreted* differently after its occurrence to fit within the belief-system developed from all the experiences, beliefs and values of the mystics of the experiencer's particular tradition.[12] Mystics' use of intentional language in describing their depth-mystical experiences would then be accounted for, not because the experience is itself intentional, but because after the experience occurs mystics themselves must use some conceptual framework to understand and to discuss both their experiences and the reality allegedly experienced. Their interpretative belief-system would then still determine how the depth-mystical experience is understood by the experiences themselves, but only after the experience occurs.

In addition, mystics cannot provide a depiction of the depth-mystical experience free from the mystics' conceptual commitments. All descriptions of the nature or importance of the experience will reflect the mystic's conceptual understanding to one degree or another—none will be a bare, neutral phenomenological description if for no other reason than that any such description will refer to the alleged source of the experience and this element will reflect the mystic's particular understanding of the nature of reality. No experience can be presented for examination, and thus no experiments are possible in this respect. All that is available to us is a diversity of descriptions from various mystics provided after the experiences occur. Nevertheless, this diversity is not evidence that the depth-mystical experience itself is structured by the mystics' conceptual systems, since the diversity may just as well be the product of different interpretations after the experience occurred.[13] The situation is comparable to seeing a colored light but not being able to examine the source. The light itself may be colored (the constructivist position), or it may be a clear light with a colored covering (the depth-mystical experience with an interpretative covering after the experience)—the colored light by itself cannot decide the issue. Nonconstructivists and mystics endorse the latter position, while constructivists argue on *a priori* grounds for the former. Since the source cannot be examined, we cannot tell on empirical grounds which alternative is correct. Our decision will have to be based on other grounds. Constructivists then can argue that their position fits within our general view of the nature of experience better than the alternative.

But it is not obvious that our notions of consciousness and cognitive experience require that there be an object distinct from the experiencer of which the experiencer is aware. We have no reason other than an *a priori* one to deny the mystic's belief-claim that the depth-mystical experience occurs. And ruling out a type of experience solely on *a priori* grounds is a risky move. From this, we should conclude that there is no reason to assert the constructivist proposal dogmatically. Instead, we should not rule out in advance the possibility that the depth-mystical experience is indeed free of all conceptual content. And the reports of certain mystical experiences (such as that referred to above from St. Teresa) is *prima facie* evidence that an experience occurs in which there is no conceptual or other content present that could shape the experience even subconsciously. Nonmystics are simply not in a position to deny that the experiences occur. In short, we should accept that such experiences are possible and in fact occur.

That an awareness free of all conceptual or other content occurs does not necessarily mean that the experience is cognitive of some reality or has the significance a particular experiencer attaches to it. The experience's alleged cognitive significance and its role in mystics' ways of life is the subject of philosophical examination.

The chapters in this book represent all the major topics within the field of the analytical philosophical study of mysticism. They are also related and organized to show how one topic leads to another—knowledge, reasoning, language, science, theology, psychology, and ethics. Collectively, these chapters illuminate the different aspects of mystical experience, mystical knowledge, and mystical ways of life. Each essay is also a revised form of an article and remains a self-contained unit. Thus, the reader need not review any of the other essays as background for understanding any one of them.

The first set of issues to be dealt with revolve around the roles of experiences and beliefs in the development of mystical knowledge. This is done in chapter 1. Despite all their talk of mystical experiences being ineffable, mystics construct interpretative systems, sometimes quite elaborate ones. One objective of this study is to show that belief-claims and doctrinal differences are integral parts of mystical ways of life and are not something to be jettisoned once a mystic has completed the prescribed path to enlightenment.[14] A second objective is to show that many of the problems arising in the contemporary philosophy of science reappear when examining the diversity and commonality revealed by the comparative study of mysticism. When mysticism and science are both viewed as potential knowledge-giving enterprises, such problems as the empiricist model of knowledge, the theory-ladenness of experience, the incommensurability of concepts, the role of models and theories in making sense of experience, and whether interpretative frameworks are open to criticism appear in both enterprises, even if the nature of mystical knowledge-claims often puts mystics' claims on the more metaphysical end of the spectrum of knowledge-claims. The contrast between our modern paradigm of knowledge and mysticism then does not seem as great as is normally supposed.

The second chapter continues the examination of the nature of mystical knowledge by discussing the role of "unlearning" all subject-object knowledge in the process of enlightenment as set forth in a classic of the orthodox Indian mystical tradition, the *Īśa Upaniṣad*.

Related to the issue of knowledge is whether mystical thought is rational. In chapter 3, issues in this area are explored: problems arising in applying standards of thought from one culture or era or set of practices to another; logic and paradox in mystics' arguments; universal reason versus differences in styles of reasoning; and relativism of systems of belief. Chapter 4 presents an illustration of the rationality of mystics' thought. In it, a detailed analysis of the nature and purpose of the arguments in the writings of Nāgārjuna, an Indian Buddhist, is presented. There is also an evaluation of whether his arguments can be convincing, either inside or outside the context of his tradition, once the logical structure of his arguments is laid out.

Issues in each of the previous chapters lead to certain issues involving language. Problems mystics encounter with language are the topic of chapter 5. A theory of how traditional mystics believe language operates is advanced to explain ineffability, silence, paradox, *via negativa,* and symbolism in mystics' use of language. The theory centers on the mistaken view shared by most people that denotative language must mirror the reality referred to in order to be meaningful. Thus, since the depth-mystical reality is not an object and since the ability to use language introduces a subject-object awareness that renders the depth-mystical experience impossible, mystics conclude that language cannot refer to the reality experienced. Similarly, since the reality experienced in the nature-mystical experience is dynamic and continuous while concepts are static and discrete, mystics claim that language cannot refer to the reality experienced in those experiences either.

In the second half of the book, the relation of mysticism to belief-claims and value-claims in certain other specific enterprises is examined, starting with science. In chapter 6, Joseph Needham's views expressed in his study of the history of Chinese science on the scientific or protoscientific nature of philosophical Taoism are examined. Problems arise as much from Needham's views on the nature of science (which are currently out of fashion) as from his attempt to show that a mystical tradition is scientific in nature. Both mysticism and science are open to analysis as allegedly knowledge-giving enterprises. And seen in this light, differences in the epistemological nature of mysticism and science are not as extreme as sometimes supposed (as discussed in chapters 1 and 3). But this chapter shows that mysticism and science still are far from identical enterprises. While some aspects of the nature of these enterprises are similar, the differences in their aims and purpose, the type of experience taken to be cognitively central, and the role of mystical experiences in total ways of life are equally important. These differences are discussed in this chapter in response to Professor Needham's views.

In the next chapter, objections from the point of view of mysticism to theology are presented. Theologians attempt to understand our situation in the world in light of a religious conception of reality. From within their commitment to a faith, they attempt to provide a theoretical understanding of, and basis for, their religious way of life. Every religious tradition has thinkers who reflect on religious experiences; and some basic understanding of any experience is needed by the experiencers themselves and others. In addition, some mystical traditions explicitly accept nonexperiential sources of justification (including sacred texts). But nonmystical theologians differ from mystics in the elaborate systems the former attempt to build from nonexperiential sources. Examining the

Ontological Argument reveals the problems of the theological enterprise from a mystical point of view. This traditional theological argument concerns the existence and nature of God based solely upon our concepts and reasoning. It is often taken to be especially mystical—perhaps because Saint Anselm may have developed the argument during an altered state of consciousness or because mysticism is often tied to speculative reasoning. But the *via negativa* and other elements of mystical traditions highlight the dangers of relying exclusively upon our reasoning and our conceptual constructions when dealing with ultimate matters. Theology directs attention away from experiences and towards systems of thought we construct with minimal experiential input. The thrust of theology is to replace a sense of awe or power or presence with our understanding, to replace silence with words. When we are confronted by mysteries in our experiences—not only mystical experiences but also the mere fact that we exist—there is the very real danger that we then will rest content with the constructs we have substituted for the mysteries. The arguments surrounding the Ontological Argument concerning whether something might exist solely because of the nature of our concepts should show how far removed from mysticism this argument is.

Chapter 8 proceeds to an enterprise that many people currently take to be very similar to Eastern mysticial traditions: psychotherapy. Carl Jung is among the most sympathetic of psychotherapists in his attitude toward religion. But his writings on Asian mystical traditions are examined to reveal the differences between the two enterprises—and the dangers of approaching another culture with a pre-established interpretative scheme. A number of different relationships between mysticism and psychotherapy are in fact possible and are discussed.

The final two chapters examine the relationship between morality and the ways of life of those mystics who have completed the path prescribed by their tradition, i. e., the enlightened. Two of the objectives here are to show that values remain integral to mystics' lives once they are enlightened and that different mystical ways of life are genuinely different. In chapter 9, whether enlightened mystics must be moral or whether they are "beyond good and evil" is examined. In place of simplistic answers, the enlightened ways of life from various traditions are examined to illustrate various issues related to moral values. In chapter 10, the moral status of the Theravāda Buddhist way of life is presented in detail to reveal its nonmoral path to enlightenment and the value options of the enlightened. From these studies it becomes clear that mystical value systems are not necessarily moral—the two sets of values are not necessarily identical and one does not entail the other.

One recurring theme running throughout these essays is that the philosophers examining mystical ways of life need not deny the existence of mystical experiences. But the philosophical examination does reveal the undeniable role of components outside of the experiences themselves in mystical knowledge-claims and ways of life.

Mysticism fascinates philosophers because of the experiences mystics take to be cognitive of ultimate reality. The role these experiences play in the development and defense of doctrinal and value systems within mystical ways of life separates mystical ways of life from all others. Thereby, mysticism presents in a clear manner some basic issues for philosophical examination of knowledge and ways of life. Whether mystical ways of life contribute to the resolution of these issues, however, is not as clear. No experience supplies its own interpretation and valuation. No interpretation of mystical experiences is obvious and unopen to examination. Choices as to how to value and understand mystical experiences must be made and these choices will occur outside of the experiences themselves. At best, the study of mysticism may only help clarify the choices we all have in the areas of what constitutes knowledge or basic values for a way of life.

But this also means that the philosophical examination of mysticism is not merely an academic matter of interest only to professional philosophers. The philosophical examination of possible mystical belief-claims and value-claims becomes of value to all who are examining their own lives. And it is hoped that the essays presented here will assist the readers as they make their own evaluations and judgments of basic beliefs and values from within their own ways of life.

Part I

Mysticism and Knowledge

Chapter 1

Experience and Conceptualization in Mystical Knowledge

The comparative study of mysticism is, on its surface, a very different enterprise from philosophy of science. But what post-logical empiricist philosophers of science advance concerning the ways theories change and the role of concepts in observation parallels philosophical problems arising in the comparative examination of mystical knowledge. First, let us consider how mystical experiences differ from other experiences normally taken to be cognitive (knowledge-giving).

Mystical Experiences

Mystical ways of life are various systems of values, action-guides, and beliefs oriented around, in Ninian Smart's words, "an interior or introvertive quest, culminating in certain interior experiences which are not described in terms of sense-experience or mental images, etc."[1] Two types of mystical experiences result from concentrative techniques (which focus attention) and receptive techniques (which de-structure our normal conceptual frameworks that structure sensory stimuli).[2] The distinction between them is brought out more clearly not by possible distinctions between extrovertive and introvertive experiences (Walter Stace) or between monistic, theistic, and nature-mystical experiences (R. C. Zaehner),[3] but by a more fundamental distinction: experiences totally free of all conceptual and sensory content ("depth-mystical experiences") and others having some conceptual differentiation regardless of whether thought content or sensory stimuli are involved ("nature-mystical experiences").

The depth-mystical experiences result, to use medieval Christian depictions, from a radical "recollecting" of the senses and a "purging" of the mind of all dispositional and cognitive content—especially any sense of "I." The resulting one-pointedness produces a stillness of mind where all sensory-conceptual apparatuses are in total abeyance. But this state of imagelessness is not unconsciousness in the sense of a total lack of awareness. Instead this emptiness permits the pouring in of a positive experience. Although this experience is often characterized negatively, it is taken to be an implosion of what is normally judged by mystics to be the ultimate reality (a permanent, unchanging "power of being"), accompanied by a sense of objectivity, certainty, and usually finality. "Objectivity" here does not denote an object or the totality of objects since nothing open to sense experience is involved; rather it means that reality, not anything subjective (dependent upon the individual experiencer alone), is present. This reality will be referred to as "the mystical." Unlike the theoretical entities of science, the mystical can be directly experienced (i.e., brought into awareness). The experiencer does not *see* the mystical but *becomes* the reality behind surface appearances. Even to say "becomes" may mislead since, according to Advaita Vedānta's construal, we always *are* the reality. There is no apprehension *of* unity, no object of awareness as in sense experience and thought, but only the objectless awareness which itself is real.

Nature-mystical experiences involve a subject-object differentiation present in ordinary sense experience or thought. They need not be sensory; an experiential sense of the presence of, or union with, God involves a differentiation, as do experiences of love or joy. If we are conscious of being in a certain situation, a dualism is set up between ourselves and something else. Within the realm of sense experience, these mystical experiences involve a lessening of the grip concepts normally have in directing our attention to aspects of the flux of experiences. The extreme instance on the continuum of possible sensory nature-mystical experiences is a pure receptive mindfulness, that is, totally de-conceptualized sensory stimuli unmediated by any sense of independent entities. In all instances of nature-mystical experiences, there is a breakdown of differentiation (as with a sense of a subject merging with an object); however, even with a sense of union, of being one with the whole of reality, there is also a sense of different nexuses within the flow of becoming. The surface appearance of the world as composed of distinct, self-contained units is seen (at least for the duration of the experience) not to be ultimate reality but a misreading of the nature of sensory data. Mystical freedom can be understood at least partially as a release from our conceptual cocoons to know things "as they really are."

The change involved in nature-mysticism is experiential, not just a change in understanding. The issue arises as to whether every concept within a theory affects or shapes every experience. In philosophy of science, it is debated whether Copernicus *saw* the same thing, with his switch from a geocentric to a heliocentric theory, that Ptolemy *saw* in watching the sun seemingly cross the sky.[4] But the emphasis upon experience in mysticism makes the claim reasonable that mystical knowledge involves an experiential change. Some mystical traditions make a distinction between two types of nature-mystical experiences: "sudden" enlightenment (in which a final and complete change in perspective occurs in one moment), and "gradual" enlightenment (in which a clarification of awareness occurs over time). However, an emphasis on experience is always there. The sensory stimuli remain the same but are structured to a lesser degree or in a new manner. Different facts then appear to the knower. One example of such a repatterning of knowledge is that one who knows reality (*tattvavit*) sees all work as being done by material constituents (*gunas*) rather than by an additional "actor."[5] The switch in perspective while viewing a Gestalt figure also produces a new fact, and sometimes a new scientific point of view or mystical enlightenment is likened to this; but scientists and mystics do not concede that all perspectives are equally valid. The analogy, though, does help to explain the experiential nature of such knowledge, that is, that experiences change, not just our understanding of them, while the stimuli remain the same.

Any reality experienced nature-mystically is not the mystical of the depth-mystical experience. Plotinus's distinction between the One and Being (the totality of phenomena) makes this distinction.[6] The depth-mystical experience involves no sensory or mental content and is temporary. Nature-mystical experiences may be temporary, but it is possible for an inner transformation of the total person to occur which affects cognitive and dispositional structures and which thus implements nature-mystical experiences into one's life constantly. Various states of enlightenment seem to involve internalizing a nature-mystical experience in this way. Depth-mystical experiences may have such a transformation as an aftereffect.

Within each mystically enlightened way of life room must be made for both types of mystical experiences; yet, mystics value each type according to their goals and beliefs, and usually one type is valued more than the other. For instance, the medieval Christian Richard Rolle valued the "ravishment without abstention from the senses" over the "rapture involving abstention from the bodily senses"; the later even sinners have, but the former is a rapture of love that goes to God.[7] A rapture without the senses may reach the ground of the individual self or of creation, but a sense of union is necessary to experience God. Thus a nature-mystical experience is valued by him over the depth-mystical experience. This contrasts with the release (*mokṣa*) of Advaita Vedānta. Here concentration (*samādhi*), leading to the stilling of all mental activity, is central, not any nature-mystical experience.

Concepts and Mystical Experiences

These evaluations of the status of the two types of mystical experiences lead to the issue of the role of concepts and beliefs in experiences and knowledge. A methodological assumption to be made here is that the depth-mystical experiences are of one type regardless of the understanding employed by individual mystics in different cultures and ages. It is an assumption since all that mystics can ever tell us is the interpretation of experience—we cannot in principle describe any experience bare of all understanding. And we cannot tell if all the symbols and other conceptualizations point to the same reality. It may be that any unusual experience will be taken to be "union with God," for example; thus little of the experiential content may be revealed by a descriptive concept alone. Although all experiences are private, still the assumption is suggested by the recurrence of certain terms in the descriptions of the depth-mystical and the fact that mystical teachers assume some experiences are of the same general type as their own enlightenment experience. This may be physiologically based, that is, whatever in our anatomy permits the occurrence of mystical experiences is the same in each individual regardless of other possible differences. Thus, when we are conditioned in the same way and all sensory-conceptual content is emptied from the mind, all people experience in the same manner.

In the case of nature-mystical experiences, concepts are absent only in the extreme sensory instance; in the other instances there is no reason not to assume that concepts play an active role in the experiences themselves, thereby producing a variety of such experiences as with ordinary experiences. The concepts inform the experiences themselves, thereby producing a variety of nature-mystical experiences; the concepts are not applied in an event occurring after the experience. Ordinary sense experiences are part of the sensory-experiential continuum. Nature-mystical experiences may involve only less structuring, a loosening of the grip of concepts upon sensory stimuli permitting more "raw sensory data" to come through the mental and physical processing mechanisms.[8] Or new structuring elements may be applied as in the case of Theravāda Buddhist insight-meditation (*vipassanā*): here the conceptual component analyzing reality in terms of the list of components comprising the experienced world (the *dhammā*) would restructure our perceptions. The great variety of nature-mystical experiences extends even to theistic concept-guided experiences, assuming love and union with God are genuinely experienced rather than added after the event as interpretations of experiences.

Conceptual frameworks do not affect the depth-mystical experience itself (since the mind is emptied of anything conceptual), but would return to the mystic's mind only after the experience is over. The position that there are any genuinely concept-free experiences is controversial. In contemporary philosophy of science the logical empiricists' assumption that there are conceptually neutral sense data, which are only interpreted differently after an experience, has been replaced, if there is any concensus at all, with a Gestalt view of observation.[9] Likewise, concerning mystical experiences, Steven Katz believes there is no "pure" experience: the experience itself as well as its expression is shaped by the concepts which the mystic brings to the experience.[10] This seems to be true of nature-mystical experiences, since they are sensory or sensory-like experiences (although it is not obvious that there is no unmediated or unconditioned element to these experiences). But if the depth-mystical experience is truly void of all sensory and conceptual content (as mystics say), what is present in the experience which could structure it? Only if the epistemological position replacing the empiricist dogma itself becomes a dogma is the possibility of concept-free experience beyond consideration. All that is available are the reports of the mystics themselves which suggest (as the quotation from Saint Teresa of Avila presented below indicates) that the depth-mystical experience itself is devoid of all dualistic content. No experiments in this regard involving the depth-mystical experience are possible, and it is not clear why the currently fashionable assumption about dualistic experiences should be used to rule out any other type of allegedly cognitive experience. Certainly Katz has advanced no reasons to believe all purportedly cognitive experiences must be of one type.

If the experience alone is given central importance, the structuring elements for the depth-mystical experience (unlike for the nature-mystical variety) become no more than, in William James's phrase, "over-beliefs."[11] Even if this experiential element is identical in every instance of depth-mysticism, still the total mystical ways of life are not identical from culture to culture and era to era. Understanding the experience is necessary—an uninterpreted experience would be unintelligible—and the understanding will reflect in varying degrees the values and beliefs of the culture in which the individual mystic lives. Concepts, doctrines, and entailed knowledge-claims are the epistemological elements involved. Concepts are any human constructs for handling experiential or mental data. Concepts and beliefs are not experiences; but, as in the case of Gestalt figures, they can enter into the experiences themselves. To speak of "beliefs" may be misleading since persons in religious or mystical ways of life speak of what they know or what is true (from their point of view), not what they believe. Doctrines are explicit statements of the knowledge contained in a way of life; but many unstated beliefs about reality also are involved which, if made explicit, a believer would accept. Thus, maintaining that the Buddha escaped the cycle of rebirths upon his enlightenment commits the holder of that doctrine to the two following knowledge-claims: there is a cycle of rebirths and one can break out of the cycle. Such claims are abstractions not conveying the total way of life; yet, they are not distortive or reductive as such.

For depth-mystical experiences, conceptualizations are *interpretations,* that is, structures of understanding consciously formulated or unconsciously imposed upon experiences *after* their occurrence. During the depth-mystical experience, all differentiations are inoperative. Once the mystic returns to a normal subject-object state of mind, reflections upon alternative systems of understanding may occur; or, as is more often the case, the superimposition of the understanding of the tradition to which the mystic belongs may take place. Mystics see their experiences through concepts: the mystical becomes a conceptual object in ordinary awareness. But the mystical is deemed ineffable: concepts necessarily differentiate and so cannot mirror a reality that cannot be experienced in a subject-object differentiation. Mystics thus become more aware than most people that the concept is not the referent. Meister Eckhart makes the distinction between God and the idea of God, and more generally he feels the soul, in coming into contact with "creatures," makes images (*Bilde*) and only gets back to things by means of these images which the soul itself has created.[12] For the depth-mystical, although giving descriptions is incompatible with having the experience, the descriptions do not necessarily distort or falsify: the mystical is not ineffable in the strongest sense of permitting no concepts to be more appropriately applied than any others, if the recurrence of some descriptive concepts (e.g., "nonduality" and "reality") is an indication. The sense of the importance of the mystical compels mystics to speak, and the claim to ineffability reduces to a stress upon the fact that the mystical's ontological status is not that of an object or the totality of objects.[13]

In nature-mystical states, the enlightened do still use concepts—only the idea of self-existent, permanent objects as referents is removed. Sense experiences and concepts are not abolished in the enlightened state but are transformed in that no distinct entities are seen; concepts are still utilized but are not taken as mirroring a world of independent entities.

Within this framework, usually mystics discuss their way of life, its values, its goal, and the reality involved. Construals of the mystical are in terms of the *reality* involved: mystics usually talk about God, ultimate realities, the self, and so on, rather than their own firsthand *experiences* of them, just as we normally talk about tables and chairs rather than our experiences of them. Mystical statements are no more about experiences than scientific statements are about sense experiences instead of planets and gravity. So too, mystical experiences, like scientific ones, are not seen as personal in the sense of being grounded subjectively rather than in reality. Mystical claims differ from ordinary empirical claims by degree because of the fundamental nature of the reality involved in mystical interpretations: mystical ontological claims are on a level of metaphysics (with the resulting difficulty in arriving at a consensus) rather than ordinary empirical claims. The discussions of the mystical are typically embedded in philosophies which are not explicit reflections upon mystical experiences or sets of scientific-like, tentative hypotheses advanced to explain the mystical. In addition, mystical systems do not involve theoretical entities, as does science; the mystical reality that is interpreted is alleged to be open directly to our experience. Mystical thinkers such as Śaṁkara and Plotinus do develop elaborate philosophies, albeit not absolutely systematic ones: such works as the *Brahma-sūtra-bhāṣya* are a series of arguments, counterarguments, and replies. But the goal of mystical ways of life is radically to end suffering or some other fundamental matter related to how we lead our lives and to our expectations upon death, not to fulfill a speculative philosophical interest. The mystics' concern is to see things as they really are and to live in accordance with that perception.

Mystical Knowledge

The general lack of discussion by mystics of their experiences has led to a problem with regard to the issue of the role of mystical experiences in mystical knowledge, that is, knowledge about the fundamental nature of reality following from mystical experiences. It is hard to distinguish those thinkers who have mystical experiences as part of their experiential background from those philosophers who advocate, for reasons other than those connected to mystical experiences, beliefs which also are defended by mystics. In fact, probably every claim asserted by a mystic has been advocated by nonmystics for other reasons. For instance, David Hume speaks of the unreality of a permanent individual self; Parmenides argues "all is one" for totally nonmystical reasons; Alfred North Whitehead's and G. W. F. Hegel's systems have been likened to those of mystics. Conversely, even the *Upaniṣads* arose out of Vedic speculation and it is difficult to identify at what point mystical experiences begin to inform the total conceptual system. Such mystical thinkers as Eckhart, Plotinus, and Śaṁkara have been portrayed as philosophers who rigorously followed their premises through to the conclusions: if God, the One, or Brahman is the ultimate reality, then nothing else is real, and so forth. No appeal to special experiences would be necessary.

Occasionally mystical experiences are mentioned. For example, Plotinus mentions in a letter that three times he had attained a state of selflessness.[14] But since these experiences are not given an explicit place in his philosophical writings it is not self-evident that they form an integral part of the total framework. The work of another Neoplatonist, Dionysius the Areopagite, also lacks specific mention of mystical experiences.[15] But it contains many elements suggesting such experiences: "ecstacy" is stepping outside oneself; the "unknowing" (*agnosia*) of mental content permitting a new positive knowledge and the "dazzling obscurity" in which one comes to know God certainly are in contrast with the "clear and distinct" Cartesian ideas of the rationalist epitemological ideal. Some mystics are philosophers also, but their total systems form fairly integrated wholes, not a series of isolated claims to be judged individually, even if the degree of this integration is not as great as the assertions in scientific theories; and the parts interact to suggest at least indirectly (as in Dionysius's case) if mystical experiences are of importance.

Mystical knowledge is not knowing that something is the case (i.e., understanding a claim and having reason to acknowledge its truth) but is experiencing the reality involved. Some mystics do not even call this "knowledge" since it may be confused with dualistic knowledge (knowledge by a subject of a distinct object).[16] It is not that intellectual propositions are necessarily wrong but just that such dualistic understanding is not the required experience. Medieval Christian contemplatives drew the distinction between knowledge of divine things coming through consideration (*scientia*) and true wisdom (*sapientia*).[17] Or according to Eckhart, to know *about* God is not to know God. In Theravāda Buddhism, Narada is said to have the same knowledge as the enlightened Musila but not to have achieved enlightenment himself: he understood and accepted the requisite truths but had not experienced them (i.e., had not internalized the beliefs so that they became his dispositional and cognitive framework).[18] The analogy is then given of a thirsty traveler who looks at water but does not drink: he understands but is not saved. Only with the internalization of mystical knowledge do we see reality rightly and live accordingly (as defined by each tradition).

The Role of Beliefs and Experiences in the Development of Mystical Knowledge

Mystical experiences give knowledge only in the context of mystical systems. What is taken to be the *insight* combines elements from the experience and from the conceptual scheme. Any *post facto* interpretation may present itself with the same immediacy and certainty as the experience itself. For example, Saint Teresa of Avila says that during the "orison of union," the soul is "utterly dead to the things of the world and lives solely in God":

> If you, nevertheless, ask how it is possible that the soul can see and understand that she has been in God, since during the union she has neither sight nor understanding, I reply that she does not see it then, but that she sees it clearly later, after she has returned

> to herself, not by any vision, but by a certitude which abides with her and which God alone can give her.[19]

Understanding applied after the experience may seem as inseparable as any occurring within the experience itself—only a great effort could convince ourselves that we are wrong. We do not normally see experiences as concept-structured events or as experiences perceived through interpretative frameworks.

In this situation two errors may result concerning the role of both experiences and beliefs. One is to conclude that the experiences provide the interpretation in a simple, straightforward manner; the other is to conclude that the experiences add nothing to the belief-framework. With regard to the former, mysticism is sometimes taken as fulfilling the logical empiricist ideal: claims about the world are confirmed by experiences alone.[20] Focusing on only the depth-mystical experiences (and again assuming they are identical in experiential character), the fact that these experiences are open to widely different interpretations should convince us that the meaning of the mystics' claim does not come from (nor is confirmed simply by) the experiences alone. Some elements of a world-view are given in a mystical experience—a sense of fundamental reality involving nonduality—but no complete interpretation is given. Śaṁkara construes the nonduality in terms of the fundamental nature of all reality while in Śāṁkhya-Yoga the nonduality is related only to the isolation (*kaivalya*) of each of many individual subjects (*puruṣas*) from all matter (*prakṛti*). Even within Christian theistic interpretations variations exist: Eckhart sees it in terms of the isness common to creature and God; Saint John of the Cross speaks of a union with a difference, using the analogy of sunlight penetrating air; Saint Teresa of Avila accepts a union of wills only, not of substance. Thus, it would appear that all interpretations are our various efforts at understanding and are not dictated by these experiences.

The problem is not only the Kantian issue of how we can go from bare experiences to concepts, nor is it that experiential claims cannot entail claims about existence apart from the experience. More than these, the problem here is that experiences related to how we fundamentally construe reality are open to widely different interpretations. For instance, even if one argues that self-awareness (the awareness of one's own immediate state of awareness) is the one certain cornerstone of knowledge which we all have, still it is open to different interpretations. René Descartes takes this awareness as evidence of a distinct, abiding, individual mental entity; the Buddha takes each act of consciousness to be separate and takes the notion of an enduring underlying self to be an unverified posit; for Śaṁkara self-awareness is the awareness constituting the ultimate reality underlying all subjects and objects. Nothing about mystical experiences, no matter how strong the sense of finality and certainty, places them in a privileged epistemological position distinct from this problem. No such experience carries with it its own interpretation. The conceptual element necessary for understanding comes from outside any one type of experience.

Thus, Ninian Smart is correct when he says that *nirvāṇa* allegedly involves the end of the cycle of rebirths and so cannot be defended simply by reference to meditative experiences.[21] Other mystics mention an end to desire, but mystics not raised with a belief in rebirth do not mention this more specialized feature. So, too, we must agree with Smart that the identification of the self (*ātman*) with the ground of "objective" reality (Brahman) in Advaita Vedānta comes not from inspecting the inner state of the mind or the mystical experience itself.[22] Similarly, branding ordinary experiences "illusions" also reflects nonexperiential judgments and reasons even if the claim appears to be given in the enlightenment experience itself. J. F. Staal notes that, although knowledge of Brahman is incompatible with ordinary awareness, preferring the nondual experience is itself an act of ordinary awareness since all knowledge and interpreting occurs in the ordinary state. Experiences are only decisive for becoming convinced of a doctrine's truth.[23]

Śaṁkara realized that the mystical experience could not establish its own interpretation: the Vedas are the final court of appeal with regard to the mystical—no experience is a means to correct knowledge (*pramāṇa*) in this area. The existence of Brahman is known on the ground that it is the self of everyone; Śaṁkara would go so far as to say it is impossible to deny that the self is apprehended because who would the denier be?[24] But the inquiry into the self is necessary because of the conflicting views of its specific nature.[25] Reason alone is incapable of demonstrating the nature of reality, as the contradictory theories based on reason reveal.[26] Nor would closer examination of the world validate any interpretation—the Vedas alone provide the right authority.

Śaṁkara's reliance on the Vedas and other mystics' denial of gaining knowledge in the mystical experience may lead some people to the other extreme mentioned above—giving full weight to the conceptual scheme. All experiences are understood in light of beliefs previously developed in a culture, and so it can be argued that mystical experiences add nothing to the experiencer's knowledge of ultimate reality—the ideas are always derived from other sources. Thus, the experiences add nothing new but at best merely confirm in a circular manner whatever beliefs the mystic previously held. In utilizing the conceptual scheme of a culture and a religious tradition of the period, mystics have a ready-made framework to give intelligibility and meaning to the experience. These conceptual systems provide the correct understanding of the construction of reality as it has evolved for that tradition, and mystics normally evaluate and place their experiences as insights in accordance with them. Seldom do mystics deny the doctrines or authority of their religious faith; even visions and nature-mystical experiences reflect only what the experiencer is prepared to discover by cultural conditioning.

There are major problems with this position, however. Although no mystic withdraws totally from the cultural setting, there are degrees of independence—for example, Jacob Böhme versus Saint John of the Cross. So, too, some mystics such as Plotinus do attempt, albeit rarely, to devise a basically original system. In addition, if the mystics sense they have come to know what they only understood before, they will not accept their tradition uncritically: their attitude to the nonmystical elements of their tradition will be reoriented. They take over the conceptual system available to them but modify it to their needs. Thus, Śaṁkara, while accepting the Vedas as authoritative in matters related to Brahman, freely interprets them to fit his system: if a passage concurs with his system, he takes its literal sense; if it conflicts, the literal meaning is dismissed.[27] There is a circularity here with his own thought, not the Vedas, gaining central importance. A basically nonmystical text such as the Bible is handled by Christian mystics in a similar manner. Eckhart, for example, sees the story of Jesus cleansing the temple as a symbolic depiction of the mystical experience (Jesus entering) cleansing the soul (the temple) of sensory concerns (the money changers).[28] Jesus' significance is also reshaped: more is said of Jesus as the bridegroom of the soul than as a sacrificial lamb on the cross.

An even more important problem with this position is that giving all weight to doctrines conflicts with a more likely explanation of the history of thought—that experiences and doctrines develop influencing each other constantly. Even if one of the conflicting revelations of the world religions is correct and unaffected by previous beliefs or by any experiences, still it must be understood in each era and culture—and this understanding will be shaped by experiences and beliefs (as with Śaṁkara). The authoritative beliefs accepted at any point are shaped by previous experiences and vice versa. The issue of which came first, beliefs or experiences, can be aptly likened to the situation of the chicken and the egg.[29] Mystical traditions evolve through interaction with religious and other ideas—mystics have some influence on nonmystical cultural phenomena and the latter influences different elements of mystical ways of life. Doctrines within mystical traditions also evolve. Mystical traditions may evolve more slowly than scientific theories, but they are not static.

Revolutions in mysticism such as Plotinus's do occur, but they are much rarer than in science. Mystics most often take their experiences as confirming the doctrines of their tradition. If the assumption that all depth-mystical experiences are identical is correct, this relative lack of revolutions is because the experiential contribution is constant. Mystics cannot run experiments which could pose problems for old views. Beliefs therefore exercise more control in the production of knowledge here than in science. Yet the lack of new experiential data does not rule out a radical change in the conceptual understanding. Depth-mystical experiences may appear as anomalies to believers who did not expect them; an adjustment in their understanding of the faith's doctrines and concepts would then be necessary. No new knowledge-claims need be revealed, but the understanding of the beliefs change. The beliefs may have previously appeared readily intelligible (e.g., "all is impermanent" or "everything is interconnected"), but they take on a new significance in mystical enlightenment, that is, with *seeing* that they are actually true of everything. Thus, mystics may fill some terms and expressions from their environment with different meanings—mystical concepts of "God," the "self," or whatever may not be commensurable with their nonmystical counterparts on the level of understanding in a way similar to how "mass," "space," and "time" for Isaac Newton and Albert Einstein may have identical referents but still differ in the understanding of the referred to reality. Or, "being" as a philosophical abstraction obtained by thinking of what is common to all entities may differ from the mystical concept "being" (the concrete content of mystical experiences).

A total break with the past is difficult, if not impossible. For example, Christian mystics—even Eckhart—were never very hostile to Christian doctrine but found it adaptable to their needs.[30] Seldom do they introduce new terms as Eckhart did; more usually, the concepts behind old terms are altered. In science there are strands of continuity with the past in radical instances of originality, since new theories arise from reflection on the current state of knowledge and its anomalies. If the history of ideas can be likened to evolution, as is often done for science,[31] still it is a form of Lamarckian, not Mendelian, evolution, since the development is not random but involves the inheritance of evolutionally valuable traits each generation acquires in adapting to its cultural environment. Thus, the history of Buddhism can be seen as a series of reactions and counterreactions to earlier developments.[32] Indeed, there are no "pure" religious traditions—every religion and every religious person is influenced by at least some other religious and nonreligious traditions. This bears upon the issue of commensurability: concepts such as "God" evolve and, although the understanding two thinkers have of the concepts may conflict, any tradition as a whole evolves through mystical and nonmystical contributions. Therefore general agreement on many concepts may result in a tradition.

Mystics' Interest in Doctrines

Before turning to the issue of the role of beliefs and experiences in justifying mystical claims, two preliminary points must be made. First, J. F. Staal's claim that mystics "are not interested in doctrines" must be refuted.[33] For Staal, the experience is all that is of importance; the added religious and philosophical conceptual superstructure is worthless if not meaningless.[34] Others make the joy and excitement of the experience everything; the different, conflicting "over-beliefs" at best aid in leading people to the experiences. According to this position, debates over doctrines or the nature of mystical experiences are pointless; inducing these experiences is all that matters, and whatever leads to being free of desire and of a sense of self is correct. The experiences are ends in themselves and the only value.

Some mystics may be interested only in the enjoyment of experiences, but this position does not reflect the interest of most classical mystics as it appears in their writings: total ways of life most often are central. Nor should we confuse the difficulties which arise in expressing mystical insights, because of the sense of otherness, with a lack of interest in them. Nor should the fact that an experience is required, rather than an intellectual acceptance of a knowledge-claim, be construed as a necessary denial of the claim itself. Mystics discuss seeing things as they really are. Even in discussing any experience, the reality that is supposedly involved (along with its nature) is a component. For example, in the case of the sun, the important scientific issues arise on a level above whatever common stimulus Copernicus and Ptolemy might receive; their understanding of the nature of the sun is what is important. The sun "as it really is" is not a set of subjective sensations free of all understanding; it really is the center of our solar system, a celestial orb circling an unmoving earth, or whatever, not just a bundle of our experiences (assuming some form of realism is correct). No one would say the experience, in that context, is all that is of importance. So, too, with mystics: their interest is in knowing how reality is actually constructed with regard to the mystical in order to fulfill their goals in life.

Doctrines go to the core of a mystical tradition, even to shaping nature-mystical experiences. Getting an accurate view of the relationship of the mystical to the rest of reality is important, too, for the other components of the way of life. How we act depends in part on how we see the world. The Brahmanical priests and Western scientists not only view the sun differently but also differ significantly in how they act regarding it: the Vedic ritual necessary to maintain the course of the universe was an essential element in the way of life in classical India but would be absurd in the context of modern society. How people value mystical experiences and place them within their way of living also differ. Usually concerns other than the experience itself are placed more centrally. For all medieval Christian mystics, mystical experiences may be a foretaste of what will occur upon death, but these experiences do not achieve that future state nor are they the basis of belief; instead mystical cultivation is only a way of loving God and of improving charity. For Theravāda Buddhists, a radical end to the suffering inherent in the cycle of rebirths is the only concern; for this, having an insight into the unsatisfying and substanceless nature of experienced reality and subsequently undergoing a permanent transformation of character is required, not enjoying any temporary experience and returning to the old condition. Different mystics not only hold different beliefs but also lead different lives.[35] Even if all mystics concurred upon knowledge-claims, expectations upon death, how to deal with others, and goals, this doctrinal component still could not be ignored. Living in accordance with how things really are, not feelings derived from isolated experiences, is what mystics deem important.[36]

"All Mysticism is One"

The other preliminary point is to refute the idea that all mystics really say the same thing regardless of different cultural expressions, that is, all mystics ultimately have one doctrine. Frithjof Schuon, standing in the tradition of perennial philosophy, contrasts the colorless essence of pure luminosity of the esoteric core with the distinct colors of the various exoteric traditions and symbols which manifest the esoteric.[37] Once we distinguish the symbol from the symbolized, the "container" from the "content," we shall see that truth is ultimately one and is only expressed differently. For instance, all spatial metaphors used for the mystical—the mystical stands "behind," "above," "below," or "through" phenomena—mean the same thing. Or the mystical is "being" while phenomena are "nonbeing" means the same as the mystical is "nonbeing" (or "nothing") while phenomena are "something": that the mystical is wholly other than phenomena and more real are the common points. The difference in terminology can be predicted once the total cultural context is seen. A variation of this position is that different exoteric configurations of practices and beliefs do not say the same thing but are complementary paths, all leading to the same esoteric truth. Each tradition is a different approach emphasizing different features; each is equally legitimate and each is equally incomplete. Ultimately, the mystical is either indescribable (with different conceptualizations dealing with different manifestations) or, if describable as it is in itself, the correct interpretation of the mystical as literally as possible is this: one reality immanent in all phenomena, having personal and nonpersonal aspects, with something in each soul joined to or identical with it; our final goal is to recognize this immanent and transcendent reality.[38]

However, if we compare this with what mystics actually say, we see that such a position is normative in two ways. One is that this interpretation of the mystical is only one scheme among many alternatives: it cannot be deduced from various theistic and nontheistic mystical claims. Second, to assert that all religions say the same thing cannot be deduced from the mystics' claims. That the relation between mystical traditions is that of clear light to colored light is an analogy that cannot simply be assumed as self-evident but must be positively argued. The dogmatic nature of Schuon's position becomes obvious when he must dismiss rebirth—a belief resulting, he says, in "some Hindu sects" through a "literalist interpretation of the Scripture"—because it would disprove all monotheism.[39] There also are methodological problems here: some diverse symbols may be symbolizing one reality, but can all mystical concepts that seem to contradict each other (e.g., Sāṁkhya-Yoga and Advaita Vedānta on the nature of the self) be treated so? We would be inclined to think of the differences as merely superficial only if we assumed in advance that there is an esoteric unity. We would need to read all the texts through a certain normative perspective.

On what grounds could we conclude, rather than assume *a priori*, that there really is commonality between traditions? It cannot be upon the assumption alone that there is one common depth-mystical experience since, as argued above, mystics take doctrines as central. D. T. Suzuki says, because of this common ground, "terminology is all that divides us [Buddhists and Christians] and stirs us up to a wasteful dissipation of energy."[40] But his religious interpretation becomes apparent when he adds that Christianity is laden with all sorts of "myths and paraphernalia" and ought to be denuded of this "unnecessary historical appendix."[41] To dismiss differences in understanding of the mystical because of the common experiential component would be as unwarranted here as maintaining that the common sensory element in Copernicus's and Ptolemy's perceptions of the sun is sufficient to discredit any divergences between their points of view. In terms familiar since Gottlob Frege, the reference of the terms may be the same but the sense provided by the conceptual background diverges substantially. The variety of nature-mystical experiences would also have to be taken into account.

Arguing that all mystical ways of life are ultimately the same because the same ultimate reality is involved will not succeed either. This is based upon an assumption with regard to the mystical. But even if it is correct, still this would be equivalent to arguing that Copernicus and Ptolemy are actually saying the same thing (i.e., their surface differences are only symbols of an esoteric truth) because a common reality is involved. Even if there were some such esoteric truth, we have no reason to believe that Copernicus and Ptolemy had it in mind: Copernicus's conceptual divergence from Ptolemy was intended. Also, we have no reason outside the normative position of perennial philosophy to think the diversity of mystical claims is not also intended. The mystical ways of life are still based on specific conceptions of the mystical and thus would diverge accordingly.

Another avenue might be to find an abstract doctrine to which all mystics would adhere. The problem here is twofold. First, finding a common core of doctrine is very difficult. Consider Sāṁkhya-Yoga and Advaita Vedānta again on the self: for the former there is a plurality of selves distinct from matter; for the latter the one self is the ultimate reality of every phenomenon. Theists and nontheists disagree over the nature of mystical experiences in a fundamental way—whether the experiencer is identical with the mystical or is united in either substance or will while our "creaturehood" remains intact, whether the mystical experience involves God, and so forth. Whether there is a neutral criterion for selecting one doctrine is highly unlikely. For example, Evelyn Underhill's seemingly innocent definition of mysticism as the "art of union with Reality" has two built-in assumptions: the mystical is ultimate reality and the process is one of uniting.[42] With regard to the latter, Advaitins would disagree: nothing is brought about—only our ignorance of the fact we have always been Brahman is overcome. Sāṁkhya-Yogins also would disagree: the isolation of selves from matter is effected, not any union.

Furthermore, it is one matter to use general terms for classes of concepts ("the mystical," "mystical experience"); it is another matter to say any general term conveys the total interpretation of specific mystics. There is no abstract mysticism but only concrete mystics and traditions. Mystics could adopt a concept of a watered-down "absolute" as an adequate interpretation, but historically none has done so. Even Zen has more specific Mahāyāna concepts inextricably interwoven within it. All mystics' conceptions of the mystical cover more than simply describing an experience and, through connections to other aspects of their ways of life, the conceptions entail more knowledge-claims than a commitment to a vague "absolute." Thus, Śaṁkara's Brahman is ultimately nonpersonal and the only reality. A more abstract mystical that encompasses more but is more vague would not satisfy his total set of commitments.

In philosophy of science, a debated issue is whether we can totally isolate theory from neutral descriptions of experiences. It may be possible here to determine a description of the depth-mystical experience which is neutral to all more doctrinal interpretations. That is, it will still be theory-laden[43] but laden with a theory neutral to all doctrinal interpretations in the way "celestial orb" would be neutral to Copernicus's and Ptolemy's use of the term "sun." This may be difficult to accomplish. For example, Agehananda Bharati claims that Advaita gives the uninterpreted content of the mystical experience.[44] Assuming the Advaita account is in fact the description of some experience, nevertheless the identification of the self with the ground of reality is more than a simple description of an experience: it is an interpretation which would not seem obvious to followers of those traditions not committed to an ontology of absolute nonduality. A sense of having come into contact with a fundamental, undeniable reality (James's "noetic quality") is usually given in the experience, but these differences reveal that no complete interpretation of the mystical is dictated by the experience itself. No complete interpretation is a minimal description of what occurs, impervious to error. None is anything other than theory-laden in the stronger sense of being integrated into more elaborate conceptual systems which give meaning to the concepts. A scientific concept has been likened to a "knot in a web," the strands of which are the propositions that make up a theory; the meaning of each concept is determined by the strands coming into that knot and by the other knots to which it is directly or indirectly connected.[45] This is true of mystical ways of life, too: concepts gain meaning in the context of the doctrinal system which gives meaning to each utterance; some concepts may be more closely related to experiences than others, but it is the complete system that gives meaning to the parts—even to the experiences themselves. For example, rebirth is not a concept that can be simply tacked on to a world-view: it changes our view of the nature of a person, replaces the uniqueness of one life and the idea of eternal post mortem existence, and may affect how we treat other people. Thus, a switch to this view would have wider repercussions within a totally integrated way of life and for how we believe things really are constructed.

Eckhart's "God," the Theravādins' "*nibbāna,*" and Śaṁkara's "Brahman" are all concepts which gain their significance within the context of elaborate religious systems. Correlating them would be no more successful than was the quickly abandoned Chinese Buddhist *ko-i* method of translating Buddhist terms by means of Taoist ones. Even if the same term is used (e.g., terms translated "self"), they may have no common concept behind them; even if the referent of each is the same, the referential and theoretical aspects of concepts cannot be conflated. Common features—overcoming a sense of duality and of self—may appear similar in isolation but not in their total contexts. Many of Eckhart's remarks sound like translations of Śaṁkara's: such phrases as "the essence of ignorance is to superimpose finiteness upon God and divinity upon the finite," "the all-inclusive One without a second, without distinction, not this, not that," and "isness-in-itself is identically unrestricted knowledge" have very similar counterparts in Śaṁkara's commentaries.[46] However, there are significant differences in their total conceptual systems and ways of life; for example, for Eckhart, there is a point in the soul that remains a creature—the soul's isness is God's isness but there is no final complete identity as with Śaṁkara's system. For Plotinus, too, there is no identity of the soul with the One even in the depth-mystical experience where the soul and the One are as indistinguishable as the centers of two coinciding circles. From each mystic's point of view, there may be something valuable in other systems, but it is vitiated by its placement within a faulty conceptual framework. To use an Indian saying, the milk in itself is pure, but it becomes useless when poured into a bag of dogskin.[47]

The variant position that each conceptual system is an equally legitimate complement can also be seen to be a normative stance at variance with the position of most classical mystics. *Prima facie* conflicting claims could be treated as complements only if the claims are viewed by their holders as incomplete, tentative, and inadequate. But classical mystics usually do not do so; they see their tradition's account as absolutely certain, if not exhaustive. The lack of any tentativeness is a central feature. Despite their disclaimers about the applicability of language to the mystical, their writings indicate overwhelmingly that they feel something can be said accurately concerning the mystical and that they have done so while other mystics have not. Even if the mystical depth is not completely fathomable by the intellect, they consider themselves the enlightened in this matter. Their word is the end of the matter, and the claims are not open to rejection in the future. They claim that, if we test the situation for ourselves, we shall come to the same conclusions they reached. In addition, the knowledge-claims are about the same subject (such as the self), and each is taken as fundamental and as complete as possible. To that extent, the situation is like the conflict between the classical Copernican and Ptolemaic theories, not like the wave and particle models of contemporary quantum physics. This is not a case of taking inexact language overly seriously: there are genuine fundamental conflicts on the issues. As with Śaṁkara arguing against the Sāṁkhya-Yogins and the Buddhists in the *Brahma-sūtra-bhāṣya,* in general, mystics in one tradition think those in other traditions are mistaken in some fundamental account of a subject.

A position of conflict is the only one that describes the classical mystics' position. It is the only one deducible from their sense of certitude and from the differing claims even if the various traditions have had no historical contact. To treat matters of whether ultimate reality is one or dual, personal or nonpersonal, and so on as complements is a religious or philosophical position external to the descriptions of the mystics themselves. To overcome conflicts by appeal to the elephant/blind men analogy employed by some Near Eastern and Indian mystics is a theological position not acceptable even to most mystics in those regions; they do not feel they are blind or that all mystical systems are of equal value. In the continuing evolution of religious thought, traditional mystical conceptual options may die out and a new fusion of ideas may occur or a sense of complementarity may develop; but this will be a new development. The more usual response to the presence of traditions other than one's own is to establish a hierarchy of teachings with one's own at the top as the final truth. The Japanese Zen master Dōgen illustrates the classical mystics' position on the alleged identity of traditions: only those from whom Buddhism has gone and who are lax in their thinking say that "the essence of Taoism, Confucianism, and Buddhism is identical, that the difference is only that of the entrance into the Way, and also that the three are comparable to the three legs of a tripod."[48] It is worth noting that Dōgen was not overly exclusivistic: he did not like the designation of a separate Meditation (Zen) sect within the Buddhist tradition.

The Role of Beliefs and Experiences in the Justification of Mystical Systems

This leads to the final topic: can any one mystical system be established as superior to others to the satisfaction of all mystics and nonmystics? This issue is important to mystics because knowing the correct status of the mystical experiences and of the mystical is necessary toward seeing things as they really are and living accordingly. Are there grounds for those who value mystical experiences to establish one conceptual interpretation as correct (or most useful or least inadequate)? How can we rationally choose between traditions when each says it has the correct account of the mystical? If one way of life is even God-given, how can we tell?

Experiential certainty—the sense that the experience is self-confirming or self-evident—is not enough. If the experience has a powerful effect upon a person, this does not exempt the experiencer from the possibility of error concerning the status and nature of the mystical. First, the immediate awareness may cause an overemphasis upon its importance. The situation may be comparable to the prisoner from Plato's cave who, in encountering the dazzling splendor upon leaving the cave, mistakes the sun (here, the mystical) as the author of all things in the universe. Second, even if no other experience can shake the sense of absolute importance attached to the mystical experience, still this certainty cannot be transferred to the accompanying interpretative system. As discussed earlier, mystics normally equate the conceptualization with the experiential component—that is, the mystics' doctrine seems to be given directly in the experience. Mystics are usually naive realists in this regard even if they are aware of alternative systems: from inside a belief system it always seems as if they are merely describing, not interpreting.[49] To give an example from Islam, al-Ghazālī speaks of getting away from secondhand belief (*taqlīd*) based upon mere authority, reaching the peak of "direct vision," and comprehending "things as they really are." But the theistic creedal principles which become "rooted in [his] being" not by argument and proof but by experience (*dhawq*) contrast greatly with those of, say, the Buddhist tradition.[50] He and the Buddha each feels that he and not the other sees things as they really are free of any theories. But it appears al-Ghazālī would be on as sound a ground in this regard for dismissing the Buddha's claims as vice versa.

Śaṁkara's appeal to the Vedas shows that not every mystic takes mystical experiences to be self-validating. While mystics do not usually take their knowledge to be conjectural rather than unchanging and given *in toto* in experience, there are instances of mystics questioning their own interpretations. Martin Buber reinterpreted an experience which he thought at the time of its occurrence was "a union with the primal being or Godhead." Later he concluded that in "the honest and sober account of the responsible understanding this unity is nothing but the unity of this soul of mine, whose 'ground' I have reached."[51] This "responsible understanding" would be dictated by his Jewish background (for which the gulf between God and creature is absolutely unbridgeable), not in the form of conscious pressure but as tacitly guiding him to what is obviously the case. To him, it would seem more like a logical conclusion than a judgment. Ordinary experiences are never accepted uncritically; for example, a stick appearing bent in water is not taken to be actually broken. Our conception of how things really are directly affects this. And the same is true of mystical experiences: the moment of ecstasy, originally taken as an insight, may even be dismissed entirely by later reflection based upon a tradition's doctrine.

If a neutral description of a mystical experience were possible, it would not support any complete interpretation. This neutralizes experiences as the sole determining factor in deciding which mystical system is best. Nor are mystical systems testable by predictions involving mystical experiences. In the process of theory-change in science, experiences occurring in new areas, as well as older anomalies, are involved. If all depth-mystical experiences are the same, more depth-mystical experiences will not enlarge the experiential base for the choice between mystical systems. For a conceptual system as encompassing and fundamental in nature as mystical ones, nonmystical experiences have little falsifying power in themselves (unless religious or philosophical considerations dictate otherwise): any nonmystical occurrences seems to be accommodatable to each system. There are no crucial experiments in this area.[52]

In science where new experiences figure into the acceptance of a theory, experiences alone do not determine theory selection (if post-empiricist philosophies of science are correct). In the case of mysticism, can the neutral mystical experiences be interpreted any way we want within the limitation of adequately accounting for all the elements (as we see them)? Are all interpretations on the same epistemological footing? Mystics do argue for their interpretation. Ernest Nagel says that a "consistent mystic cannot hope to establish his claims by argument" since "argument involves the use of analytic reason, and on the mystic's own view reason is incapable of penetrating to the substance of reality."[53] However, while mystics would insist an argument is no substitute for the necessary enlightenment, still the proper understanding of the mystical and accepting the proper way of life are necessary—and these may legitimately involve arguments. Saṁkara's arguments with the Sāṁkhya-Yogins and Buddhists are a good example. Argument is an unmystical activity but is not completely negative for being so.

Are there any useful criteria for comparing and selecting mystical systems? Within science such criteria for the acceptability of a theory are: empirical accuracy, simplicity (ontological and mathematical), internal consistency and systematic organization, coherence with other accepted theories, scope, fruitfulness in leading to new empirical findings and new theories, familiarity, and the intuitive plausibility of the most basic elements of the theoretical framework. Whether even these criteria taken collectively can determine rationally one unique solution is debatable.[54] Mystical systems, though, have broader concerns than understanding the world through sense experience; within this broader context, while many of the same considerations apply, agreement is harder to establish. For example, all mystical systems claim to be of the same scope: each comprehends all aspects of reality that are fundamental from its point of view. Or consider simplicity: Advaita Vedānta is committed to the fewest number of ontologically irreducible elements—one—but this does not satisfy theists and others; such simplicity is rejected in favor of other values and considerations. Coherence with other beliefs (religious and nonreligious) is important, as Buber's reinterpretation indicates; but this shifts the problem to justifying the other beliefs or the belief-framework as a whole.

One criterion relates to the fruits of one's mystical experience—joy, paranormal powers, character changes, and actions toward others—but these are relative to the broader mystical positions. For example, many mystics de-emphasize the significance of paranormal powers. So, too, proper enlightened mystical action may be helping others with this-worldly concerns in Christianity or it may mean taking no action at all, and consequently starving to death, as is the Jaina ideal upon enlightenment. As with differing doctrines, it is too facile to say that such differences merely complement each other—instead they compete.

A proposal of a more general religious criterion is the adequacy of the solution offered to the perennial religious needs of humanity.[55] Yet, there does not appear to be any one set of such needs: overcoming estrangement with other persons, realizing one's unchanging true nature, escaping a cycle of rebirths, and reaching heaven as primary goals are objectives which, if not all conflicting, are not identical. Determining one set of social or psychological needs may be just as difficult. Taking history seriously is integral to Judeo-Christian traditions, but that whole area of concerns is screened out in most traditional Indian systems. Taking this criterion as the deciding factor is therefore inadequate.

More limited enterprises such as science may be able to find a common framework within which to resolve disputes, but the problems are greater at a level describing the fundamental structures of reality. Each such scheme determines by its very nature the criteria deemed relevant towards justifying a conceptual scheme. To anyone within a given mystical framework, any view advanced from outside that framework is an unintentional or intellectual misinterpretation of what is real. Once the prescribed enlightenment experience has occurred, one's internalized point of view no longer appears to be a view at all but the way things really are. This is not so much audacity as simply part of the logic of such belief: the mystical way of life provides the broadest court of appeal and thus, unlike more limited scientific theories, it is very difficult (if possible at all) to stand truly outside it in order genuinely to consider alternatives.

Any experience occurring in this situation tends to be taken as confirmation of belief, thereby leading to conviction. All experiences confirm the doctrines from inside the circle of faith somewhat as Ptolemaic astronomy was verified by every predicted eclipse before a plausible alternative interpretation was advanced. Clifford Geertz sees religious systems as defining a reality which believers use in turn to justify the systems themselves.[56] Paul Feyerabend says the same about science: empirical evidence is created by a procedure which quotes as its justification the very same evidence it has produced.[57] But science does progress in a way the world's mystical systems have not; this points to the greater control of doctrine in shaping world-views in the case of mysticism. The self-fulfilling nature of this situation means that any mystic's vision of the nature of reality is verifiable in the way all are: the vision itself sets up a framework for facts which determines in advance what will be the objective facts and what will count as verification. In valuing experiential, social, and historical phenomena differently, each tradition will construct problems differently. Refuting one system in such a situation is only possible from the point of view of a rival set of commitments: mystical experiences are neutralized, and phenomena deemed negative from one point of view are handled differently by another system.

What is deemed rational in different ways of life will depend upon the total conception of reality. Thus, for those Christian theologians who take the Christ as the central fact, any attempt at understanding reality which ignores this fact as central is not being *objective*. Reasonable actions will depend also on what is deemed real; for example, if belief in rebirth is accepted, repercussions of action upon future lives become a concern. The very ground that permits comparisons (i.e., a common level of interpretation) rules out any adjudication between the systems. This may lead to skepticism (no means of determining which mystical system is best) or relativism (each viable system is no better than any other). Each system can consider criticism from other systems, but in the end grounds internal to the system will decide such issues as how much weight to give each desideratum. Justification in the sense of advancing reasons acceptable to all parties appears to be ruled out when there is no theory neutral way of determining fundamental ontology.

If there are no timeless, neutral standards, to whom do we have to justify our commitments? Certainly not to someone, whether mystic or nonmystic, who endorses another set of commitments. The most that can be done to make a particular mystical conceptual system acceptable to other people is complicated and ultimately inadequate. Ninian Smart feels the truth of a doctrine depends on evidence other than the mystical experience.[58] However, probably the justificatory process is similar to the discovery process: elements from experiences and the concern for understanding interact in devising a conceptual apparatus which adequately accounts for all experiences in light of the concerns. Having reason to believe an interpretation will depend on both considerations. The central principles within a mystical system need not be accepted uncritically any more than are those of science—alternatives and possible objections are discussed by mystics such as the Buddha and Śaṁkara. Mystical experiences alone are not evidence for one position since alternative interpretations are possible. But they are not irrelevant either: they make up part of the pool of allegedly cognitive experiences out of which world-views arise; they are usually considered especially prominent and can adjust our understanding of doctrine. The religious experience argument for good grounds for belief in some absolute is damaged by the fact that mystical experiences are not a unique source of experience for establishing doctrines. This does not, however, reduce religious thought to speculative metaphysics independent of experiences. Knowledge-claims are justified by clusters of factors from both experience and conception. An experience may be decisive for convincing one of a doctrine's truth, but neither the doctrine nor the experience is the basis of the other; rather, the understanding of the experience is consistent with the tenets of the system.[59] In philosophy of science, W. V. O. Quine and other argue for a holistic position in which the basic unit of empirical inquiry is a theory as a whole or even science as a whole. The same way may be even more applicable to mysticism; that is, it may be that evidence for a position will be the adequacy of the conceptual unit as a whole: the parts may not be totally isolatable, and so cumulative weight and basic decisions—not formal justification—will prevail.

One consequence of this is that, contra William James, the acceptability of a mystical position would not be greater for one who has undergone a mystical experience than for those who have not.

Mystical experiences may be replicable by all other people, but no new experiential data will in principle be produced. Even if only those who have had such experiences have the psychological motivation to endorse a mystical position, the experience is not conclusive proof of a position—a web of arguments is necessary. Because of this, if it is reasonable for some people to make certain decisions, it is reasonable for all, although the problem returns concerning what is reasonable. The mystical experience does not place some people in a privileged epistemological position in this regard.

Vindication of a whole conceptual and value system may rely upon an appeal to a way of life to which we are committed. The most that can be done to justify any system is to invite others to adopt it, to ask whether these ideals reflect what they want to see realized in the world and how they want to live.[60]

Are rational choices between alternative ways of life ideally possible? Probably not. If for each way of life, its possible effects and the means necessary to bring it about could be known, there would still remain disagreements over the value of each, over the ultimate construction of reality, and hence over which way of life ought to be pursued. Of course conversions do occur. Often psychological and social causes and persuasion are involved, or a mystical experience may occur while a person is under the influence of one system and the experience is taken as proof of that system. Rarely does one convert by means of rational consideration of doctrines and experiences alone.

In the last analysis, the different religious and mystical traditions of the world that have historically survived have earned the status of being legitimate options at present. Various theistic and nontheistic systems, nondualisms, and pluralisms have proven adequate to a significant number of people, whatever their philosophical problems or the survival value of mysticism for an individual or a culture. Not all mystical positions have survived; for example, Buddhist and Advaitin texts discuss mystical traditions that have since died. So, too, the popularity of options has varied from period to period; for example, in India, Advaita Vedānta has gained widespread acceptance only in the last few centuries. Because of the role of group decisions, there has been a weeding out process, but there has been no convergence upon one point of view, or a "progressive problem shift" as in science.[61] The options that have survived account for the experiences and basic values: any one will appear invalid only from the viewpoint of other belief-commitments. No one can be singled out as compelling or strongest in some absolute sense, or even as more probable or plausible since probability calculations simply cannot be applied in matters of basic choices. Judgments will be made and all positions will be without ultimate foundations. Antimystical positions,[62] whether nonreligious or religious, will remain options, too, since even any unanimity among mystics does not guarantee validity (e.g., all people might suffer the same persuasive delusion under the same conditions) or determine the significance of the experience.[63]

In the evolution of human thought, the present options may prove to be temporary and obsolete; other religious positions or conceptual systems may develop in light of other cultural factors. A consensus may form, although consensus does not guarantee truth—before the sixteenth century all European astronomers were Ptolemists. The alternative is that a pluralistic situation will continue: different human constructions will survive, each accounting for all the data in light of different fundamental beliefs, values, and concerns—and each providing a way of life for different people.

Chapter 2

Knowledge and Unknowing in the Īśa Upaniṣad

Translating *Īśa Upaniṣad* 9–11 is not difficult to do:

> 9 They enter blind darkness who worship nescience (*avidyā*), and into even (*iva*) greater darkness than that [enter they] who delight in knowledge (*vidyā*).
>
> 10 Other indeed, they say, than knowledge; other, they say, than nescience. Thus we have heard from the wise ones who have announced it to us.
>
> 11 Knowledge and nescience: who knows (*veda*) both together, having crossed over death (*mṛtyṃ tīrtvā*) by means of nescience (*avidyayā*), he reaches immortality (*aṃṛtam*) by means of knowledge (*vidyayā*).

Understanding this passage, however, is difficult. "*Vidyā*" in the *Upaniṣads* is usually taken to mean knowledge of Brahman or the Self (*ātman*), that is, final and unalterable knowledge of reality, unless it is explicitly connected to a more limited topic. "*Avidyā*" in Indian thought in general usually means either (1) absence of knowledge, that is, ignorance of some doctrine or fact (as is the most natural interpretation of "*avidyā*" in *Chāndogya Upaniṣad* I.1.10), or (2) an active falsification impeding *vidyā* (as in *Yoga Sūtra* II.5 or *Aṅguttara Nikāya* IV.52).[1] It has been variously translated as "ignorance," "blindness," "unwisdom," "no-knowledge," "non-knowledge," "un-knowledge," and "nescience"—all with negative connotations. But employing these definitions of the terms "*vidyā*" and "*avidyā*" here leads only to problems: How can knowledge of Brahman lead to darkness (v. 9)? Why is the result of nescience needed too (v. 11)? Why can we not be satisfied with the result of knowledge alone? Letting "*vidyā*" mean everyday knowledge (thereby coming close to the second variety of *avidyā*) does no better: How does this mundane knowledge effect immortality? And again, why is the result of nescience needed?

For Śaṁkara, *vidyā* here cannot be *brahmavidyā* since knowledge of Brahman cannot lead to any darkness, let alone a greater darkness than that connected with nescience. In his commentaries upon these verses, he equates *avidyā* with rituals (*karman*), as does Rāmānuja, and *vidyā* only with knowledge of the gods (*devas*).[2] The immortality obtained is not true immortality; it is only becoming one with these gods. Śaṁkara has to give different meanings to "nescience," "knowledge," and "immortality" to reconcile this passage with his nondualistic system; but equating *avidyā* with the Vedic sense of *karman* does show that he saw a positive, if limited, intent of *avidyā* here.

Contemporary commentators have tried other ploys to show that both knowledge and nescience alone are insufficient. For example, Paul Thieme sees ignorance serving a purpose, too: for living our mortal lives, we need to acknowledge separateness, as it were.[3] This would be the only instance in the *Upaniṣads* which stressed needing separation. Also this gives a new meaning to "*avidyā*." Nescience is not simply making distinctions. The "wise ones" who know how to communicate needed to make linguistic distinctions. Distinctions per se are not nescience, but the misreading of their status, that is, being unaware of a reality behind the surface appearances or taking the appearances as the final reality. *Vidyā,* to use the Advaitic explanation, shows distinctions to be similar in status to the images in dreams: they occur, but are not indicative of reality. No endorsement of the nescience-governed life—a life without *vidyā*—occurs anywhere else in Indian literature. Nor does Thieme's interpretation explain how knowledge leads to darkness, unless such an endorsement is to be implied.

In the standard English translations of the *Upaniṣads*, the problems of understanding this passage are indicated but not resolved. Thus, Robert Hume translates "*avidyā*" in verse 9 as "ignorance" (his customary translation of the term), but in verses 10 and 11 switches to "non-knowledge" as the translation.[4] This clearly suggests that he thinks the usual sense of the term is not intended. Sarvepalli Radhakrishnan and Charles Moore leave Hume's translation unaltered.[5]

In general, the established understandings of this passage by both Western and Indian scholars can be summarized along these lines: The problems with verse 9 are neutralized in the following ways: (1) The term "*vidyā*" is construed as "*brahmavidyā*" and "*iva*" (following Śaṁkara) as "as it were" (that is, those who are attached to *brahmavidyā* enter a realm which only seems like greater darkness to someone within the realm of nescience). (2) "*Vidyā* is construed as "sophistry" (that is, an erroneous "knowledge" of some kind). If "*vidyā*" is meant to denote any sort of sophistry, then "*iva*" need not be interpreted in the preceding manner: for those persons who are aware of their own ignorance of something may not go as far wrong as those who are actually wrong but think they are correct. Still, how this flawed "knowledge" is to be differentiated from *avidyā* is never explained.[6] The *Kaṭha Upaniṣad* I.2.5 (as well as *Muṇḍaka Up.* I.2.8, *Maitrī Up.* VII.9) refers to those people who think themselves to be wise (*dhīra*) and learned (*paṇḍita*), but it does not explicate the role of *avidyā* or this sophistry in attaining immortality. (3) Another maneuver is to maintain that the sense of "*vidyā*" changes from verse 9 to verse 11 (from sophistry to *brahmavidyā*). This sounds like an ad hoc reaction, but may be correct. (4) Finally, this passage is sometimes taken as a condemnation of one-sidedness, as the first half of the *Īśa* can also be understood: we need both *brahmavidyā* and everyday knowledge or works (*avidyā*)—knowledge both of the one and the many—to function properly. However, as mentioned earlier, this would go directly against the other strands of Upaniṣadic thought.

In addition to problems already mentioned, the stumbling block for all these interpretations is verse 11. When "crossing over death" (*mṛtyuṃ tīrtvā*) was discussed in the *Bṛhadāraṇyaka Upaniṣad* (I.3.11–16), it was considered to be something positive occurring as part of a process of transformation accomplished by knowledge, as is true, too, in the images contained in *Chāndogya Upaniṣad* VIII.1.3 and VIII.4.1,2. That is to say, there is at least a temporary transcendence, overcoming, or escape from the power of death. Here, "crossing over death" cannot be equivalent to "gaining immortality," or else why would both be mentioned and connected with different operations (that of *avidyā* and of *vidyā*); but it is part of the process of gaining immortality. Within the context of Upaniṣadic thought, how could ignorance, the falsification hiding knowledge, or acknowledging apparent separateness succeed in achieving this? If "crossing over death" is meant to convey a continuation of the process of rebirth by means of a "redeath" (that is, crossing over the intermediate state to a new rebirth), then such nescience would certainly accomplish this. But how is it to be coupled with knowledge in reaching immortality? Why would such nescience be needed?

And why is "crossing over death" said to be accomplished by destruction (*vināśa*) in verse 14, if the continuance of the cycle of rebirths is intended?

Verse 11 cannot mean simply that we need to know two facts—that by nescience the cycle of rebirths continues and that by knowledge one attains immortality. This is so because the verse tells how one person reaches immortality: (1) crossing over (*tīrtvā,* in form an indeclinable participle) mortality by means of nescience (*avidyayā,* the instrumental case), he reaches (*aśnute,* finite verbal form) immortality by means of knowledge (*vidyayā,* instrumental again). If two isolated processes were merely being mentioned, the verbs would be of the same grammatical form, not of forms connecting them. Knowing (*veda*) *vidyā* and *avidyā* may mean: (1) knowing their nature, (2) controlling them, or (3) knowing what is knowledge and what is not; but nevertheless, the verse says death is crossed not by knowledge of *avidyā,* but by *avidyā* itself, and immortality is gained by knowledge, not knowledge of knowledge.

There is an alternative possibility of what this portion of the *Iśa Upaniṣad* means which is based upon the following premises: *vidyā* is *brahmavidyā* throughout the passage and of utmost importance; escaping the cycle of rebirths and attaining immortality is the goal, as it is in the rest of the *Upaniṣads*; "crossing over death" is positive; and the *Īśa* means what it says in claiming that *both* knowledge and nescience are necessary.[7]

This alternative interpretation is suggested by the works of a middle Eastern Christian Neo-Platonist. In *De mystica theologia,* Dionysius the Pseudo-Areopagite spoke of a "divine ignorance" (Greek, *agnosia*), whereby we "un-know" or "unlearn" the normal content of our awareness in order that an awareness of God may flow in.[8] In Dionysius' words, we need to unknow "this" and "that," thereby permitting God's "ray of darkness" to enter in. To apply this to the *Īśa Upaniṣad,* we need to empty ourselves of all dualistic understanding (the *a-vidyā* phase), and to be filled by the knowledge of Brahman (the *vidyā* phase). Each phase has its unique result, and both are required. Emptying does not itself achieve immortality, and if we become attached to the knowledge without seeing the necessary role *avidyā* plays, we shall end up in greater darkness: without the emptying phase, the mind is filled with dualistic clutter and the enlightening knowledge cannot occur. Unknowing (emptying the mind of all normal content) and knowledge (the positive replacement) lead to immortality only together.

The key to the justification of this interpretation lies in *Bṛhadāraṇyaka Upaniṣad* IV.4. That there is a close relationship between the whole of this early *Upaniṣad* and the later *Īśa* is undeniable: both belong to the *Śatapatha Brāhmaṇa;* two of the *Īśa's* seventeen or eighteen verses (verses 9, 15) are found in the *Bṛhadāraṇyaka* (IV.4.10 and V.15.1 respectively) and a third (verse 3) is very close (to IV.4.11). No other such correlation can be made between the *Īśa* and another *Upaniṣad.*

In the *Bṛhadāraṇyaka Upaniṣad* IV.4.1–2, an instance of the emptying phase is discussed. When the inner self turns away from sense-experience at death, there is an unknowing or nondistinguishing of forms (*arūpajña*).[9] The next verses make it clear that the compound "*a-rūpa-jña*" is not to be interpreted to mean "knowing the formless" (*arūpa*): the dying person is becoming one (*ekībhavati*); he cannot sense, think, or understand. He is becoming one with understanding (*vijñāna*) itself, and consequently one with Brahman (IV.4.4–5). Upon death, one throws away this body and dispels ignorance (*avidā avidyā*) (IV.4.3–4). Thereupon one's knowledge determines what occurs (in conjunction with one's previous actions for those persons without *vidyā*). If a dead person does not know Brahman, he is returned to the cycle of rebirths; he is not tranquil and his desires create a new rebirth (a reemergence from Brahman), just as on a larger scale desire (*kāma*) was a creative force for the emergence of the entire cosmos in some Vedic speculation. But knowers of Brahman (*brahmavidas*) are not reborn (IV.4.8). Those who know Brahman before death become immortal, while the destruction (*vinaṣṭi*) is great for those who do not (IV.4.14), that is, the latter are reembodied out of the merging with Brahman. Brahman can only be seen by the mind because there is no diversity there: he goes from death to death who sees diversity (IV.4.19). This is to say, an unknowing of diversity is a necessary prerequisite for the filling accomplished by the knowledge of Brahman. At death, for such a person there is immortality, not rebirth. Having understood (*vijñāya*) Brahman, a wise Brāhmaṇa cultivates discernment (*prajñā*) (IV.4.21) for, as the discourse ends, "who knows thus (*ya evaṃ veda*) becomes (*bhavati*) fearless Brahman" (IV.4.25).

That this passage in the *Bṛhadāraṇyaka* is relevant to *vidyā* and *avidyā* in the *Īśa* may be revealed by the fact that verse 9 of the *Īśa* is found here (*Bṛhadāraṇyaka Up.* IV.4.10). More particularly, this is one of only three occurrences of "*avidyā*" in the whole *Bṛhadāraṇyaka* (the others being in IV.3.20 and IV.4.4), although elsewhere it does employ other forms of the prefix "*a-*" plus the root "*vid*" to indicate the lack of knowledge. Thus, perhaps a connection of the two ideas was noticed.

This section of the *Bṛhadāraṇyaka* also helps clarify the passage following *Īśa Up*. 9–11:

> 12 They enter blind darkness who worship destruction (*asambhūti*), and into even greater darkness than that [enter they] who delight in merging (*sambhūti*).
> 13 Other indeed, they say, than merging (*sambhava*); other, they say, than destruction (*asambhava*). Thus we have heard from the wise ones who have announced it to us.
> 14 Merging and destruction (*vināśa*): who knows (*veda*) both together, having crossed over death by means of destruction, he reaches immortality by means of merging.

The passage is exactly the same as 9–11, except for the substitutions for "*vidyā*" and "*avidyā*." "*Sambhūti*" is sometimes translated as "rebirth" and "*asambhūti*" as "lack of rebirth."[10] But the same sort of problems as with verses 9–11 recur: Why do those who worship a lack of rebirths enter darkness? Is that not the objective?[11] And again why are both rebirth and a lack of rebirths necessary? The primary meaning of "*sam-*" affixed to the root "*bhū*" is "coming together," "meeting," or "merging." "*Vināśa*" in verse 14 makes clear the intended meaning of "*asambhūti*" and "*asambhava*": the dissolution of the individual as a separate unit. "*Sambhūti*" should be construed as "merging with Brahman," if the treatment in *Bṛhadāraṇyaka Up*. IV.4.14 of destruction (*vinaṣṭi*) of the person as a unit and the subsequent becoming what we know is a trustworthy guide: merging with Brahman occurs routinely in dreamless sleep and after death, but only one who *knows* Brahman remains immortal, and conversely remaining merged with Brahman is the only route of becoming open to one who knows.

The *Bṛhadāraṇyaka Up*. IV.4 and *Īśa Up*. 12–14 deal with the unknowing of forms (*arūpajña/avidyā*), which occurs naturally at death with the dissolution of the bodily unit. But to bring knowledge to this event, we would need to see no diversity beforehand. The *Bṛhadāraṇyaka Up*. IV.4.19 claims we should see no diversity here (*iha*, in this world), and verse 14 confirms that knowledge is possible here (*iha*). Thus, an unknowing of diversity or an emptying of this or that is possible in this life, too.

With all this in mind, we can make a structural study of verses 9–14 of the *Īśa Upaniṣad*. Looking at the structure of 9–11 and 12–

14, we see that *vidyā* is correlated with *sambhūti* (*sambhava*), and *avidyā* with *asambhūti* (*asambhava, vināśa*). In addition, by looking at verses 11 and 14, we see that "crossing death" is accomplished by nescience and dissolution, while immortality is achieved by knowledge and becoming/merging. These findings can be summarized in a table:

emptying phase:	→	*filling phase:*
unknowing of forms (*avidyā*)		knowledge of Brahman (*vidyā*)
dissolution		merging
↓		↓
crossing death		immortality

The results of each process (the emptying and the filling) are different, and both are necessary. The middle entries (dissolution and merging) occur automatically at death, but the others must be accomplished. The entry in the left column is the prerequisite for the occurrence of the event in the right column on the same line, but it does not bring it about: only with unknowing is one in a position to gain knowledge, and only by escaping the power of death can one become immortal.

Therefore, the intent of *Īśa Up*. 9–14 as one unit, with *Bṛhadāraṇyaka Up*. IV.4 as the key, is this: There must first be an unknowing of forms (*arūpajñā*/*avidyā*) so that knowledge of Brahman (*vidyā*) may occur; if this happens, then with the automatic destruction of the bodily unit and merging with Brahman, death will be escaped by the unknowing and dissolution, and immortality will be gained by the knowledge and merging. "Crossing death" means one is in a position to escape rebirth if one has the knowledge: to gain immortality knowledge and merging are necessary, and to achieve these unknowing and dissolution must occur first. Both phases are required—attachment to only one will not succeed.

Other passages in the *Bṛhadāraṇyaka* lend some support to aspects of this analysis. A common formula throughout the book is "who knows thus (*ya evaṃ veda*) becomes (*bhavati*)": who knows *x* or the nature of *x* becomes or obtains *x*. Thus, for example, *Bṛhadāraṇyaka Up* I.4.9: by the knowledge of Brahman (*brahmavidyā*), one becomes all. The *Bṛhadāraṇyaka* in contrast to the *Chāndogya* has much that is negative in tone (*asat* versus *sat* more often beginning the cosmogony, "great sayings" of "*neti neti*" versus "*tat tvam asi,*" being desireless versus having all mundane desires fulfilled, etc.) and more on the process of becoming/merging. The *Bṛhadāraṇyaka*

Up. IV.3.19–32 asserts that in deep, dreamless sleep, we cannot sense, think about, or understand because there is no duality there; but the Self which understands is still there—indeed, we have become the nondual seer. An unknowing of objects has occurred, but the *knowledge* of Brahman is not present when we are in that state.

To deal with another passage, *Bṛhadāraṇyaka Up.* II.4.12–14 says that the Self (*ātman,* the Lord or One of the *Īśa*) consists of nothing but understanding (*vijñāna-ghana*): We arise out of it and at death vanish into it. After death, there is no ideation (*saṃjñā*), since all ideas are of a dualistic nature. Where there is duality (*dvaita*), one senses, thinks about, and understands another. Where everything has become the self, there is nothing by which one can sense or understand. An unknowing of forms has again occurred. By what can one understand the one who understands (the inner controller, the self)? The words for *understanding* come from "*vi-*" plus forms from the root "*jñā.*" "*Jñāna*" without a prefix does not occur in the *Bṛhadāraṇyaka;* it means to know by acquaintance (Fr. *connaitre,* Ger. *kennen*).[12] The prefix "*vi-*" emphasizes the separation: "*x* understands *y*" conveys this. *Vidyā,* cognate with the Latin "*video,*" contrasts with this as direct, nonreflective knowledge gained in experiences. It also has the power to transform the experiencer: whether ignorance or desire is the cause of rebirth, *vidyā* (and only *vidyā*) will end the process. It is the ability to realize, in the sense to accomplish or obtain, something: One becomes what one knows. The difference between the two concepts is roughly equivalent to discriminating (understanding) the meaning of a claim, and seeing (knowing) that the claim is true. When there is a merging with understanding itself (II.4.12,14), that is, where everything has become the self, the space required for understanding (or sensing) is obliterated. The self is beyond the dualistic situation (compare, *Īśa Up.* 4). Thus, the connection between merging and the absence of awareness of this or that is again reiterated.[13]

Even the famous passage concerning becoming like a child has at least some relevance (*Bṛhadāraṇyaka Up.* III.5.1): To become a true Brāhmaṇa, one must become disenchanted (*nirvidya*) with learning (*pāṇḍitya,* not *vidyā,* but "pedantic" worldly wisdom again), and desire to become like a child; having become disenchanted with the learned and childlike states, one becomes a silent one (*muni*); having become disenchanted with the nonsilence and silence, one becomes a Brāhmaṇa. The roles of unlearning and silence, and the need to go beyond them are what is of significance from this passage for the purpose at hand.

Whatever support or complications the rest of the *Bṛhadāraṇyaka* and *Īśa* may bring, the connection between *Īśa Up.* 9–14 and *Bṛhadāraṇyaka Up.* IV.4 still remains illuminating. Using the term "*avidyā*" to designate a positive role in the process leading to immortality should not appear too startling. There was no fixed religious vocabulary at the time of the *Īśa's* composition, the more established uses of the term "*avidyā*" coming only later. Furthermore, the *Upaniṣads* themselves had no settled way to indicate a lack of knowledge—the *Kena,* even in a verse almost identical to *Īśa Up.* 10, used another word (*avidita,* I.4). The *Īśa's* attempt to give *avidyā* anything other than a totally negative role may have been the only such attempt—it is certainly not readily understood and easily leads to confusion. In the West, Dionysius' effort to give "*agnosia*" a meaning other than its established one never became overly popular in mystical circles.

But in defense of the suggestion advanced here, it must be pointed out that it is the *Īśa Upaniṣad* itself which ascribes *avidyā* a positive and necessary function in conjunction with *vidyā*. The question is how to interpret this function. Pointing out fatal difficulties in past attempts to understand this passage adds nothing to the plausibility of the alternative offered here, but it should make us more open to new possible interpretations of the familiar. In the work of Dionysius and in the *Bṛhadāraṇyaka,* unknowing has a positive role in the mystical process. If we make the problematic, but not implausible, assumption that the same holds here (coupled with the less controversial assumptions stated earlier and the value of consistency of meaning throughout the passages under study), everything within the passage at issue falls into place, and the passage is seen to be consistent with the more common Upaniṣadic doctrines.

Part II

Mysticism and Reason

Chapter 3

Rationality and Mysticism

Do standards of rationality vary in different historical and cultural contexts? Or is there only one way of thinking which qualifies as being "rational"? The study of mysticism offers an opportunity to address these questions in a way which in one important respect is superior to the history of science or cultural anthropology, namely, the narrow range of allegedly cognitive experiences that is mysticism's central experiential focus. The term "mysticism" has been used to refer to everything from mythology to metaphysics. But here the term will refer only to the values, action-guides, and belief-commitments constituting those ways of life oriented around experiences (both sensory and introvertive) which lessen the sensory and conceptual structuring of ordinary experiences and thereby allegedly permit an insight into the nature of reality. Examples will be presented from a variety of systems developed around the range of these experiences.

The discussions that have become important since the work of Walter Stace concerning the distinctions drawn between types of mystical experiences and of the role of concepts in mystical experiences will not be entered into here.[1] Instead, as discussed earlier, the experiential component of some mystical experiences may remain constant regardless of the historical or cultural setting, and all mystical experiences may have an experiential component with many features in common, regardless of whether cultural structuring informs the experience itself or is independently applied (consciously or unconsciously) after the experience itself by the experiencer. In this situation, the historical and cultural variations in mystical interpretative systems can then be studied as human constructs bearing directly on the issue of whether there is one standard of rationality or many.

To be rational is to be reasonable. But there is an amazing lack of consensus on just what this means, or even what the issues involved in analyzing rationality are. Here, the general topic of "rationality" will be broken down into four somewhat more manageable subtopics: (a) the possibility of understanding other cultures (translation); (b) the structure of reasoning when operating unconnected to facts (logic); (c) the interaction of reasoning and factual claims (styles of reasoning); (d) and the problem raised by the comparison of competing beliefs (relativism). As will become apparent, these subtopics are integrally interwoven and so cannot be totally separated.

The issues will be approached first by setting out problems posed by philosophers and anthropologists concerning any alleged universal rationality, and then by discussing what mystics themselves say, if anything, about the issues and what bearing the comparative study of mysticism may have upon them.

Translation and Incommensurability

If different languages involve different standards of rationality, how is translation possible? Conversely, if translation between languages is possible, must there not be only one standard of rationality? Both vocabulary and grammar present potential difficulties. Concerning vocabulary, different languages contain different categories for ordering experiences and thus contain different inventories of what constitutes reality. If there is no neutral vocabulary to express each conceptual system, then the different systems are incommensurable (i.e., lacking a common ground into which systems can be translated without loss).[2] It may not be that all terms gain their meaning from the doctrinal system in which they are embedded as a whole; instead, most terms may be easily translated. Nevertheless, it is not possible to define all high-level theoretical terms of one belief-system in the vocabulary of another. This problem is broader than that between different natural languages since it also encompasses the problems of translating one metaphysical or scientific theory into terms of another (e.g., "sun" in the Ptolemaic and Copernican systems does not mean the same thing although the referents are the same). Both the dimension of meaning (the sense of terms) and the referential dimension of terms (the range of application) present problems. Benjamin Whorf advances a thesis concerning grammar which would produce a further problem for translation: there is an "implicit metaphysics" in the grammatical structure of different languages such that the background linguistic system shapes ideas, not merely voices them.[3] Thus, in "Standard Average European" things (objects) predominate while in Hopi events do; mutually untranslatable languages are thereby produced.[4]

Basic problems can be raised as to whether untranslatability can determine the general issue of rationality. First, if conceptual systems are incommensurable, this does not help decide whether the holders of any of them are rational or not. We could not tell which systems were rational from this fact alone. Rationality involves more how the terms are handled than whether they can be mapped from one language into another language. Second, even if different languages cannot be translated, still speakers of different languages can understand each other. Thus, Thomas Kuhn thinks that holders of different scientific theories can understand each other, compare the theories, and genuinely discuss the differences. So too, Whorf is able to express in English how the Hopi see the world; the expressions may be awkward, but he is not bound by the grammar of English. Our native language may contain our habitual categories for dissecting the world; these categories, however, have not presented an absolute barrier in understanding others or in the development of science. Thus, untranslatability would not present a barrier to determining if the other speakers were rational.

The study of mysticism can illustrate the above problems. For example, the rapid failure of the *ko-i* method of translating Indian Buddhist texts into Chinese by substituting Taoist terms for Buddhist ones highlights the problem of the incommensurability of terms central to highly developed doctrines in various mystical systems. This presents difficulties not only for advocates of "perennial philosophy" but also for translation more generally. Translating core concepts such as "*puruṣa*" from Sāṁkhya-Yoga and "*ātman*" from Advaita Vedānta with the English word "self" does not circumvent the problems involved in removing highly refined concepts from the context which gives them meaning. Even when two mystical systems use the same term from within one language-group (e.g., "*ātman*" in Advaita Vedānta and in Buddhism), each mystical system still may use it with a unique sense and reference. "Self" may seem a convenient shorthand for the further explanations that are necessary when discussing concepts from a particular doctrinal system, but it is misleading as a translation without an explanation since various Western philosophical and unphilosophical ideas will be read into the term. Many terms may be incommensurable with any contemporary English terminology (e.g., *karman* or *nirvāṇa* or Plotinus's *nous*) and thus remain in the transliterated form when texts are translated; others may require explanations for whatever English placeholder is conveniently substituted (e.g., "wisdom" or "insight" for *prajñā*). Explaining the terms is possible in English even if they are not translatable in a convenient one-to-one fashion into any contemporary European language.

The Whorfian idea of an implicit metaphysics within a language is not supported by the fact that very different mystical systems have been conceived by speakers of the same language (e.g., Advaita Vedānta and Sāṁkhya-Yoga in Sanskrit). The variety of explicit metaphysics statable in the same language renders at best unhelpful this notion of an implicit metaphysics forcing certain concepts or producing one mystical system as the most natural reflection of a language's grammatical structure. Highly specialized sets of categories and uses of terms unique to particular mystical groups often develop. So, too, concepts behind terms evolve (e.g., "*brahman*" evolving through Vedic texts to Advaita Vedānta) rather than remain fixed. Languages may present natural ways of looking at the world and experiences, thereby making certain responses to culturally-invariant mystical experiences seem natural and also affecting the cross-cultural adaptation of religions.[5] But while accentuating different aspects of the world may affect the formation of ideas, historically this has not prevented the creation of fundamentally different systems within one language (even contemporaneously). Nor has it prevented the understanding of those systems by others both inside and outside that language.

The problems which incommensurability and grammar present for translation do not address the basic problem which mystics find with language—that language by its nature objectifies a reality which is not in fact distinct from the speaker nor divisible into separate, independently existing parts.[6] The metaphysics implicit in language in this sense in common to all languages rather than varying with different language-groups. Thus, mystics could not devise new languages without this problem remaining. Furthermore, mystics still find language useful, that is, they can use the particular language present in their culture without projecting whatever divisions it makes onto the actual nature of reality. In this fundamental sense, no language is more "mystical" than any other. Mystics can utilize any given language for the particular metaphysical systems they devise. Since this approach involves the underlying issue of how concepts work rather than issues of specific concepts and grammars, translation is not a fundamental problem in this regard.[7] Nor can the issue of the mystics' view of how language works be easily related to the issue of rationality. That is, the writings of mystics can clearly illustrate the problems of translation discussed above because of the experiential component common to mystical systems, but whether the mystics' attitude toward language is rational, irrational, or expresses an alternative standard of rationality cannot be determined without looking at the other issues involved in discussing rationality.

Logic and Paradox

Basic to the idea of rationality are the notions of consistency and coherence. That is, part of being rational relates to the structure of one's beliefs rather than to its content—rational systems of belief must be non-contradictory, both in small segments and as a whole. Thus, logical relations become central to the notion of rationality. In particular, certain principles of logic are usually deemed necessary to rationality: identity, non-contradiction (nothing can be both x and non-x), excluded middle (everything is either x or non-x), and truth-preserving inference (if A is true, what is "deducible" from A alone is also true).[8]

Just as all physical objects tacitly obey the law of gravity, are these principles of logic implicit in any language or any communicable system of thought even if the speaker is not aware of them? Or are the principles embodied in the grammar of certain languages only? Whorf asserts that these "laws of correct thinking" are not universal but only reflect the background character of Indo-European languages.[9] Others would argue that logic is not the reflection of a particular language but is merely an explicit articulation of the rules by which any language works.[10] Thus, it is possible to find examples of ideas which can be consistently stated in one symbol-system but not in another, although each symbol-system in itself still operates by these same rules of logic.[11] A third position is that we must assume that other belief-systems are not incoherent or inconsistent—we must impute rationality, for otherwise no understanding is possible.[12] This last position appears to impose dogmatically an answer to what should be an empirical question concerning alternative standards of rationality. Nevertheless, it can be rightly asked whether we would ever accept inconsistent translations or whether we would instead persist until attaining a translation which makes sense to us (thereby fulfilling our basic principles of logic) before rejecting or accepting another belief-system for other reasons.

All of these positions concerning logic raise problems for the claim that we can empirically answer the question of whether logic is universal or culturally bound. The study of mysticism can contribute to this discussion, however, since mystical writings are often taken to be the paradigm of irrationality: it is often claimed that because mystics place soteriological goals (related to the meaning of life or to the end of suffering) in a central place in their ways of life, they are uninterested in such mundane concerns as logic. Or it is claimed that mystical experiences transcend all duality and hence transcend logic. Mystics are said to feel unconstrained by logic or to delight in paradoxes. And it is certainly true that other considerations keep logic from being a topic of major concern to mystics. While mystics may be familiar with the thought of contemporaneous thinkers who deal with laws of argument, the most likely reaction is that of Chuang tzu to the sophists of his day—to play off their work to reveal its limitations.[13] Thus, if mystical works can be understood as implicitly conforming to the principles of logic, this would be some *prima facie* evidence that any belief-system communicable to other people may be logical and, hence, that logic is indeed universal rather than Western (although the possibility that commentators are merely imposing their own order on the mystics still cannot be ruled out).

To show that mysticism and logic are not incompatible, it first must be understood that logic applies to statements, not to experiences or alleged realities. No experience or reality, mystical or otherwise, is itself "logical" or "self-contradictory." Rather only claims about the mystical made while mystics are operating in the realm of distinctions are logical or illogical. The issue thus becomes whether mystics implicitly follow the canons of logic or not in their statements.

It is undeniable that enlightened mystics can resort to arguments structured by "Western" logic if the occasion demands it, even when mystical topics are being discussed. In the *Milindapañha,* the Buddhist monk Nāgasena addresses questions often reflecting a concern with the direct violation of the principle of noncontradiction in the form of two-pronged dilemmas. For example, he reconciles the apparently conflicting statements that the Buddha claimed to have no teachers and to have five teachers by asserting that none of the Buddha's teachers instructed the enlightening knowledge and thus he had no teacher of that (*Mlp* 235–236). Many passages also implicitly involve the principle of excluded middle in the form, "if *x,* then *y;* if non-*x,* then non-*y.*" We may not find all the reconciliations convincing, but this is not to deny the logical skeleton tacitly in the structure of the argument.

Other sorts of argumentation can also be shown to be not illogical. To focus simply on the Buddhist tradition, various strategies are open to the charge of irrationality. The skillful means (*upāya-kauśala*) employed by the Buddha in leading listeners to enlightenment, and the distinction between conventional truth (*saṃvṛtisatya*) and absolute truth (*paramāthasatya*) may be thought at best to reflect logic as a means to an end and, therefore, of no final significance. But giving a provisional answer to listeners unprepared to understand the ultimately correct answer or distinguishing between levels of truth is not to assert contradictory claims. The issues are whether the claims in their context are logical and whether any ultimate claims can be stated in a non-contradictory manner. And in terms of these issues, these Buddhist strategies are not *per se* illogical.

One Buddhist strategy which has been accused of being irrational, or of proposing an alternative to two-valued logic, involves the "four alternatives" (*catuṣkoṭi*). This strategy consists of rejecting any answer to certain questions—claiming that none "fit the case" (*upeti*)—even though the proposed alternative answers exhaust the logical possibilities. Thus, in response to the question of whether a Buddha exists after death, the Buddha rejects with the answer "Not so" (*mā h'evam*) the alternatives that a Buddha exists, does not exist, both exists and does not exist, and neither exists nor not exists (*Majjhima-nikāya* I.485–487). This appears clearly to violate the principle of non-contradiction, and numerous attempts have been made to show that it does not.[14] (Indeed, so many different applications of symbolic logic to this strategy have been proposed in order to show its rationality that these applications are especially open to the charge that we are imposing our logic upon other belief-systems.) Another option, which does not ascribe too much sophistication to early Buddhists, is to view the Buddha here as concerned only with ending attachments and not with logic.[15] The Buddha is simply stating as strongly as possible that no terms, which might be taken as referring to an independently existing entity, are applicable to a Buddha after death. The four alternatives would then be an instance of skillful means used when thinking of an object or of its absence would be misleading to the unenlightened. The style of reasoning is different from that of modern Western thinkers, but the strategy is not illogical for assuming that it would be misleading to describe *x* by predicate *y* or by the denial of *y* because either way the listener would still be thinking in terms of *y*.

Other Buddhist strategies are also implicitly logical in structure. For example, Nāgārjuna is often assessed as using logic (without advancing any substantive views of his own) to destroy the views of others. Whether this assessment is correct is open to question, but at least it can be shown that Nāgārjuna's argumentation readily conforms to the principles of logic, whatever the ultimate purpose or valuation of this argumentation.[16] In general, as J. F. Staal concludes, the idea of Buddhist irrationality does not withstand examination.[17]

Examples of ways of arguing could be presented from other mystical traditions, but it may be more profitable simply to turn to the matter most fundamental to mystics' supposed irrationality—their use of paradox. Paradox is not an inadvertent inconsistency, but is, instead, the conscious use of self-contradiction. It can be used as a soteriological device whose purpose is to free the listener from thinking in terms of distinctly existing entities. Zen *kuans/koans* are examples of deliberately absurd statements, some of which are paradoxical, employed as part of religious training. To be effective for the listener, this strategy must presuppose that the listener accepts the applicability of the principle of non-contradiction to mundane matters—otherwise there would be no need for a special paradoxical strategy, when it comes to the mystical, to direct the listener's mind away from the mundane. The issue at hand, however, is whether the cognitive content of paradoxical statements can be stated consistently, if the occasion calls for it, or whether self-contradiction is dictated by the nature of mysticism.

Probably all mystical paradoxes can be given non-contradictory interpretations.[18] Each paradox must be examined to determine the proper method for defusing the apparent conflict. The most common resolution is to interpret the apparently conflicting claims as referring to two different subjects and thus not actually conflicting. These interpretations would be open to the charge of imposing logical order on true paradoxes, if mystical statements in principle had to be self-contradictory because of the experiences or realities involved. That is, if, when the human mind attempts to comprehend the ultimate, our concept-systems all fail, then Tertullian's "*credo quia impossible*" would be the only proper response. From the mystics' point of view, any statement made in any language will involve distinctions, and, thus, could not mirror a reality which is free of all distinctions.

The problem with the mystics' position on paradox, however, is that it itself is another instance of the problem which mystics find with language in general: just as mystics can use a language without projecting its distinctions onto reality, so here they should be able to speak of the mystical without such a projection. Because the mystical is "wholly other" than the mundane, the unenlightened may be especially susceptible to being misled when the mystical is discussed, and thus paradox may seem the natural way of speaking about it. But words need not reflect the subject to which they refer in a one-to-one manner to make meaningful statements about it. And since logic (and hence paradox) is a matter of language rather than a matter of experiences and realities, paradox is not required by the nature of any experiences or the realities. In these circumstances, the possibility of non-contradictory interpretations of apparent paradoxes should not be ruled out. Thus, if some statements by mystics do not tacitly follow the principles of logic, it may very well be because of considerations unrelated to the issue of the possible rationality of mystical belief-systems, not because mystics or their belief-systems are inherently irrational.

Styles of Reasoning and Universal Reason

The step beyond the logical structure of arguments is to look at full arguments themselves. Rationality involves more than logic—it involves the use of factual claims and the relation between beliefs in justifying one's beliefs. It may be that the mental steps each person subjectively employs in reasoning are unique to that person, but are there common (and hence objective) standards in the process of reasoning? Do people in different cultures reach different conclusions merely because they argue from different premises and have different values or interests, or do they actually "think" (reason) in different ways? That is, are there criteria of proper reasoning applicable in any context or are there in fact alternative criteria? And as a counterpart to the problems mentioned above, would we be able to recognize and acknowledge standards of reasoning which were truly completely different from our own?

The standard of rational thought in the West is often thought to be the certainty of logical deduction and mathematical proof. But problems have been advanced concerning both such basic logical operations as *modus ponens* and completeness in mathematics (e.g., by Gödel's theorem). More generally, no proof is final even in mathematics—"the proofs of one generation are the fallacies of the next."[19] Concerning the application of standards of proper reasoning to more clearly factual matters, natural science is taken to be the paradigm of rationality. The nature of science, however, does not fit an empiricist image. No set of neutral sense-experiences determines the choice between competing theories in a simple manner. Not only is there no one "scientific method," but standards of reasonableness appear to vary with different theories rather than to be timeless.[20] Rationality thereby comes to involve not merely coherence of beliefs or holding one's beliefs open to criticism, but what is "plausible" in light of underlying beliefs and values; metaphysical issues related to the nature of reality become intertwined with the standards of rationality. What is accepted as a "rational," "natural," or "logical" explanation becomes tied to the cultural beliefs of a particular historical period about the nature of the world. Because of the absence of a neutral algorithm determining a choice between competing scientific theories, the currently most popular models of rationality stress both the need to weigh various factors important to science and the role of community in decisions in the evolution of scientific ideas.[21] Science is seen more as a human activity than as a mechanical reading of nature. Argument becomes more a matter of persuasion rather than of compulsion. This lack of factors compelling a decision between competing theories and the role of a "conversion" in a scientist's final decision do not introduce "irrationality" into the core of what is usually taken to be the most rational of activities, but rather redefine what exactly "rationality" is.[22]

An image of rationality which encompasses the historical context of reasoning, the role of judgment and choice, and the role of communal decision-making does not require that all thought be deemed rational. Some people may go beyond reasonable disagreement and adhere to beliefs for which there is no experiential basis, which is adhered to despite all evidence and argument to the contrary, and which cannot be accounted for by any coherent explanation. Not all nonscientific activity falls into such irrationality. Western philosophy and legal decision-making are kinds of activity which can be rational in the above sense although they are not natural sciences.

Turning to activity in other cultures, are there features of reasoning common to different cultural contexts which indicate that rationality is a universal component of belief-systems, or does the study of other belief-systems indicate that rationality is in fact tied to certain beliefs about the world? To Paul Feyerabend, the self-proclaimed Dadaist of philosophy, there are many canons of rationality, no privileged class of good reasons, and no restrictive preferred paradigm.[23] On the other hand, E. E. Evans-Pritchard in describing Zande witchcraft—a cultural system which most modern Western thinkers would find absurd—indicates that the Azande use patterns of inference which follow the same logical rules as we use in reasoning.[24] So, too, in Indian philosophy all schools accept some form of inference (*anumāṇa*). The Nyāya employ a syllogism which, although not Western in form, obeys Western rules of deduction. The premises employed by these nonmodern groups do not affect this structure. What are the limits to rationality in such a situation?

The study of mysticism is valuable in this regard. If in their various styles of reasoning mystics reveal a fundamentally different way in which facts are handled or in the application of reason to facts, they would be exhibiting an alternative standard of rationality or a form of irrationality. This possibility is heightened by the mystics' own sense that their cognitively central experiences transcend language and, hence, reason. In the words of Ernest Nagel, a "consistent mystic cannot hope to establish his claims by argument" since "argument involves the use of analytic reason, and on the mystic's own view reason is incapable of penetrating to the substance of reality."[25] An argument can be made that mystical experiences, like all experiences, underdetermine theory, and, therefore, mystics must provide arguments for their particular interpretations.[26] But more to the point of the present issue, mystics can consistently claim both that reason is no substitute for any experience and that reason can be part of an enlightened way of life (since distinctions are present outside of mystical experiences even after enlightenment). Advancing an argument, perhaps involving reference to mystical experiences, to establish the superiority of one mystical position would then not be inconsistent with being a mystic or evidence of irrationality. Being a mystic would not necessarily be an alternative to being a philosopher.

With regard to the styles of reasoning in mystical texts, one notices that many texts do not appear argumentative in nature. For example, many texts are poetry (partially because of the need to use symbolic language to point to the non-mundane) which is of value to followers, but which is free of any arguments. The *Tao te ching* is an example of a text which, while containing arguments, also contains logical forms to give the appearance of coherence to a disconnected collection of sayings. On the other hand, many texts contain explicit arguments in support of certain positions and against other traditions. For example, the *Yoga-sūtras* and the *Brahma-sūtras* contain only summary statements, but the classical commentaries contain full arguments. Śaṁkara's commentary on the latter contains arguments against the Sāṁkhya-Yogins and the Buddhists which point out the inconsistencies and conflicts with general experience which appear when their doctrines are examined from an Advaitin point of view. The approach is "rational" by the standards discussed above. It is also worth noting that no appeal is made to mystical experiences as a means to correct knowledge (*pramāṇa*). Indeed, in most classical mystical texts, there is no appeal to special experiences as a basis of an argument. Thus, for example, Plotinus's *Enneads* is similar in style to classical Greek and Roman philosophical texts, even if the topics and premises are not the same.

Mystics reflect the concerns of their culture but are not necessarily irrational. Thus, Meister Eckhart, standing in the medieval scholastic tradition, agrees that reason can find proofs for truths revealed in Scripture (although God dwells beyond the limits of the mind).[27] In Buddhism, argument (*tarka*) is rejected as a means to enlightenment, but the Buddha does produce arguments. Appeals to ordinary experiences and conceptual analysis are the basis for arguments in favor of the no-self doctrine (*an-ātman*). Other means of arguing are also employed as aids to the religious quest. Neither skillful means nor the four alternatives discussed above are in principle irrational. Conditioning one's teachings to the level of understanding of the listener is not irrational if some teaching is advanced as the final truth. (Here, the cycle of rebirth, the role of *karman,* and the end of the cycle are not ultimately denied.) So, too, dismissing some questions unanswered, while other questions are dealt with in other ways (*Dīgha-nikāya* III.229; *Aṅguttara-nikāya* I.197, II.46), is not irrational if the teachers have reason to believe that the listeners will be misled by any answer.

In the *Milindapañha,* Nāgasena, in response to very Western-style questions concerning the consistency and plausibility of Buddhist doctrine, answers, not with analogies of attribution or proportionality as were popular in the West, but with similes. For example, the material components of what we take to be a distinct person, "name and form" (*nāmarūpa*), are said to arise together and to depend upon each other just as a yolk and eggshell do (*Mlp* 49). Arguing by simile is usually not very convincing. At best, similes give other instances which make the problematic aspects of the situation in question seem at least plausible. Sometimes this is very valuable in itself, as in explaining that monks do not love their bodies but care for them during the quest for enlightenment, just as they care for unwanted wounds to ensure their continuing health (*Mlp* 73–74). Or sometimes the simile is very closely parallel, as with using the parts of a chariot to explain the idea that names of persons have no independent referent (*Mlp* 25–28). But similes usually do not provide any reason for believing that there is a connection between the matter to be explained and the simile employed (e.g., using the inference of the existence of deceased warriors from the presence of weapons to justify inferring the existence of the Buddha from the presence of teachings attributed to him) (*Mlp* 329–330). This severely limits this style of reasoning, although it does not make it irrational. Indeed, it reveals a concern with relations and an awareness of the problematic aspects of claims, none of which is at all irrational. Mystics may not deal with claims we find problematic (as when Nāgasena explains by simile how rebirth works (*Mlp* 72) but does not deal anywhere with the basic claim of rebirth itself) or may rely on beliefs which we do not accept, but this does not make the structure of their reasoning irrational.

Often mystics appeal to self-evidence or to an article of faith. Śaṁkara finds reasoning to be an unstable foundation for understanding matters that should be realized from Scripture (*śruti*); philosophers constantly contradict each other (*Brahma-sūtra-bhāṣya* II.1.10–11). To the objection that this is itself an instance of reasoning, Śaṁkara replies merely that the Vedas, being eternal, provide the necessary knowledge. This defense involves a premise undefended in this passage concerning the Vedas and is ultimately circular.

Śaṁkara's response may appear irrational and dogmatic, but it should be noted that even in science a degree of dogmatism about the fundamental belief-commitments of a theory (e.g., Newton on forces) may be necessary to research. In addition, science as an enterprise is not merely a trial and error method in empirical matters: science as an approach to reality has metaphysical presuppositions (e.g., reality is objective and can be physically analyzed into discrete entities and processes without distorting its nature), and scientists are no more open-minded about the metaphysics underlying their enterprise than are mystics about theirs. Indeed, a circularity similar to that in mysticism has been attributed to science: empirical evidence is created by a procedure which quotes as its justification the very same evidence it has produced.[28] Similarly, Clifford Geertz sees religious systems in general as defining a reality which believers use in turn to justify the systems themselves.[29] Circularity in one enterprise, of course, cannot be justified by circularity in another, but it may be that some circularity or assumptions cannot be avoided at a basic metaphysical level of any enterprise. To say that fundamental beliefs are irrational because of circularity may require condemning the more basic aspects of natural science, and thereby undercut the metaphysical basis of the paradigm of rational activity. Thus, accepting some circularity at a basic level as rational may be the lesser of two evils. To fulfill the standards of rationality in this situation, all that may be possible is to open one's presuppositions to some criticism and examination, as Karl Popper suggests[30]—if one can accomplish the often difficult task of revealing one's presuppositions as presuppositions. Mystics can be as critical in their context as scientists can be concerning the metaphysical dimension of science. Mysticism differs in degree only, because it involves total ways of life. Thus, its fundamental belief-commitments are more encompassing than those of the limited concerns of science and are correspondingly harder to uproot and discuss critically.

Mystics do not always see the nature of their reasoning in a way that philosophers unconcerned with soteriological goals do. Often both mystical and nonmystical thinkers do not admit (or perhaps even see) the active role of their premises. But the point for the issue at hand is that the mystics' styles of reasoning do not reveal a unique "logic" to mystical thought. Mysticism is not science, since it has different concerns and values. Nevertheless, the primary contemporary philosophical image of science suggests a rationality whose nature would not exclude as irrational how mystics deal with their experiences and beliefs. The premises with which mystics work differ from the paradigm of Western rationality, but mystics do not "think differently." They, too, deal with highly complex systems of beliefs, and for the issue of standards of rationality, there is nothing unique about mystics' reasoning. Their concerns are different, their premises may mix factual and evaluational elements, they may differ in the experiences taken to be cognitively supreme, and they may weigh different cognitive considerations differently. But, as the examples discussed in this section suggest, how mystics handle these elements is not necessarily irrational in this regard. Mystics cannot be condemned as irrational simply because they do not have the same concerns as scientists or any other group.

A complete justification of the rationality of mysticism would also have to justify the premises with which mystics operate. That is not being dealt with here. Rather, all that is being argued is that mystics handle their premises within their accepted frameworks in a rational manner. The beliefs accepted and the way they are handled are interrelated, but the rationality of the latter may be apparent without showing the rationality of the former. In addition, there are limits to rational argument about matters of ultimate belief-commitments. Holding one's beliefs open to criticism is a sign of rationality, but it is difficult for anyone—mystic or nonmystic—to step outside one's basic commitments in order to gain a perspective from which to criticize one's own most deeply held beliefs and values. Debating the basic premises of one's ways of life may not prove especially profitable with respect to the issue of rationality. Subjecting such premises to examination and criticism may be at best of only limited value in this regard, since the criticism may be ultimately circular, and the basic commitment will remain ultimately beyond the realm of rational criticism.

Relativism

The last point leads naturally to the issue of whether any set of premises is more rational or more reasonable than another or whether all sets must be treated as cognitively equal. This is the issue of cognitive relativism: each way of life or system of beliefs internally sets its own standards of truth and rationality; these systems conflict; there is no independent, external standard by which to judge one system against another; and, therefore, at least certain competing belief-systems each can claim to be equally good.[31] Relativism goes a step beyond the topics discussed above by expanding the theory-dependent nature of what is "reasonable" to a denial that there is any way to adjudicate between competing belief-systems. Not all relativists think that all belief-systems have an equal claim to acceptance, or that every criterion of rationality is completely dependent upon a particular system—some criteria may be culturally invariant,[32] and by these criteria not all systems are equally good. Relativists, however, deny all forms of absolutism (the theory that there exists some absolutely certain basis for knowledge which provides a universal, theory-independent criterion for truth and rationality). Non-relativists may believe that truth is only a goal which we can never completely reach or may be skeptics concerning whether any particular claim is ultimately correct, but they do believe that there are claims about the world which are in principle true or false independent of individual belief-systems. Relativists, on the other hand, view truth and falsity and rationality as internal to belief-systems, and thereby are often charged either with denying any real truth at all or with irrationality. Holders of different belief-systems accept their systems as the most rational or the best reflection of reality and also produce arguments justifying their choices, but no such system (including the relativists' own) has any special status—none can be ranked as more rational or closer to reality by any theory-independent criteria. Any idea, it is claimed, which may make, say, magic as acceptable as modern science appears to question whether any truth or knowledge is possible at all. It is feared that cognitive relativism is the epistemological equivalent of a moral relativism which would require its adherents to tolerate violence and torture in other cultures. Only with the comfort of an absolute standpoint (such as some assume is provided by science) is there any point to attempting to justify one's beliefs at all.[33]

The characterization relativists' opponents give them is not necessarily accurate. Relativism does not follow merely from the fact that there are many different belief-systems, or that truth necessarily involves formulation in concepts and thus may be open to revision. Nor does it follow from the need to examine concepts within their context in order to understand both them and what constitutes a justification for the system's holder. Rather relativism involves the additional premise that there is no way to adjudicate between all competing systems, and that, therefore, there is no way of telling if at least some of these conflicting systems are no better than others. Conceptual relativity (the view that different cultural groups produce different social constructions of reality by ordering their experiences according to differing concepts) and perspectivism (the view that there is a plurality of complementary frameworks each of which reveals something of reality that others miss) do not preclude the possibility of absolute claims about reality, and, hence, do not, by themselves, entail cognitive relativism. Similarly, the incommensurability of terms or the evolution of standards of rationality does not preclude comparison, and so does not entail relativism. Relativists can concede that communication between holders of different belief-systems is possible—translation of most concepts may be possible, with only the most theoretical core concepts producing relativism of total belief-systems. Simplistic relativists assert that our constructs are totally unconstrained by any external world. But advocates of a non-thorough-going relativism may concede that there is a context-independent "human nature" which produces a core of culturally invariant simple beliefs; only total belief-systems would then be relative. Furthermore, relativists need not deny that there is a reality existing independently of all conceptual systems, but they do deny that that reality determines one system or set of systems as the uniquely accurate picture of reality.[34] There are no standards of truth or rationality transcending all cultures and practices. Our concepts and interpretations always permeate how we see reality; reality is never free from our conceptions to determine which conceptions are "better."

The situation relativists see for belief-systems is comparable to having a series of conflicting map projections with no possibility of building a globe—there is no way of providing information independent of the projections and no absolute standpoint (the world "as it is in itself") from which to compare the projections. Each projection represents reality in a particular way; the projections share some features, but are incommensurable since there is no way to get to reality free of conceptual systems. The distinction here between "reality in itself" and "reality as conceived" is important to relativism: there is no theory-neutral way to reconstruct phrases like "really there,"[35] and comparisons between belief-systems are always comparisons between conceptions of reality. Thus, in the view of relativists, belief-systems cannot justify themselves against the world of theory-neutral experience, and thus there is no non-circular way of justifying the foundations of our ultimate beliefs about reality.

Mysticism cannot contribute to a resolution of the issue of relativism. Nelson Goodman finds mysticism to be a form of absolutism in that mystics hold that there is one definite way the world is, although this way is not captured by any description.[36] Indeed, mystics do adhere to an absolutism: mystical enlightenment involves a frame of reference which consists in part of implicit knowledge-claims concerning reality that are considered by the enlightened to be immune to correction. Thus, if relativism is taken to be a form of irrationality, mysticism cannot be criticized on this point. In addition, although many mystics would deny any final and complete description of the mystical reality, mystics are concerned with truth. For example, the Buddha uses skillful means to lead followers to enlightenment, but he is not concerned merely with what works. Instead he is concerned with that subset of knowledge which is useful in attaining a particular soteriological goal. Falsehoods may be temporarily helpful to certain listeners on the path, but nothing in the Buddha's total teaching suggests that there are no doctrines which are the final word on certain subjects related to the cycle of rebirths. Similarly, there are components of the experienced world (the *dharmas*) even if they are impermanent; and for all Buddhist traditions "dependent arising" (*pratītya-samutpāda*) is the ultimately correct description of the relation of these dependent, impermanent components of the experienced world. More broadly, mystics do not adhere to a solipsism which would make reality dependent upon an individual—reality is not an object distinct from the experiencer, but it is not reducible to any experiencer's individual existence either.

The doctrines which mystics advance are usually held to be the highest statable truth. Mystics who have produced writings have been aware of other doctrines, both mystical and nonmystical. They have been aware of criticism and other options, and they have responded. Central doctrinal concepts may be incommensurable between different mystical traditions, but mystics do believe that they can understand mystics from other traditions. Debates occur between rival teachers in many cultures, although there is a very real possibility that teachers are merely talking past each other rather than genuinely debating common issues. Mystics do not normally reject other mystical traditions totally, but instead rank mystical doctrines into a hierarchy with one particular doctrine at the top. The hierarchy may be arranged historically (indicating an evolution of doctrine) or by means of some other criterion. But the result is the same: the mystic making the ranking places his or her sect's teaching alone at the top. Doctrines from both within and outside the mystical tradition in question are included, the doctrines from within the tradition being both the teachings of other sects and the doctrines taught to the less spiritually advanced which are to be corrected by the final teachings. The popular Middle Eastern and Indian simile of the blind men giving differing descriptions of an elephant has the implication that all rival belief-systems are equally valid. This, however, does not reflect how mystics usually see their own doctrine—theirs is uniquely the most complete or best answer attainable, not merely one among equals.

If mystics see themselves as absolutists, the comparative study of mysticism raises doubts concerning absolutism in mysticism. The commonality of the experiences and any reality involved permits comparison of the mystics' belief-systms even if core concepts are incommensurable. The problem which becomes apparent is that the different mystical ways of life conflict with respect to beliefs, values, and goals.[37] Reality may be open to direct mystical experience, and mystical experiences may be open to descriptions at a basic experiential level where descriptions are neutral between competing belief-systems. Nevertheless, there appears to be no set of culturally invariant criteria for the level of fundamental belief by which to judge the relative superiority of one mystical system over another.[38] The criteria which each mystical tradition employs to make judgments concerning both experiences (including non-mystical and different types of mystical experiences) and the views of other traditions are internal to that tradition. Each tradition will characterize facts, problems, and solutions differently in varying degrees. In addition, the experiences themselves, as with all experiences, underdetermine any total interpretation and thus do not verify any one complete theory. The fundamental premises of a belief-system will be open to examination, but ultimately there will be no non-circular way to justify them. In light of this, it is difficult to speak of any one set of highly-laden doctrinal mystical concepts as "corresponding to reality." The traditional mystical systems that have survived can in principle be internally coherent and can handle all the experiential data. The concepts from different traditions may have the same referent, but the characterization of "reality" and of the final nature of any experiences will reflect highly intricate belief-systems, and we are left with no theory-neutral way to decide between the competing characterizations. Judgments of the superiority of one tradition over another by any means of ranking will be normative. Similarly, the view that all mysticism is the same, as adherents of perennial philosophy claim, will involve judgments not deducible from mystical experiences or the various mystical traditions themselves.

Thus, mysticism cuts both ways on the issue of relativism: mystics themselves espouse absolutism, while the comparative study of mysticism presents *prima facie* evidence against absolutism. It may be that both absolutism and relativism are points of view which are not themselves the results of empirical study but instead represent stances taken prior to any such study. Tying rationality to either point of view may also represent an *a priori* judgment.

Conclusion

Cross-cultural studies of rationality have a certain inconclusiveness about them because we cannot eliminate the possibility that we are merely assuming the rationality of other people. The above examination of mysticism's bearing on the sub-issues of rationality, however, leads at least to the conclusion that there is a very real possibility that mystical thought is rational. Not everyone may be rational, nor may anyone be totally rational; but the obvious instances of mystical strategies which, on the surface, appear to be irrational can be seen upon closer examination to be rational. The survey of examples from mystics in this paper may not be comprehensive enough to warrant broad generalizations, but it should present difficulties for any generalizations about the "mysterious Oriental mind" or other characterizations of mystics from any culture which present mystics as operating irrationally or with inscrutable alternative standards of rationality.

Chapter 4

The Nature and Function of Nāgārjuna's Arguments

This chapter sets out to provide an overview of Nāgārjuna's reasoning in order to understand the many claims in the *Mūlamadhyamakakārikās,*[1] the *Vigrahavyāvartani*(VV), and the *Ratnāvali*(R) which seem on the surface to be rather odd. For instance, if fire is different from kindling, it would exist without kindling; or, one who moves cannot rest. What will be maintained here is that such claims are logical in the context of Nāgārjuna's way of arguing and that the arguments make sense only if the premises and definitions he employs are adhered to strictly.

Nāgārjuna's Religious Purpose

Nāgārjuna's work is not a mere philosophical analysis, but has a soteriological intention. His opponents, he feels, take language to be reflective of the nature of the world so that if we have a word for something, it must exist (VV 9). Such entities (*bhāva*) we take to be real (that is, independent of other entities), and we crave them. But for Nāgārjuna these targets for attachment are no more than reifications of our own fabrications (*saṃkalpa*) abstracted out of the arising and falling of experience. Since we react to them, fabrications are the source of the three roots of unskillfulness (greed, hatred, and delusion, 23.1). To become freed from suffering, the mental props must be undermined. By ending, or "pacifying" (*upaśama*), our conceptual proliferation (*prapañca*), defilements and motivated action (*karman*) cease (18.5). Voidness (*śūnyatā*) serves precisely this function in the religious quest (22.11). His analysis attempts to show that what our terms denote lack what is essential for them to be considered real and desirable. The result would be that we would see that entities are not independent and consist of nothing to which to become attached. In this vein, Nāgārjuna speaks of the peaceful cessation of conceptual proliferation (25.24) and of the Buddha seeing no real entities nor speaking any words (establishing the existence of real entities) in expounding his doctrine, the Dharma. Elsewhere he states that those who see entities, or the absence of entities, or self-existence, or other-existence do not see the Buddha's teachings (15.6). In fact, for Nāgārjuna *nirvāṇa* simply is the suppression of any notion of real entities or their absence (*abhāva*) (R 1.42).[2] According to Candrakīrti, *nirvāṇa* is the quiescence of all conceptual proliferation (*niṣprapañca sarvaprapañca*).[3] Āryadeva probably means the same when he refers to *nirvāṇa* as the extinction of all words.[4] It is freedom from our obsession with our own conceptual fabrications. With the end of that obsession, our desires for what is unreal ends, and thereby our suffering ends.

Nāgārjuna's Method

To introduce the peculiarities of how Nāgārjuna goes about his task, consider his claim to expound no views (*dṛṣṭi*). Indeed, he says that one who holds voidness, the remedy of all views, as a view is incurable (13.8). Of course by any commonsensical definition of "view," he has many, starting with the first verse of the *Kārikās.* But he asserts that he has none (27.30), not simply a lack of wrong ones. Or, he proposes that where all is void there can be no propositions (*pratijña*; VV 29); this is so because, if voidness were usable in an argument (4.9), it would be made into a thesis, and if voidness were a thesis, its antithesis (non-voidness) would be derivable from it (R 2.4).

Nāgārjuna's claim becomes understandable once one realizes that his notion of *views* is always connected with the eternality or annihilation of real entities (15.10; 21.14; 24.21; 27.1–2, 13–14, 29–30; R 1.43–46), and as voidness neither "is" nor "is not" (22.11), by definition it is not "real" and therefore cannot be associated with any view. This may seem an odd way to get out of a problem, but as will be seen, many of Nāgārjuna's arguments follow the same pattern: first giving a very narrow definition to a term and then showing his position does not fall into that category. Thus, by his definitions, Nāgārjuna is in a position of maintaining that he has no positions and of stating such *prima facie* strange remarks as merely "making known" the unreality of things without affirming or denying them (since there is nothing real to affirm or deny). Further more, affirming or denying causes the state of affairs in question to come about (VV 64) by the rule that if there is a word for something, it exists. He asserts "We have already established [in detail] the voidness of all things" (VV 59), while in the commentary upon the verse remarks " . . . your criticism is directed against something which is not a proposition." Voidness is not a "right view." It is right in a broad sense, but not a view in his usage of the term.

His method is not to advance a thesis and to adduce supporting reasons but to show that no other position can be maintained which accepts the premises he ascribes to his opponents. By this means he can knock down one position without establishing its opposite in the process. Two such premises are "To exist an entity must be eternal" and "Real things cannot affect other things." He proceeds to show either that they conflict with ordinary sense-experience—as in the appeal to observation (for example, 13.3),[5] or to seeing the removal of perception (VV 67), or to seeing that the world does not vanish or remain immutable (R 1.63)—or that they are inconsistent. Thus, both logical and ordinary empirical arguments are made with no appeal to meditative experience or specifically Buddhist doctrine. The arguments therefore rest on grounds easily intelligible to Westerners.

His basic argument for establishing the nonarising of all entities through self-existence relies on this reasoning: if a statement is a real entity (the commentary clarifies that only the voidness of statements is established first and that then the same method applies to all things), it is either identical or absolutely different from its causes and conditions (VV 21). But a statement is not absolutely different, i.e., independent of its conditions. And it is not identical: if it were in the totality of causes and conditions, it could be grasped there. In experience, however, it is not so grasped (20.3). Hence, entities and their causes are not real entities but are void of self-existence.

Although logic (theories of deductions or valid inferences involving the forms of statements) is never explicitly dealt with, from inferences repeatedly made in the *Kārikās* the forms employed can be abstracted. For example, if paraphrasing questions as statements is permissible, verse 19.6 ("If time depends on an entity, how can there be time without an entity? And no entity whatsoever exists—how could there be time?") could be arranged to show its formal validity:[6]

(1) If there is time, then some entity exists.
(2) Thus, if there is no entity, there is no time.
(3) There are no entities whatsoever.
(4) Therefore, there is no time.

(1) is a restatement of "time depends on an entity," (2) of the entire first question, and (3) and (4) of the next two clauses. (2) follows from (1); (4) is entailed by (2) and (3).

Nāgārjuna's method of arguing appears to involve the basic ways of reasoning found in the West. Inferences such as the preceding one occur throughout the *Kārikās*. Dichotomies between *p* and not-*p* are central in every chapter; and Nāgārjuna's arguments are designed to exhaust all the possibilities he sees open to his opponent. In verses 2.8 and 14 it is explicitly asked what third alternative there is between a mover and a nonmover. An instance of this rule used implicitly is verse 3.6: "No seer exists apart from seeing nor not apart from seeing; there being no seer . . . "—a seer can exist only either apart from seeing or not; there is no third possibility. This same procedure recurs frequently (for example, 1.4, 4.6, 6.10, 8.1). Similarly, he states *p* and not-*p* cannot occur together (7.30, 8.7, 25.14) as they are contradictory. Nāgārjuna is consistent in his usage of the logical laws of noncontradiction and excluded middle throughout his work.

This being so, there seems to be little justification for maintaining that Nāgārjuna denies either the law of noncontradiction or the law of the excluded middle or that somehow he is "using logic to destroy logic," since such reasoning is how he establishes the voidness of entities, and so forth. He merely ascribes a set of premises to those who use "is" or "is not" and proceeds logically, relying on logic or empirical experience.

Richard Robinson cites what he considers a logical dilemma:[7]

> If a cause is void of a result, how can it produce the result? If a cause is not void of a result, how can it produce the result? (20.16)

This, says Robinson, has the form, "If *p*, then *q*; if not-*p*, then *q*," where *p* stands for the cause being void of the result and *q* for the inability to produce a result; *q* would be established quite trivially.[8] But looking at verse 1.6, one sees Nāgārjuna intends something more substantial:

> There is no condition either of an unreal (*asat*) or a real (*sat*) thing. Of what is unreal, is there a condition? If it is real, how can it be so through the condition?

Conditions cannot produce something unreal because an unreal thing does not exist (that is, no thing is produced) nor something real because the real is unproducable; if "unreal" means a change in a nonvoid entity, still conditions cannot bring this about (24.33). The sense is similar to verse 2.24 which states that both a really existing (*sadbhūta*) mover does not move (since the real cannot change) and a not really existing (*asadbhūta*) mover also does not move (since there is no thing real to move). Thus, verse 20.16 can be paraphrased nontrivially as:

> If the cause is void of the result, how can the real cause produce a real effect through a casual connection? If the cause is not void of the result, how can there be a change in a real cause necessary to produce a real, independent effect?

If the cause and result are both real, they are independent and cannot be causally related. If the cause is not devoid of the result, then either the result is not real (and thus no thing is produced), or it is within the conditions and causes (VV 21) and thereby not produced. The first sentence concerns the process of producing (if entities exist via self-existence, the process is not possible) and the second the result (if the process is possible, no real entities can enter into it); the phrase "how can it produce the result" likewise is concerned with both. In any case, no real result is produced nor is any real referent involved.[9] Under either interpretation the process and concepts involved are seen to be fabrications corresponding to nothing real. This is a paradigm of Nāgārjuna's argumentation and other verses with the same form can be dealt with in the same manner.

Basic Terms

To arrive at the implicit premises Nāgārjuna feels his opponents hold, the next step is to see the characteristics of the basic terms involved.

Svabhāva: "self-existence," that is, self-generating, causing its own nature (essence), self-maintaining, existence by reason of itself. From chapter 24, what exists by means of self-existence is permanent, fixed, unproduced, unstopped, and unchanging (*kūṭastha*); elsewhere it is said to be independent and underived (15.2) and uneliminatable (22.24). Unlike the Buddhist Logicians for whom efficiency is the criterion for existence, for Nāgārjuna only entities with self-existence exist or are real (*sat, sadbhūta*). A real entity is in the causes and conditions or totally independent of them (VV 21).

Parabhāva: "other-existence," existence by reason of or from another. An entity existing by means of other-existence relies for its existence on the self-existence of some other real thing. In this way, other-existence must rely upon some self-existence: other-existence means the self-existence of the other-existent (15.3), and if there is no self-existence other-existence is not possible (1.3, 15.3, 22.9).

Anyathābhāva: "otherwise-existence," for example, milk existing as curds (13.6). Since, for Nāgārjuna, only real entities can become otherwise and real entities cannot change, he easily disposes of this concept in chapter 13 (but only after he has made sure the meanings of other concepts that he ascribes to his opponents are interconnected with this one).

Sahabhāva: joint-entity of two real entities.

Bhāva: an entity. An entity lacking self-existence is not real or existent (*sattā,* 1.10; *asti,* 13.3).

Abhāva: the absence of an entity (15.5). If there are no real entities, then, of course, there are no entities to be absent (25.7)—something must exist to be absent.

Śūnyatā: emptiness, voidness, that is, void of independent existence. What is lacking self-existence and arises dependently is indicated by "voidness" (24.18). Every entity is void of self-existence and thereby not real but is like a dream or a magical illusion. Since voidness is not a real entity itself (but is itself void), voidness cannot be said to exist or not exist. Nāgārjuna uses the adjective "*śūnya*" (empty)—as a modifier of words denoting entities—more often than he uses the abstraction "*śūnyatā*" (emptiness). The concept of voidness is employed only for informing us of the fabricated nature of our fabrications (22.11); it cannot be used for refuting (4.8) since it is the conclusion, not a premise.

Asti and *Nāsti:* It is extremely important to note that even "is" (*asti*) and "is not" (*nāsti*) are technical terms for him, as becomes clear from 15.10–11: "Is" refers only to what exists through self-existence, that is, only to what would be real for Nāgārjuna. "Is not" is the notion of annihilationism (*uccheda*), the destruction of the real. "Is not" does *not* designate what does not exist by self-existence. Nor does the phrase refer to what is totally nonexistent such as a hare's horn or a square circle. Candrakīrti affirms that the phrase "son of a barren woman" is "mere words" corresponding to nothing in reality that could be an entity or the absence of one: denying such sons involves no real negation because it is "a mere denial of the possibility to imagine them as real."[10]

"Is" and "is not" are thus interconnected terms—is-not-ness cannot occur without there first being is-ness (R 1.72). These terms are the only terms that can designate real ontological status.[11] "There *is nirvāṇa* lacking self-existence" (*asvabhāvo nirvāṇam asti*) would be a contradiction in terms for Nāgārjuna. What is void of self-existence neither "is" nor is absolutely unreal (like a hare's horns). Once this is understood, saying that what exists through voidness neither "is" nor "is not" is not so much paradoxical as Nāgārjuna's code for saying merely that the entity neither has self-existence nor is the result of the destruction of self-existence: it is an unqualified denial of eternalism and annihilationism and that entities are real in this sense. Since self-existence is the criterion for being real for him, this is reasonable. In this sense, those who see is-ness and is-not-ness do not see the cessation of the seeable (5.8). Nothing concerning three-valued logic is being introduced since "is" and "is not" are not mutually exclusive and exhaustive categories. Instead they are restricted to denoting only what exists by means of self-existence. Dependent arising (*pratītyasamutpāda*) is outside the realm of self-existence and thus is outside the realm of existence (is-ness and is-not-ness) of entities; it is the "middle way" between "is" and "is not" (R 1.67).

Nāgārjuna thus substitutes talk of entities arising dependently in the place of talk of existence ("is" and "is not" in his sense). All elements of experience (*dharmas*) are like dreams or mirages (23.5). No *dharma*—no object, not the Buddha nor anything else we can imagine—arises nondependently. The question of self-existence versus dependent arising occurs only within the framework of both the existence and arising of entities—it is these fabrications that are devoid of self-existence.[12] Self-existence deals only with what would make *entities* real; self-existence and voidness have no meaning outside this context. Once the subject shifts away from questions related to entities, Nāgārjuna does speak of *reality* (*tattva,* not *astitā*): reality is nondependent, stilled, undiffused by means of conceptualizations (*prapañcair aprapañcitam*), free of our fabrications and undifferentiated (18.9). There is no mention of reality existing by self-existence since it is not an entity.

Relationships

Besides these distinctions among terms, the arguments in the *Kārikās* succeed only if a very restricted range of relations which Nāgārjuna believes entities with self-existence are able to undergo is understood.

First, nothing can be done to something existing through self-existence. For example, it cannot be created (24.33), eliminated (23.24, VV 67), or attained (24.39). A person with demerit would never be able to remove this self-existent demerit and thus would be permanently in that state. Images in the mind or perceptions would be forever before the mind. There could be no real actions (17.21–22): if an action lacks self-existence, it is not real and if it has self-existence, it does not occur (that is, it is eternal and thus never is completed). Besides being unaffectable, real entities cannot affect other things. Thus, an actually existent actor can neither do an actually existent action (because it, too, is real) nor do a not actually existent action (since it is unreal). There is no activity of a real entity; the actor and action would exist independently (8.1–2). Cause/effect obviously is among the proscribed relationships.

He sees his opponents as advocating a Humean world of loose and separate real entities (confer 1.9 against continuity [*saṅtāna*]). The only possible relations between real things are *identity* and *absolute unrelatedness* (for example, 2.21, 6.5, 18.10, VV 21). If *nirvāṇa* and *saṃsāra* were real, they would be totally unrelated, and thereby enlightenment would be impossible. Difference for Nāgārjuna requires things existing through self-existence. If there are no self-existent entities, there is no true difference. The consequent of the conditional of verse 20.4 makes sense only if one thinks in terms of unrelatable real entities: "If the effect is not in the complete collection of causes and conditions, the causes and conditions would be the same as non-causes and non-conditions." If the result is not in the causes and conditions, it is not related to them at all. Similarly, if fire is not identical (*ekatva*) to fuel, it is distinct and thus exists without fuel (10.1); the same with a mover and motion (2.20), and so forth. A remark by Āryadeva which seems at least odd is correct from the standpoint of this way of reasoning: "If the whole and the parts [of an elephant] are not different, the head must be the foot, because both of these thing would not be different from the elephant."[13]

Behind this view seems to be the idea that an entity existing through self-existence is analogous to a physical object. Thus, light is seen as coming into contact with darkness, light destroying darkness, and darkness covering itself (7.9–12). Darkness is not mere absence of light but an object present when light is absent. If present and future are dependent upon the past, for Nāgārjuna they must be things back there with the past (19.1–2). Action, motion, passion, and so on become reified things distinct from persons.

Self-existence is for him a reified property controlling its entity. For example, if a perception constituting a mirage exists through self-existence, it would be irremovable (VV 67); if self-existence were merely the essential property making perception, then a perception could be removed without destroying its essential property. But if this essential property is itself an object in its own right then the perception (the entity with self-existence) would be irremovable. The reified property would be the controlling factor. Thus, verse 5.2 can state that there is no entity without a mark (*lakṣaṇa*), and then turn around to ask if this is so, where can the mark apply? The mark is reified into an entity distinct from the mark's entity. In this way, the mark is not applicable to that which is the unity of an entity and its mark.

What lacks self-existence cannot be related in ways entities with self-existence must be. Thus, if *nirvāṇa* and *saṃsāra* lack self-existence, they are neither different nor identical—they are not the type of things which can be related in these ways. Verses 25.19–20 assert only that there is absolutely no difference between *nirvāṇa* and *saṃsāra*. This does not entail their identity, however, since only the real have properties which can be different or the same.[14] To put it another way, because the world (*loka*) and *nirvāṇa* are equally nonexistent, how can the difference between them be real (R 1.64)? The case is the same with the "I" of present and past births (27.9). This pattern is transformed into arguments throughout the *Kārikās:* If the oneness of two entities (for example, cause and product, 20.19) or their absolute difference is not possible, they are void of self-existence and thus not real.

Another relationship employed in arguing is the interconnection of terms denoting real entities. One group consists of such terms as "*bhāva*" and "*abhāva*" whose definitions overlap.

A second group is created by the fact language denoting objects operates by making distinctions (e.g., if there is not something other than light, then the word "light" would have no meaning), and hence, for Nāgārjuna if an entity does not exist through self-existence then neither does its opposite (if "light" is meaningless, then the question of light versus darkness is senseless). If the self (*ātman*) is not found, then neither is the nonself since "nonself" would be without meaning. The same is true with the other wayward views (23.22) and even with void and nonvoid entities (13.7). Plurality and unity (R 1.17), long and short (R 1.48), and other contrasting pairs are dealt with in the same manner. The claim in verse 2.15 that a mover (*gantṛ*) and a nonmover do not rest reflects this:

A real mover does not exist apart from motion (2.9) and therefore there is no real ex-mover to rest; and a nonmover never moved and so cannot stop moving to rest.[15]

A third group is based upon reified properties seen as real entities. Previously pointed out were examples of separating persons and their properties or actions into distinct entities which can be neither identical nor unrelated (and thus not real). Here the problem revolves around an entity gaining a new property or description. For instance,[16] when a man has a child, he gains a new property—that of fatherhood—but obviously the man himself is not physically dependent upon the child. But Nāgārjuna would see this process in a rather odd manner: if a father is an entity existing through self-existence, then either he is identical or unrelated to the man before the birth of the child. If he is identical, no change could possibly have occurred (since the real does not change), that is, no birth. If the father is different, then a change occurred, that is, the child created the *father* by producing his fatherhood. The first alternative is rejected since a birth did occur; the second involves a change and production—neither of which can occur to what exists through self-existence. Thus, the man is neither identical nor distinct from the father and thus neither exist. And if the father does not exist, then the child does not exist (a child by definition is dependent upon a father). So there are no real fathers or children.[17]

Other arguments in the *Kārikās* rely upon this strange kind of reasoning. Verses 14.5–7 contain this somewhat confusing passage:

> [What is] other depends upon [something] other; another is not different from [something] other without the other. And what is dependent does not occur distinct from it. If [what is] other is different from [something] other, it would exist without the other. And without [something] other, that [which is] other is not [something] other. Hence, it does not exist. Otherness is not found in [what is] other nor in [what is] not other. And when otherness is not found, then there does not exist the other or the that [to which something is other].

The thing, which is other, exists without anything else; but its otherness (seen as a reified entity, analogous to a physical object) does not exist without there being something else. Therefore, for Nāgārjuna, like the father and child, neither is real.

The Four Alternatives

The final form of arguing is the four alternatives (*catuṣkoṭi*). These occur in several places in the *Kārikās*,[18] but those occurring in the chapter on *nirvāṇa* will be explicated here since that chapter has the most detailed discussion. (Since the form of the four alternatives is the same in every case, they can be dealt with in the same manner in each instance.)

In chapter 25, the four alternatives are "*Nirvāṇa* is an entity," "*Nirvāṇa* is absence of an entity," "*Nirvāṇa* is both absence and presence of an entity (*abhāvo bhāvaś ca*)," "*Nirvāṇa* is neither an entity nor the absence of an entity (*naivābhāvo naiva bhāvo*)." Each alternative is denied. *Nirvāṇa* cannot be an entity existing through self-existence, because then it would be unattainable; nor can it be dependently arisen since it would then be connected with old age and death, composite and dependent (25.4–6). It cannot be the absence of an entity because of the interconnection of terms: where there is no entity, no absent entity can be found (25.7: *yatra bhāvo na nābhāvas tatra vidyate;* confer also 15.5). To be rid of the notions of becoming and annihilation cannot be characterized as an entity or its absence; *nirvāṇa* is thus not an entity nor its absence (25.9–10).

The rejection of the third alternative is based upon the facts that both entities and absences are composite (*saṃskṛta*) and that opposites such as light and darkness cannot be found together (25.14). Candrakīrti agrees that nothing can be entity-absent-entity "since such mutually contradictory (characteristics) cannot exist in one thing, and because, if they did, they would be subject to both of the above strictures together," or since a *bhāva* and an *abhāva* "are mutually incompatible, they cannot possibly exist together in one place, in Nirvāṇa."[19] Verses 7.30, 8.7, and 27.17, 25–27 likewise affirm the logical impossibility of the presence of opposite properties in one place. The *Brahmajāla Sutta* of the Pāli Canon rejects the third alternative by denying the existence of one feature (the universe being infinite laterally) and the nonexistence of another feature (the universe being finite vertically). Rejecting the existence of x and the nonexistence of y is substantially different from rejecting *one* reality allegedly composed of contradictory properties.[20]

The fourth is denied based upon the third alternative:

> The proposition (*añjanā*) "*Nirvāṇa* is neither an entity nor the absence of an entity" is established (*sidhyati*) if [the proposition] "It is both an entity and an absence" is established. (25.15)

Verses 27.18, 28 also contain the claim that if a thing conjoined with its negation is proved, then the fourth alternative follows. Consider also a comment by Candrakīrti on whether the Buddha exists after death: "Since both these solutions are unimaginable singly, they cannot be right both at once, neither is the negation of them both, therefore, imaginable."[21]

The way Nāgārjuna proceeds is reasonable: he rejects *nirvāṇa* as an entity and shows that the second alternative is dependent upon the first; the third is logically impossible and understanding the last one depends on understanding the third. And since it is meaningless to talk of the existence of *nirvāṇa* apart from these terms, *nirvāṇa* cannot be treated as an entity.

Those who claim that in the four alternatives Nāgārjuna is denying a property, then its negation, as well as the conjunction of the first two and the conjunction of the negation of the first two, are introducing inadvertently logical paradoxes that are simply not in the text. Under this interpretation, the denial of the first alternative contradicts the second denial, and these two together are equivalent to the third, as is the fourth. What is being denied by Nāgārjuna is not the isolated terms but different statements. This is a major distinction. For example, the word "self" can only be negated as "non-self," but statement (1) has two possible negations:

(1) The Buddha taught there is a self.
(2) The Buddha taught there is *no* self.
(3) The Buddha did *not* teach there is a self.

(2) and (3) do not contradict each other, but they do not claim the same thing. The one is the statement that the Buddha actively taught the nonexistence of the self (which at least in the conversation with Vacchagotta he did not do)[22]; the other simply states that the Buddha taught nothing affirming the existence of the self. (1) and (2) can be consistently denied if the Buddha was silent on the matter; (1) and (3) cannot be consistently denied.

The four alternatives resemble this situation: "Thus the view 'I existed in the past,' 'I did not exist,' both and neither does not occur" (27.13).[23] The form is: "That x is p does not occur and that x is not-p does not occur." It is similar to saying: "That the unicorn is white in color does not occur and that the unicorn is nonwhite in color does not occur." These denials do not contradict each other since there are no unicorns. If there is no "I," the situation above is parallel.

"*Śūnya*" being an adjective, a translation of part of verse 22.11 is "Neither 'It is void' or 'It is not void' may be said. 'It is both' and 'It is neither' [may not be said]."[24] The alternatives in chapter 24 are similar in form also.

Nāgārjuna is claiming "It is not the case that *x* is *p*, nor that *x* is not-*p*, nor that *x* is both *p* and not-*p*, nor that *x* is an entity which is neither *p* nor not-*p*," where *x* is an alleged real entity and *p* is any predicate. These denials are true and consistent if there are no real entities.[25] There is no real subject which "is" (in Nāgārjuna's technical sense of the term) and thus any predicate is without a referent—the problem is switched to the "it is" from what it is supposed to be.[26] In other words, a category mistake is involved in ascribing properties which presuppose existent subjects to what, in fact, arises through voidness. If we understand the nature of things, the predicates "is," "void," "eternal," and so on are all dissipated (9.12), since there are no real things to which to apply them, just as those who realize the true nature of a mirage no longer think in terms of whether there is water (R 1.54–56).

Candrakīrti's comments provide a summary:

> Because this tetralemma [eternal, non-eternal, and so on] is not applicable [to the Buddha who is appeased by nature and void of self-existence], just as the son of a barren woman cannot be said to be either black or white, it is not defined for men by the Buddha.[27]

Nāgārjuna's Consistency and the Two Types of Truth

Through these methods of arguing, Nāgārjuna attempts to remove *idola mentis*. He sees possible relations between entities with self-existence as so restricted that one is compelled (based upon his definitions and lines of reasoning) to turn to voidness—only then do things work (24.14).

One final topic needs mentioning, though. Some statements are at least in *prima facie* conflict. Consider these fragments of two verses: "Without self-existence and other-existence, how again can there be an entity?" (15.4), and "All entities are always characterized by old age and death" (7.24). The first denies that entities exist and the second seems to affirm them. But by remembering that "is" is a technical term denoting existence by means of self-existence, the tension can be dissolved. The two quotations together could be: "All entities which are characterized by old age and death lack self-existence and therefore are not permanent or independent—in a word, not *real.*" That is, no entity "is" in Nāgārjuna's specialized sense. Entities within the realm of dependent-arising are not "mere words" like "son of a barren woman"—they resemble dreams and thereby do not fit into the category of existence for Nāgārjuna. Existence is unqualifiedly denied; but "existence" is a highly specialized predicate for him.

What is involved here are two types of truth (*satya*): conventional truth (*saṃvṛtisatya*) and absolute truth (*paramārthasatya*).[28] From a conventional point of view, entities exist (hence 7.24), but from the ultimate ontological point of view, there are no entities since there is no self-existence (hence 15.4). Thus, the enlightened can use entity-language (such as "I" and "table") with all its convenience without getting involved in conceptual proliferation because they know the ultimate status of such entities: they do not ascribe ontological status to "entities" because of grammatical status (confer *Dīgha Nikāya* 1.195f). Further, the enlightened need not contradict themselves: what is true in one context (for example, "There are tables" from a conventional point of view) may be false in the other (ultimately there are no entities termed "tables" nor any other entities). In other instances, claims may be true or false from both points of view: "There are no unicorns" is true from both points of view and according to the *Ratnāvalī* (1.47) the notion of birth cannot be conceived from the conventional or from the absolute point of view (*tattvatas*). The emphasis placed on keeping the distinction between the two types of truth clear (24.9) points to the importance of knowing within which context a claim is made.

Nāgārjuna barely mentions the doctrine of the two types of truth; more elaborate views are set forth by later writers. In fact, all he says is that the absolute truth is based upon the conventional and that recourse to the conventional is necessary for enlightenment (24.8–10; VV 28). Nothing in Nāgārjuna's works suggests that he thought that absolute truth was beyond language. The difference between the two types of truth is merely that conventional truth deals with ordinary matters and ultimate truth deals with the ultimate fruit (*parama-artha*), i.e., *nirvāṇa*.

It might be asked whether the claim that voidness as the doctrine of dependent arising is itself void is a case of something being true from one point of view and false from another. The voidness of voidness is not an attack upon dependent arising but instead is an attack upon viewing it as a real entity rather than as a fabrication whose function is to counteract other fabrications (22.11).

An Assessment of Nāgārjuna's Program

Even if Nāgārjuna is logical and consistent, two questions (among others) can still be legitimately asked: (1) Does he succeed in establishing the dependent arising of things? (2) Can his technique "still" or "pacify" our mental fabrications once his method of arguing is understood?

To answer the first: if Nāgārjuna succeeds in establishing that entities arise and fall, he certainly does not establish in the process the Buddhist formula for how entities are related (that is, dependent arising) since there are many other alternative kinds of interdependence. Everyday experience may invalidate the position that entities are unchanging and independent, but is not enough to establish only one alternative explanation. Of course to assume initially dependent arising as a premise and then argue that there are no independent entities—a procedure directly opposite to what he is doing—would be pointless and question-begging.

Regarding the second question, his conclusions sound a good deal more dramatic and radical than he can adequately maintain. What he has done is to fabricate, for those who accept self-existence, a world-view which is obviously incompatible with ordinary experience and then merely pointed that out. Historically would any Indian tradition accept what he supposes to be the condition of reality for such entities as pots and *dharmas*? To cite an anachronistic example: Śaṁkara rejected objective entities or any phenomenon as being real in the sense of nondependence (and his characterizations of Brahman sound reminiscent of Nāgārjuna on *tattva*).

But ignoring the issue of whether he is attacking straw figures, problems still remain concerning his method of stilling our fabrications.

Nāgārjuna's scheme reduces to a paradox. He begins with observing change and proceeds by arguing that if any process of change is possible, then no real entities can enter in—and if no real entities are involved, he concludes that the process is *not* possible. He cannot use observations to attack the possibility of real entities and then use the lack of real entities in turn to attack what is observed without a circularity becoming involved which destroys his position. When he goes, for instance, from saying that there is no seer apart from or not apart from seeing to the claim there is no seer, act of seeing or object seen (3.6), one must remember that it is only in his technical sense of "exists" (total independence) that these do not exist. In any normal sense of "exists," (for example, what produces an effect or what is publically observable), just because the act of seeing involves more than one isolated subject does not invalidate any claim to existence of the object and subject independent of the act of perceiving—and it certainly does not attack that there was a perception.

Consider his argument concerning a mover. For him, if the mover and the motion are real, each must be totally different from or identical with the other—but in fact they are related. The problem would evaporate and the argument would collapse if any definition of "mover" other than "one who is in the process of moving" is employed. For example, if a mover is simply one who moves in a tenseless sense of "moves" (that is, in the sense "I eat" does not imply I am eating at this present moment), then a mover could rest: "The one who was moving is now resting" (2.16) is not absurd. No appeal to the idea of an unchanging substratum denoted by "person" is necessary—what produces an effect is constantly changing. The one who moves does exist in any usual sense of the term before that move because of which the mover is called "a mover" (2.22); that is, the one who moves exists before and apart from the act of moving. Similarly, the one who sees may exist before any acts of seeing which confers the label "seer" (contra 9.6), and the one who sees can be the one who hears without there being a multiplicity of subjects (contra 9.8).

People tend to divide experience along linguistic lines, such as taking adjectives as denoting "secondary properties" and nouns as denoting "primary properties." W. V. O. Quine has a thought-provoking remark that may be on this point:

> We tend not to appreciate that most of the things and most of the supposed traits of the so-called world, are learned through language and believed in by a projection from language.[29]

Bertrand Russell gives what could be an example of this projection:

> "Substance," in a word, is a metaphysical mistake, due to the transference to the world-structure of the structure of sentences composed of a subject and a predicate.[30]

Nāgārjuna unfortunately undercuts the thrust of this type of assault upon such metaphysics by connecting the problem of abstracting parts of the flux of experience and labeling them "real entities" with the supposition of his method that for an entity to be real it must be permanent and independent. Nāgārjuna is correct in pointing out that there is a continual change of attributes of persons and that we should not view these attributes as a string of real entities. There is nothing permanent in the sense that the contents of consciousness are always changing. (What makes up "persons" and "consciousness" apart from our concepts might be the reality [*tattva*] of which he speaks.) Even though we tend to reify attributes, the changes are not merely human fabrications. The words "birth" and "death" tend to isolate distinct occurrences out of a process, but they do no more than that towards causing the situation labeled thus. Showing that the reality lies not in the conceptual understanding or that there is a linguistic basis to the idea of identity does not entail that what is labeled by our concepts is "unreal" in any normal sense of the term. To go from saying that no words denote independent, unchanging, eternal entities to saying that they are without referent cannot be done. But for his method to work, this is the situation Nāgārjuna believes his opponents are in.[31] Even his description of entities being actually like dreams, mirages, or reflections shows the limitations involved: dreams are not nonexistent (R 1.38), except in his sense of the term, but are real (people do have them). He cannot conclude they are totally nonexistent in any significant sense but only that they (and those who have the dreams) neither "are" nor "are not," when these terms are given his normative definitions.

Nāgārjuna complicates the situation further by failing to distinguish *physical* dependence from *conceptual* dependence. In attacking the reification of "loose and separate" words into a world of loose and separate entities, he relies upon a parallelism between a conceptual interdependence and an ontological interdependence among entities. However, such a parallelism does not exist. As discussed in the next chapter, Nāgārjuna attacks one form of "grammatical realism" but falls prey to another. Problems discussed previously contain an element of this. Giuseppe Tucci's comment on *Ratnāvalī* 1.47 reflects Nāgārjuna's position and the problem:

> Since the cause is called a cause in so far as it produces an effect, if it exists before the production of this effect, that cause cannot be the cause of this effect, because it would have no relation to it.[32]

"Cause" and "effect" are conceptually interdependent, but what is labeled "the cause" certainly may physically exist before the conceptual rearrangement involved by the process it enters into. Once this is pointed out, Nāgārjuna's argument is destroyed.

Consider next the argument concerning fire and kindling: "Fire does not exist dependent upon kindling; fire does not exist independent of kindling. Kindling does not exist dependent upon fire; kindling does not exist independent of fire" (10.12). If this is interpreted solely in light of Nāgārjuna's criterion that real entities can only be related by means of identity or absolute difference, the first and third clauses make sense: fire is not identical to its fuel—where there is kindling, there need not be fire (10.13). And the second and fourth clauses point out the empirically obvious: fire does not exist totally independently since it needs fuel (10.14). So Nāgārjuna concludes there are no real entities here.

But taking any other definitions of "exist," the first and fourth clauses would be false: fire is physically dependent upon some fuel (among other things). It is only conceptually that "fire" and "kindling" are not identical nor completely distinct—wood becomes "kindling" only in relation to "fire." But then "kindling" is dependent upon "fire" and vice versa. So again two of the four clauses (the first and the third) are false. In either case, all four clauses are not true under one consistent interpretation of either physical or conceptual dependence. The argument appears forceful only in Nāgārjuna's artificial situation.

The passage cited earlier about the "other" relies more clearly upon the ambiguity between conceptually being an "other," while not being physically dependent upon the something else. Āryadeva's example of the father and child does the same: the child is physically dependent upon the man, while the attributes of "fatherhood" and "childhood" are mutually related.

Nāgārjuna cannot argue that interdependence of definitions (for example of "straight" and "curved") renders the words meaningless or that physical dependence of x and y makes both unreal in any sense other than his highly restricted one.

Other objections could also be raised. For instance, why must the future be in the past for temporal relations to obtain (19.1), or why if vision cannot see itself can it not see anything else (3.2)? But behind all these arguments lies the mistaken premise that relational properties dependent upon more than one object (for example, up/down) must be treated as distinct objects. As Ben-Ami Scharfstein puts it: "Relationships are not objects or physical parts of them. Relation-words mimic the language of physical possession and containment, but why should we confuse them any more than we confuse a parrot and a man?"[33]

All of this shows that Nāgārjuna succeeds at best within a very limited scope. Nāgārjuna ascribes certain claims to his opponents and then uses logic and ordinary experience to show that these claims cannot describe reality. However, he is not convincing because of the artificial nature of the claims he creates. By refuting those claims Nāgārjuna certainly does not establish that all views are false or establish the fundamental Buddhist metaphysics of dependent arising. As Richard Robinson also concludes, Nāgārjuna's procedure is a variation on the old shell game.[34] Serious doubts thus arise about whether he can accomplish his religious intention by his method of stilling our conceptual preoccupation (and thereby ending suffering) once these problems are pointed out.[35]

Part III

Mysticism and Language

Chapter 5

A Philosophical Analysis of Mystical Utterances

> If Jacob [Boehme] saw the unutterable,
> Jacob should not have tried to utter it.
> —Samuel Johnson

In one of his typical remarks about the Godhead, Meister Eckhart declares "Everything in the Godhead is one, and of that there is nothing to be said."[1] Well, did he not just say something about it? The same difficulty arises with most mystics. For instance, while discussing Brahman, Śaṁkara bluntly says Brahman is unspeakable (*avācya*) and inexpressible (*anirukta*).[2] This situation will be explicated by dealing with (1) why mystics deny that any language is applicable to the mystical, and (2) the meaning of their linguistic responses in the light of this denial.

Before delving directly into these problems, what is meant here by "mystical experience" and "the mystical" needs to be made explicit. Ninian Smart's definition of "mysticism" will be convenient: Mysticism consists primarily "in an interior or introvertive quest, culminating in certain interior experiences which are not described in terms of sense-experience or mental images. . . . "[3] The process involves a "fasting of the mind" until we become "clear," as Chuang Tzu would say. One moves away from the normal cognitive situation of a "subject" knowing a mental or physical "object" set off from the subject in some sense. More exactly, the result is a state of consciousness without an object *of* consciousness. Such a state is totally other than that which constitutes normal sensing or conceptual activity, where "normal" merely denotes anything involving a subject-object framework. Under Śaṁkara's conceptual scheme, the new knowing is itself the mystical—the awareness is Brahman.

"Nature-mysticism," that is, any of a range of experiences which involve the suspension of the concepts which normally structure our experience, will not be considered. These latter experiences still involve perceptual or internal images to some extent, and they do not involve a sense of "something other" than the experienced universe itself. The distinction between these types of experiences is indicated by Plotinus when he says "the One" rather than "Being" (the totality of all particular things) is involved in the mystical experience.[4] This "something other" will be designated "the mystical." In calling what is realized in this type of sensory-free and concept-free experience "the mystical," mystical experiences are being treated as mystics treat them when they "return" to the normal mode of awareness: they depict them as experiences *of* something, and then disclaim the experiences can be so characterized since no *object of* awareness is involved.

Religious uses of language often present problems. For example, unusual terms are used to indicate the complete otherness of the ultimate reality. Mystics mistrust language because by it we create mental objects that take us out of the present. However, the linguistic problems of concern here are those encountered after the mystical experience (especially the depth-type which is totally other than any state of sensing) when mystics attempt to communicate allegedly profound insights into the nature of the world. In short, of interest is that element of mystical discourse paralleling the fact-stating function of some ordinary uses of language. Mystics do not claim to have discovered new empirical material related to why one state of affairs, and not another, is the case. Their knowledge concerns something about the status of any "fact." The contents of sense-experience do not count for or against claims about the status of sense-knowledge. However, although they do not make empirical claims, mystics are *assertive* about the world and the mystical. Claims are advanced about what there is, not merely about experiences; and they are advanced as true, not false. Seldom do mystics refer to their own experiences per se, nor do they take them to be grounded subjectively. Thus, such statements as Eckhart's cited earlier are intended to be cognitive, that is, giving knowledge of something other than mental states.

This is not to reduce mystics' discourse to only one component. In addition, at least, instructions are given on how to attempt to generate one's own mystical experience. But to maintain that all such statements are merely transformative or soteriological is simply wrong. Eckhart closes one of his sermons with the comment: "If anyone has understood this sermon, I wish him well! If no one had come to listen, I should have had to preach it to the offering box."[5] This he would have done not out of concern for the salvation of the offering box, but to proclaim something he felt to be true and of the utmost importance.

Ineffability

The dilemma again is of uttering the unutterable in discussing the mystical. What sense can we make of Śaṁkara claiming that the whole of nescience (*avidyā*) arises entirely from speech alone?[6] According to him, even the words "Brahman" and "self" (*ātman*) are superimposed upon Brahman.[7]

This raises the question of ineffability. To be "ineffable" cannot mean merely that something cannot be described adequately. Such an attribute can be ascribed to anything, and thus when applied to the mystical is too vague to be very illuminating. Nor can ineffability mean that no words apply to the mystical: "ineffable" at least applies even if the mystical were not extensively discussed. Nor does it mean the mystical is not directly experienceable by other people.

"Ineffable" does mean that something is in some way incommunicable in words. Unfortunately *all* experiences are ineffable in various ways. In one sense, we can only communicate our understanding of an experience, not the experience itself. Thus, it is impossible to communicate the experiential aspects of any sense-experience to someone who has not already experienced it, or to communicate the degree of emotion or importance accompanying any experience. So also we can be so absorbed in an experience that any communication would break us out of it. Mystical experiences, of course, share these problems. Similarly, any object of sense-experience is ineffable in one sense: no attempt to depict what is unique about anything—what absolutely differentiates it from everything else—will be successful since descriptive words involve commonality and generalizations. Dignāga and other Buddhist Logicians emphasized this. But any object is also not ineffable: it is accurately to call my pen "a pen." For most contexts this characterization is not only accurate, but also adequate. Therefore pens are not considered to be "utterly beyond words."

What then separates the mystical so that it is considered ineffable in some unique sense? Why do mystics deny "the One" or

"Brahman" works for the mystical the way we suppose "pen" adequately and accurately communicates? The answer is that unlike talking about objects, any discussion of the mystical introduces a mode of awareness foreign to experiencing it. A mystical experience is not one sense-experience among others—it and its content are "wholly other." To speak about the mystical is to switch from the awareness of it to our customary awareness. In the case of speaking of objects, we merely rearrange the content within normal (dualistic) awareness; the awareness involved is the same as in the experience of the objects. Language has arisen within and as an integral part of the nonmystical point of view oriented around sense-experience. The duality set up between subject and object permitting perception is likewise necessary for thought and linguistic phenomena: language can operate only where distance is placed between the seer and the seen—a "space" for encoding is required.[8] The abolition of this dichotomy is the reason for the label "ineffable" as this Upaniṣadic passage indicates:

> . . . where knowledge is of a dual nature (implying a subject which knows and an object which is known), there, indeed, one hears, sees, smells, tastes and also touches, the self knows everything. Where knowledge, being devoid of effect, cause or action, unspeakable, incomparable, indescribable, what is that? It is impossible to say.[9]

Only by removing that duality by which language operates can one realize the mystical.

The Mirror-Theory of Language

Mystics' discontent with language is compounded by their misreading of the nature of language. Language differentiates: it conceptually isolates the item under consideration by contrasts and comparisons. More specifically, all determination is negation as Spinoza says. To say "This is *x*" or "Do *y*" necessarily entails not saying "This is not *x*" or "Do not do *y*." This process of creating dichotomizing categories underlies all linguistic functions, not just the assertive one under special consideration here. The distinctions and classifications language makes direct awareness by calling attention to those features of reality which a culture deems most important, necessary for survival, or just convenient. Different languages reflect different conventional codifications of reality.[10]

The error comes into play when we let grammatical status dictate the ontological status of the referents. We go from the fact that denoting terms are distinct to believing in a world of Humean "loose and separate" entitites, each real and independent. For instance, because we have such terms as "I," we tend to believe in a distinct mental entity which corresponds to it—otherwise why are there such terms? Or from the phrase "the blue book," it seems natural to suppose that because "book" is a noun while "blue" is only an adjective that the book-ness is the primary (essential) property and the blue-ness is only a secondary (accidental) one. Galileo thought the only reason we feel colors are as real as primary properties is because we have terms for them.[11] Bertrand Russell sees the whole idea of substantive entities arising in the manner: "'Substance', in a word, is a metaphysical mistake, due to the transference to the world-structure of the structure of sentences composed of a subject and a predicate."[12] More to the issue at hand, it may be absurd to maintain that words about water must be *wet* in order to apply. But to maintain that "static" concepts cannot in principle apply to "dynamic" reality, or that applying a name or a predicate "imposes a limitation" upon what is being referred to, is only one step away. Under this theory, for knowledge-claims to be accurate or useful, they must involve a correspondence between statements and reality in the sense of mirroring. Many philosophers today deny that it makes sense to claim that our concepts match some reality which is totally free of conceptualization. But most people unconsciously accept such a position.

That the deep structure of language and world share the same form is termed "Grammatical Realism" by Arthur Danto.[13] Although nothing necessitates this view, it seems to be accepted by most people. Danto mentions that every metaphysical system he knows of presupposes it. Certainly Ludwig Wittgenstein's *Tractatus Logico-philosophicus* with its thesis concerning the shared logical form between the structure of language on the level of statements and the structure of reality on the level of facts making up the world (and that this structuring itself cannot be expressed) is a case in point. The opposite of a metaphysics of "atomic facts" is also a variety of this "mirror-theory" of what language does: to go from the fact that language is an interconnected fabric—terms operate only in relation to each other—to the conclusion that what is designated is also relative.

The Buddhist Nāgārjuna is guilty of this latter move. He is attacking the other variety for soteriological purposes. The version of the mirror-theory he is arguing against is stated in the *Vigrahavyāvartani*: people who accept the notion of self-existence (*svabhāva*) feel that language reflects the nature of things—if we have a word for something, then it is an independently real part of the world.[14] His works are an analysis of the interrelation of concepts to show that no entity (*bhāva*) or factor of experience (*dharma*) whatsoever is real (*sat*), because each is void of self-existence.[15] The problem as he sees it is that we project all grammatical distinctions unto reality and become attached to the fictitious real entitites. Only by undermining all mental props can we be freed from the suffering entailed by taking a fabricated world to be real. We become detached from verbal idolatry and thereby extinguish the fires of desire, hatred, and delusion.[16] One characteristic of reality (*tattva*) is its being free of all conceptual projection (*prapañca*), and *nirvāṇa* is simply the cessation of this tendency.[17] That is, *nirvāṇa* is the cessation of seeing the world as constructed of multiple entities because of grammatical distinctions.[18] The result is not an undifferentiated awareness, nor a lack of linguistic ability. To cite the Theravāda canon, the enlightened can make use of current forms of speech without "clinging" to them and thus are not led astray by them.[19] They can use "I" without believing in a separate, enduring entity. This would be in accord with the Buddhist view of the world. Denotative words and phrases are taken then not to refer to permanent objects but to fairly stable configurations in the flux of experience which we group together and separate for attention. We can use the word "blue" without supposing all "shades" of blue to be variations of one underlying, unchanging color. We do not need to convert ideas into entities. Language does not entail an ontological commitment—only a theory of language does.

But these Buddhists are not usually assertive concerning the mystical; in their soteriological program they use other techniques to induce enlightenment. Mystics who do discuss the mystical adhere to the mirror-theory. The problem is that of using something—language—which supposedly mirrors the structure of what it refers to in order to depict something essentially alien to that structure. For ordinary experience, mystics, like most of us, do think the mirror-theory holds: if all denotative words were considered "conventional designations" or constructions void of reality, then discourse about the mystical would be in the same boat with all discourse about objects. But any word denoting the mystical has the identical grammatical structure as terms denoting objects. Thus, although the mystical is ontologically incommensurable with the results of dualistic awareness, any words grammatically objective in nature may be taken as indicative of the mystical's ontological status, that is, the mystical is reduced to one differentiated object among other objects. In other words, because we take most denotative words to refer to *objects,* all must. Therefore, the mystical is declared ineffable. Plotinus clearly indicates this position:

> The [One] is only thus, as it is, and not otherwise. But even the expression "it is thus" is *inaccurate,* for thereby it would be *limited* and thereby *made* into a *definite* something (and an *individual* having number). For then it would again take *its place amongst things* of which it can be said they are thus or not. But the [One] is exalted above all these things.[20]

The discussion in the *Tao te ching* concerning the role of naming in the recognition of opposites, and thereby the carving up of the "uncarved block," also reflects this notion. Taoists react to the Confucian concern with the "rectification of names" and the general notion of language as a medium that can exactly express the values central to a Confucian way of life. For Taoists, heaven does not speak (TTC 73) and the Way is nameless(TTC 1, 32, 37). The Way is formless and beyond the senses and comprehension; hence, it is unnameable (TTC 14). Names come into play only with the opposition of objects (TTC 32). That is, concepts arise only when we are aware of opposites, as with beauty and ugliness or good and bad (TTC 2). But the Way is an "uncarved block" (*p'u*) free of all opposites and hence free of all names (TTC 37). Thus, the sage teaches a wordless doctrine (TTC 2, 43), even though the sage is forced to refer to the Way and so must use some word to refer to it (TTC 25). But since language by its very nature bifurcates into categories and since the mystical is "undifferentiated" (that is, not one thing among others), language cannot actually apply to it.

The problem with regard to the mystical is not the reification of abstractions into concrete entities (another by-product of the mirror-theory), but the transformation of the ontological status of what is involved in an experience. Mystics speak of the mystical as more than subjective, and normally there is only one alternative—therefore we construe the mystical as an external entity. Even the idea of a referent denoted by mystical uses of words is misleading to the extent that a referent is an object. As the mystical is not an object among objects, it cannot be pointed out in the manner of referring procedures for objects. What is identified by a mystical utterance is something given in the mystical insight itself, and only by having the experience would we know what is being identified.

Treating "the One" or "Brahman" as names is no better, since obviously we take names to be names of objects. Plotinus tells us that it is precisely because the One is not an entity that "strictly speaking, no name suits it."[21] Also because of its syntactic form, the idea of Brahman as an entity is superimposed (*adhyāsa*) upon the name "Brahman," according to Śaṁkara.[22] Lao Tzu's distinction between an intimate name (*ming*) and a public name (*tzu*)—there is no first such name for the mystical, but "Tao" is used in the second sense—does not overcome the difficulties.[23]

The agrammaticality of the mystical according to the mirror-theory must also be the reason William Johnston asks " . . . how can unity be expressed in dualistic language?"[24] Not only the differentiation entailed by holding this theory, but also the objectification, creates puzzles. Hence K. S. Murty's question: "How can Vedānta sentences have their *object* Brahman, which is said to be the eternal *subject*?"[25] If descriptions were treated as no more a substitute or a copy of what is being referred to than a set of instructions is a substitute for what is to be carried out, this impasse would not arise.

But if talking about the mystical is felt to be reducing it to an object, why talk about it at all? Because of the importance mystics attach to it. How can mystics speak at all? To answer this, it must be noted again that mystics do not speak during the mystical experience, but only afterward. When the mystic has returned to normal awareness, the mystical is looked back upon. Plotinus speaks of afterward seeing an "image" of what is experienced.[26] But he makes clear that this seeing (which involves duality) of an image of the One is distinct from being "oned" with it; no retained memory of the latter experience is possible. This image is of necessity objectified—some mental distance is placed between the seer and the seen—as are mental images of physical objects. The mystical is "wholly other" than any objectified conception we could have of it in the unmystical state of awareness; to this extent, it is "unimaginable." Some concepts are more appropriate in the sense that *if* the mystical *were* an object, it would be denotable by them in the same way objects are. Some words reflect better the image, but since any image is in the same class as object-images and since the mystical is not in the class of objects, any description reflecting the image is held to be distortive. There is something in common in how images are formed, but not in what they represent.

Some features do seem definitely to be given in the experience. For example, "oneness" or "nonduality" occurs frequently in descriptions, although it is interpreted differently (for example, as the ground of awareness or of the world and the person). If absolutely no features were given, there would be nothing retained and nothing to express. But the features which are given are totally incommensurable with those of objects. Thus, "oneness" is meaningful when discussing normal experiences in contrasting plurality. But this numerical sense of oneness is the "positive sense of oneness" which Plotinus denies is applicable to the mystical: "One" is used only to start the mind toward simplicity, not to designate one thing among many.[27] Even the phrase "one-ing" to indicate "union" with the mystical would only indicate to the unenlightened a state of being one *with* some other object. Using "the One" implies commonsensically the universe considered as a complete set of all objects or as a kind of organic whole—each idea a product of normal awareness only. If "the One" is said to be wholly other than "empirical objects," still we think of some *thing* wholly other than "ordinary" objects. In sum, we react to this attribute in terms of our normal frame of mind. In every case, we make oneness an attribute of objects—whenever we talk about it, we talk about an *it* which is ipso facto wrong. To the extent one takes grammatical distinctions as indicative of ontological ones, one still "has time and place and number and quantity and multiplicity, he is on the wrong track and God is far from him."[28] One is still in the realm of normal awareness and, as Eckhart again says, to "be conscious of knowing God is to know *about* God and self,"[29] not to realize the intended experience.

If the mirror-theory were carried out fully, even "is" would not be applicable to the mystical since objects *are*. Saying "There is the mystical" would reduce the mystical ontologically to the level of objects. Only if mystical utterances can refer to the mystical without reducing their grammatical object to an ontological one do they succeed. In other words, the mirror-theory must be rejected. Otherwise language appears to be a Procrustean bed, and the mystical is declared to be ineffable.

An Analogy

To further elucidate the problem, perhaps an analogy that parallels the situation in one important respect will help. Ignoring how such a situation could ever arise, consider describing a cube to people who have never seen a three-dimensional object. (Plato's analogy of the cave in *The Republic* could be used as well, but the present analogy can be handled a little more easily.) We could make

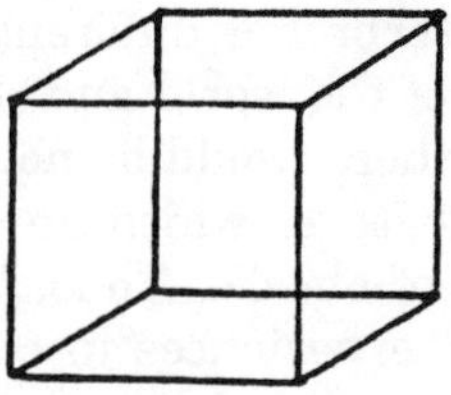

a two-dimensional drawing. In fact, this is all we can do—we cannot present the cube itself to a people who can experience only two-dimensionally. For such people the cube would not even be the object of thought insofar as the drawing (Plotinus' "image") is the focal point for them, not the cube itself. If we were to talk about the cube, the situation would seem worse. We might say, "Well, the cube really is not like this. It is not *flat* (a term these people might understand by analogy, that is, three dimensions are to two dimensions as two dimensions are to one). Its mode of existence is different. And the angles are all really the same size, although in the drawing they are not. And the edges intersect only at the eight outer vertices (although they do not all appear to be on the outside), not also at interior points as the drawing indicates." We might even conclude that the cube itself is ineffable since the drawing seems to reduce it to two dimensions.

Now such a predicament parallels that of mystics in one way (and perhaps only one way since an object and the mere collapse of one dimension is all that is involved): just as these people tend to reduce the referent of the drawing to something familiar, likewise the unenlightened reduce the mystical to some kind of object when mystics speak of it. In each case, the lack of the enlightening experience is the problem. The drawing is certainly an accurate representation of the cube as far as it goes—accurate, that is, as long as we realize that it is only a drawing and that there is a dimension not conceptualizable in "two-dimensional language" the way the other two are. Those who are sympathetic may come to understand that the drawing is not really the cube, and therefore not assimilate the drawing to their normal reactions. But without actually having the experience of the cube, they cannot know why this drawing and not others is appropriate and in what sense it is accurate. Studying the drawing itself will in no way substitute for this experience—there is no direct way to get to three-dimensional objects by looking at the drawing. Only with such an experience will the odd, if not contradictory, features be understood in a nondistortive fashion. For those without it, the drawing may remain something like M. C. Escher's drawing of the four waterfalls flowing into each other—something which can be drawn but cannot correspond to anything in the world.

The situation is similar with mystical utterances: because of the "drawing," the mystical is relegated to the familiar status of an object. But just as some features of the drawing of the cube are accurate if viewed correctly (for example, straight edges, eight vertices, and some right angles), so may be some features of the descriptions of the mystical (nonduality and a sense of reality), if we overcome the tendency to project grammar along ontological lines. The linguistic drawings do not completely falsify, but they do introduce another mode of awareness. This mixture of correct description with distortive structures accounts for the hesitancy of mystics to affirm the adequacy of conceptualizations of the mystical. The mystical's ontological status is not "captured" by the grammar. Its mode of existence is missed in some sense. The negative phrases are accurate, but studying them does not cause the required insight. As the cube is different from the drawing, the mystical differs from any conception we may have of it. Having a mystical experience reorients how we see the utterances, parallelling seeing the drawingness of the drawing upon seeing the cube. The language is no longer as confusing, but it remains the only language mystics could employ if they want to conceptualize the mystical.

On one issue the situations diverge. In the case of the cube and the drawing, we cannot *draw* the fact the drawing is a drawing. All we can do is produce another drawing—we can show a picture, but we cannot picture the process of picturing, as Wittgenstein would say. However, if we reject the mirror-theory of language, language can be treated as one art able to reflect back upon itself to "draw" the fact that drawings of the mystical are only drawings. Words are not pictures in this sense.

With this explanation of mystical ineffability in mind, consider then four traditional linguistic responses to the mystical: silence, negation, paradox, and positive descriptions.

Silence

Logically, if mystics accept the mirror-theory, absolute silence concerning the mystical would be the proper response. But this is hard to sustain. Mystics do *speak* of silence in two senses: the silence necessary in inducing the experience, and a silence in Simone Weil's words "which is not an absence of sound but which is the object of a positive sensation, more positive than sound."[30] Or from Eckhart: "The central silence is there, where no creatures may enter, nor any idea, and there the soul neither thinks nor acts, nor entertains any idea, either of itself or of anything else."[31] Or there is the famous example which Śaṁkara cites from a now unknown Upaniṣad of Bāhva, who when asked to explain the self, said, "Learn Brahman, friend" and became silent; when the questioner persisted, he finally exclaimed, "I am teaching you, but you do not understand. Silence is that self."[32] But speaking of this silence, unlike remaining silent, reintroduces the problems with language. As in the Weil quotation, we make the central silence into an object and all the dangers thereby reemerge.

Negation

The *via negativa* is another traditional way of attempting to direct the listener away from the realm of objects. Under this approach, every possible positive description of the mystical is denied (since the mystical is wholly other than what we normally experience). This process of undescribing is represented by Śaṁkara's discussion of the Upaniṣadic "not this, not this" (*neti neti*). What we consider normal (the sensory-conceptual mode of awareness) is considered by him to be the operation of the nescience (*avidyā*), that is, the condition wherein limiting adjuncts (*upādhi*) are superimposed upon the only real (*sat*); since describing the real without recourse to limiting adjuncts is an "utter impossibility," words like "Brahman" and "self" are superimposed.[33] But, since in its true nature the real is free of all differentiation, we are left with describing it as "not this, not this" in order to remove all terms of name, form, and action.[34] He says this process of negation leaves something real, because we can only negate something by reference to something real.[35] Thus, because of his adherence to the mirror-theory, he wants to maintain that there is a real basis to the superimposed while asserting that Brahman as an object of consciousness is a product of nescience—either in its lower form as Īśvara (Brahman as qualified) or in its higher form (Brahman as the opposite of all qualifications).[36] He even labels his position "nondualism" (*a-dvaita*) instead of "monism" to remove the possibility of mistaking the real as an objective thing. Only negations finally apply, he believed. Similarly, Plotinus tried to use "the One" to indicate only a lack of plurality, not one object.

Theravāda Buddhism carries this approach further. What is indescribable according to this tradition is not *nibbāna* (the state in which the "fires" of hatred, greed, and delusion have been extinguished, thereby ending the cycle of rebirths),[37] but such matters as whether the enlightened exist after death. Each of four alternatives (the enlightened exists, does not exist, neither exists nor does not exist, and both exists and does not exist) is rejected because when all factors making up our experiences (*dhammā*) are removed, there is no means of knowledge and therefore no means of description.[38] All alternatives reflect properties applicable only to existence before *parinibbāna* and therefore are negated; affirming any one would show a misunderstanding (and would also give us a prop to which we can become attached).[39] With regard to the mystical, Plotinus says the same: any property (for example, being in motion or at rest) is a characteristic of Being, not the One, and so all properties are denied.[40]

Such an approach is reasonable if language is accepted as a mirror of reality. But here again there are difficulties. We can say the number five is not green, not red and so on, because numbers are ineffable with respect to color terms. But to say "The mystical is not an object open to conceptualization" itself involves a conceptualization. When Eckhart says that the spark in the soul is "neither this nor that" or that we should love God "as he is, a not-god, a not-ghost, apersonal, formless,"[41] the danger remains of merely separating one object from others by means of negation. Even attributing "nonbeing" to the mystical or saying it does not *exist* still produces in the mind the image of an entity set off from other entities. Perhaps this is why Dionysius the Areopagite says neither affirmation nor even negation applies to the mystical.[42]

Paradox

The third approach, that of paradox, provides a link between the negative and positive descriptions. It should be noted that not all mystical utterances are paradoxical, nor do all mystics speak paradoxically. But paradox is significant for many mystics. It may involve the mystical as in saying "God is everywhere and nowhere" or the mystical experience as in the depiction of the realization in the *Kena Upaniṣad:*

> It [Brahman] is conceived of by him who does not conceive it. Who conceives it does not know it.
> It is not understood by those who understand it.
> It is understood by those who do not understand it.[43]

Or from Eckhart: " . . . no man can see God except he be blind, nor know him except through ignorance, nor understand him except through folly."

"Paradox" is not merely any perplexing claim, but is the conscious use of what is strictly contradictory, that is, any statement asserting the conjunction of one claim, *a*, with its logical negative, not-*a*. Mystical experiences, like all experiences, are themselves nonrational—only claims about them can be consistent or inconsistent with each other or with other claims.

Paul Henle advances one theory of mystical utterances centering upon mystical paradox. He affirms that the mystical is ineffable with respect to the conceptual scheme which our language and thought embodies: something is involved which cannot be imparted using our present concepts.[44] It might be that the mystical is not ineffable as such but is actually expressible in some other scheme. In support of this idea, Henle devises an example of a primitive mathematician entrapped within a mathematical system where quite usual operations for our arithmetic lead to self-contradictory statements in his symbol system. Thus, an idea may be logically quite ordinary within one conceptual scheme but contradictory by nature in another. To give more credence to this, he could have cited an actual historical instance as an illustration. The ancient Egyptians had no words for compass directions. Instead their words for "to go north" and "to go south" meant literally "to go downstream" and "to go upstream" respectively (because of the flow of the Nile). Thus, when they encountered the Euphrates (which flows the opposite direction of the Nile), they had to express this situation by calling the river "that circling water which goes downstream in going upstream."[45]

Such examples do establish that something well-formed in one language can be inherently paradoxical in another. What is fatal to the applicability of these examples to the mystical is the lack of attempts at constructing a new language on the part of mystics. Would not the primitive mathematician, if he encountered a contradiction which he still considered to encompass something of value, adopt or develop a new system? (The very example shows the relativity of being absurd or commonplace in mathematical systems.) Similarly, would not mystics attempt to devise a new language to express the mystical, if it were possible, since it seems to them so real and so important? Henle's reply to this point is that one cannot force a new language—a "flash of inspiration" is required and such a discovery is always fortuitous. If something were given in the mystical experience which revealed the necessary ineffability of the experience itself, then, as Henle points out, this would be an insight not only into religious matters, but semantics.

But still when philosophers and mathematicians encounter such paradoxes as Russell's, flashes of inspiration usually eventually occur. In the case of mysticism, though, no efforts ever have been made to create new languages. Not even such thinkers as Eckhart, Plotinus, and Śaṁkara endeavored to do that. New uses are given to old words (for example, "one") and some new words are coined (for example, being "oned" with the mystical), but the denials of the applicability of any language to the mystical go on unabated. It certainly indicates *prima facie* that the problem mystics see with language lies with something inherent in language or with how mystics view language. If the explanation lies with the mystics' adherence to the mirror-theory of language, mystics would not bother to invent an entirely new language (if this is even possible), because the same problem would always be involved: we would tend to project whatever categories the new language differentiates, and unenlightened people would still make the same reductions. The fuzzy and imprecise natural languages we now have are as good as any in this regard. It also follows that no language is any more "mystical" than another. All suffer from the same basic problem. Therefore, mystics use whatever language is available to them, although they may give new meanings to old terms. They also tend to favor the passive voice; Nāgārjuna, who was discussed in chapter 4, is a good example.

However, the problem remains of why mystics speak paradoxically upon occasion. If they accept that the mystical is not ontologically similar to the referents of ordinary linguistic usages and therefore denotative terms cannot be employed, should mystics not consistently deny that any term applies? The use of paradox may, in fact, indicate that mystics do see that certain concepts are applicable to the mystical (although not when the everyday sense of these concepts is intended). The assertions would then be only paradoxical on the surface, since, in reality, two different senses of the key terms are being employed. For example, the mystical is unknowable in the way objects are (that is, implying duality), but knowable in another sense (that is, experienced or apprehended through the mystical mode of awareness). Thus, Eckhart can speak of an "unknowing knowing,"[46] which sounds paradoxical because the contexts of meaning are not specified: the experience involves an unknowing of all sensory and mental images, but is still apprehending the mystical in the only way possible. Similarly, "see" means two different operations when Plotinus says we see and do not see the One: the experience is not perceptual in nature (that is, not dualistic) but is still cognitive, and therefore "seeing" is an appropriate locution. To paraphrase part of the *Kena Upaniṣad* quotation cited earlier: Brahman is not understood by those who take it to be an object but is understood by those who pass beyond such understanding.

Even "is" presents difficulties, as alluded to earlier. Mystics would not say the mystical *is,* because we would then conclude that the mystical exists in the sense a physical object does. From the point of view of common sense, we think something either *exists* or *does not exist* without qualification. But, to mention only one example of the problems concerning the use of "exists" in connection with the components making up our everyday world, it seems that the sense in which a dream exists is not the sense in which a physical object does. And mystics would say the manner in which the mystical exists is not that of anything else—to know its mode of existence would of course require a mystical experience. (For some mystical systems, the fundamental importance attached to the mystical makes "is" inapplicable to anything but the mystical.) A Christian mystic may say "God neither exists nor does not exist," when what is meant is that God neither exists in the manner objects do nor does not absolutely not exist—God's mode of existing differs from that of objects or anything else.

Śaṁkara's explanation of paradox has similarities with this view. Paradoxes he feels result from superimposing attributes upon Brahman which are known to be false in order that no one will believe Brahman does not exist. These attributes are then negated (*apavāda*) to show that they, in fact, do not apply.[47] His acceptance of the mirror-theory would account for the latter move. His misapprehension of the nature of language also explains why he makes the status of the world paradoxical, or inexpressible (*anirvacaniya*): it is neither real (*sat*) since not anything present in dualistic awareness but only Brahman is real, nor totally unreal (*asat*) as is, to use the Indian example, the son of a barren woman. Anything describing the status of the world which is not self-contradictory would tend to indicate it is an objective entity—which it is not—so its status according to Śaṁkara must be inexpressible.

That what seems paradoxical should result from mystics' brief elliptical passages is not too surprising, even assuming mystics are clear on how the paradoxicality arises (subscribing to the mirror-theory would make this difficult). A real paradox results only when a statement refers to one subject in a contradictory manner. But what is involved in mystical utterances are different views of the world—not, say, the shape versus the color of an object, but what is perceived in normal awareness and what is realized in mystical awareness.

If this explanation is correct, a consequence would be that mystical utterances can be given nonparadoxical paraphrases which lose none of their assertive import. Not all paradoxes arise in the same manner and thus no one procedure for restating them will work. Some may arise simply through confused thinking. Even such major thinkers as Plotinus are not always consistent. He claims, "The One is everything and not everything," but in the same tract he says the One is *other* than everything because all comes from the One and the One *is* everything again because everything comes from the One.[48] Other mystics may purposefully emphasize paradox for soteriological reasons—the oddity of the claims reflects the otherness of the mystical, and thus helps the unenlightened realize the mystical.

But most paradoxes probably can be handled similarly to an example from the *Prajñāpāramitā* literature. There the *bodhisattvas* think: "Countless beings should I lead to Nirvana and yet there are none who lead to Nirvana, or who should be led to it."[49] This can be made logically coherent: only things which have self-existence (*svabhāva*) are considered real for these Buddhists, and therefore, since no object exists through its own self-existence, there are in reality no beings. On the other hand, such things as people are not totally nonexistent (as are unicorns or square circles) and thus there is something to lead to *nirvāṇa*. In other words, if "things do not exist" means only "they are unreal as we imagine them to be,"[50] then the claim made above merely juxtaposes two senses of "beings": beings in the sense we ordinarily mean (and as a version of the mirror-theory supposes) do not exist, but still there is some reality present. Things and persons are compared to magical tricks (or "illusions," *māyā*), that is, something not totally nonexistent but which is deceptive if taken at face value. There is no separate and enduring object to lead to *nirvāna,* but the reality underlying the illusion is there.

Such will be the pattern for the resolution of a large class of paradoxes. The common plenum/vacuum paradox may be treated simply: the mystical is void of any multiplicity (as in sensory-experience), but is full in its own right. In the words of the *Tao te ching,* "what is most full seems to be empty."[51] Or Eckhart on detachment (*Abegesheidenheit*): "to be full of things is to be empty of God, while to be empty of things is to be full of God."[52] This difference of senses can also be seen in the matter of "depth": God is here (in the "depth" dimension of "being" of the world revealed by the mystical experience) and is nowhere (on the "surface," that is, what is revealed through sense-experience). Hence Eckhart remarks: "All that a man has here externally in multiplicity is intrinsically one. Here all blades of grass, wood, and stone, all things are one. This is the deepest depth."[53] This causes confusion among philosophers because they imagine the mystical in terms of an object related to other objects. For instance, Professor William Wainwright maintains that if this doctrine, which he considers monism, were true, then "God would be identical with the world, and each item would be identical with every other apparent item."[54] But it is not a question of identity on the surface—here objects are obviously different. In Eckhart's words, the "creaturehood" of objects is distinct, but in their "is-ness" (*Istigkeit*) they are the same.

Some paradoxes may be recalcitrant to such paraphrasing because the context of some paradoxes does not make it clear what the author had in mind. Or it could be that all such paraphrases, in fact, miss the point of mystical paradoxes—they remain real, not *prima facie*. If this turns out to be the case, the experience about which nothing nonparadoxical can be said would remain central. Coming up with consistent claims to believe would not be a major concern. But to speak of "believing what is self-contradictory" is misleading. The situation would be comparable to the "paradoxes" of the drawing of the cube. No new language is generated, but, just as the drawing does not affect our relation to the cube, the verbalization of the mystical cannot adversely affect our relation to it (although this may gravely hamper our further understanding of it). When "drawn," the mystical appears not as experienced, and no longer is there a question of believing the verbal construction (confer Henle's mathematician). We would be forced into a Tertullianesque situation of affirming the impossible while interest remains focused upon the mystical insight.

Positive (Symbolic) Characterizations of the Mystical

Whatever the case, as part of what appears to be paradoxical descriptions, mystics ascribe positive properties to the mystical. If nothing else, the mystical is real and unitary (although again not in the mode of objects). To reiterate what was discussed previously, some descriptions are more accurate than their opposites, but the danger of misunderstanding the nature of the mystical is of tantamount importance. The device mystics use to avoid the reduction of the mystical when employing positive descriptions is to maintain that these remarks only "point to" rather than "directly describe" the mystical. Plotinus says we speak of the One to give direction, to point out the road to others desiring the experience of the mystical themselves.[55] And Śaṁkara says "reality-truth" (*satya*) cannot *denote* Brahman, but only can *indirectly* refer to it.[56] Words, he explains, do not properly describe or signify Brahman, but imply or direct our attention toward it.[57] The view of Sureśvara, one of his chief disciples, on this matter is that Brahman is indirectly signified in the manner the statement "The beds are crying" indirectly refers to the children upon them; but this type of suggestiveness (*dhvani*), based upon literal meaning (*abhidhā*), he concedes only inadequately implies the self since whatever is used to refer to the self becomes confused with it.[58]

It is adherence to the mistaken view of language that causes mystics to make such a distinction between direct and indirect reference. If they rejected the mirror-theory, the direct accuracy of certain remarks could be affirmed. But symbolic uses of language are necessary in giving meaning to the positive descriptions of the mystical because terms with established nonmystical uses are employed.

The term "symbol" has been used to mean almost anything, but here it will be restricted to mean what Mircea Eliade has in mind when he speaks of religious symbolism: its function "is to transform a thing or action into *something other* than that thing or action appears to be in the eyes of profane experience."[59] Such a distinction between literal and symbolic is what causes the term to be used in connection with mystics' discourse. The author of *The Cloud of Unknowing* in discussing spatial terms says:

> And therefore, be careful not to interpret the spiritual in material terms. It is necessary to use such words as "up," "down," "in," "out," "behind," "left," and "right," for regardless how spiritual our subject, we are men and must rely on the vocabulary of ordinary human language for communication. . . . Does this mean, however, that they must be understood in a literal sense? Of course not. As human beings we can go beyond their immediate significance to grasp the spiritual significance they bear at another level.[60]

Plotinus likewise notes that we need to add "as if" when speaking of the One, and Śaṁkara says the same about using "self."[61] The distinction between literal and symbolic may be hard to find. Philosophers today raise the issue of whether all denotative discourse is permeated with metaphors. Mary Hesse argues that even in science, analogy, not univocity, is the norm; and additionally because likeness, but not identity, between instances is the means by which generalizations are brought in, all discourse is metaphoric.[62] But as the preceding quotation indicates, mystics assume some terms apply literally sometimes when the mystical is not involved. Thus, such terms have established literal meanings. Mystics see linguistic problems arising only when assertive language is used for purposes other than for what it was originally designed (the description and analysis of physical objects).

Metaphoric statements are literally false and their meaning is governed more by the context in which they appear. They reorganize our view of the true referent by associating it with something else. This is important for advances in scientific theories and for our understanding in general. But since symbols are not analogies of proportionality, we are not enabled to know exactly the applicability of the property being ascribed.

Mystics do often speak figuratively about the mystical. To cite Plotinus on the One again: "Consider a spring which has no origin, which pours itself into all rivers without being exhausted, and which remains always as it is, undisturbed."[63] So also mystics use symbols of light and dark (even combined in such odd phrases as Dionysius the Areopagite's "ray of darkness" or the *Tao te ching's* "dark brightness") in connection with the absence of dualistic knowledge. In such cases, however, the principal subject (the mystical or mystical knowledge) can be specified nonfiguratively.

But in such direct attempts at denotation, transformation of normal meaning must occur if attention is to be directed toward the mystical. Thus, "the One" is not a colorful image, but to know what is meant by unity in mystical discourse we must go beyond its immediate significance, that is, uproot the idea of unity within normal awareness where it refers to objects (either unity of two previously distinct objects or the relation of the whole to its parts). Words point to the mystical in the sense the drawing of the cube points to a cube when it is uprooted from the usual implications such an image would hold for those who have never seen a three-dimensional object. In effect, a normal term is emptied of its normal connotation and filled with a new one given by the mystical insight.

A question immediately arises: if the mystical is totally distinct from the everyday world, how could anything from the latter be used symbolically to refer to the former? The answer is that although the two are ontologically incommensurable, they do have structural similarities. As the drawing and the cube have features in common even though their "modes of existence" differ, so also distinctions made within the normal world can be used metaphorically to explicate the mystical. This is why "one" and "reality" are more applicable than their opposites. If these attributes were open to revision with changes in the theory of the nature of the mystical, the reference problem would remain. If these or other attributes do survive shifts in theories, then one can argue that mystical discourse is a medium of representation and (ignoring the problems with realism) that in some sense it is anchored by reference to a reality existing independently of any language system.

But using symbolically what is apparent in everyday (dualistic) awareness is the best that can be done positively. Plotinus' figure of the One as an ever-full spring shows the problem. We all know what a spring is but how are we to understand a spring which has no origin and is never emptied, the source of all rivers, ever-flowing and yet always full? Because of this limitation, the positive remarks will always be indirect, not a direct presentation. So also with nonfigurative descriptions. Even to make the notion that the mystical involves a different "mode of existence" intelligible, the everyday distinction between "mental" and "physical" needs to be relied upon. An analogy such as the dreamer being "more real" than the characters in a dream and being the source of whatever "reality" they have is also required to make sense of saying the mystical is more real or more fundamental than the everyday world and that it is the "ground of being" upon which the everyday world is dependent. As mentioned before, the Indian illustration of a magical trick is intended to show the world's dependent existence and its outwardly deceptive character. Saying the mystical is "behind" the everyday world in the way the scientific world of particles and forces is "behind" appearances (this itself an analogy) entails the spatialization of the mystical, that is, using spatial metaphors to explicate the aspatial, and so is not clear and obvious. The idea of a "common depth" likewise needs explanation by means of a metaphor. To speak as Eckhart does of an "is-ness" in the context of a way of seeing the world not oriented around conceptual distinctions will certainly not make sense of "common depth" to philosophers for whom the only sense in the notion "is" is that of instantiation of a concept.

To take one final illustration, Śaṁkara tries to explain the idea of the ultimate nonduality of the world by means of analogy: the world appears multiple in normal perception just as the moon appears multiple to someone with a diseased eye, when in fact only one reality in each type of perception is actually involved.[64] We can understand the latter instance easily enough, but without a mystical experience its applicability to the matter of the relation of the world and the mystical is in question.

This highlights the issue of whether nonmystics can understand mystics when they give positive characterizations. All metaphors require some such imagination, but sympathy is not enough. A metaphor used to communicate any experience only becomes clear after the intended experience has occurred. Whether mystical utterances are meaningful to the unenlightened will ultimately depend upon whether such metaphoric discourse supplies a "meaningful" content. Arguably it does. The unenlightened can understand the point of a metaphor even if they do not know why it is applicable. But the unenlightened will always rely upon their nonmystical understanding of such characterizations of the mystical as "one" and "reality." To that extent, positive characterizations of the mystical will always be based upon metaphor. To use an analogy to explicate the role of analogy in mystical discourse, mystics cannot present the mystical for dualistic investigation any more than a cube can be presented for two-dimensional inspection. Nothing better can be supplied by mystics. Metaphors remain irreducible to any more literal description because of the role of a new experience in reorienting the sense and use of pertinent terms.

To make one final point, this survey of the four types of reactions to the mystical shows differing relations to the view that linguistic structures mirror the reality referred to. Silence and the way of negation affirm it; paradox shows perplexity concerning it; and the positive descriptions involving indirect reference implicitly reject it by accepting a commonality of some features comprising the mystical and the ordinary world—Śaṁkara, for instance, could not otherwise give a good reason why certain "limiting adjuncts" are more useful than others.

Conclusion

To conclude then, in such statements as Eckhart's at the beginning of this chapter something must be wrong: either the claim about everything in the Godhead being one accurately reflects Eckhart's belief, or the assertion that nothing can be uttered about it does—they both cannot be correct. And the usual alternatives (either rejecting mystics' claims out of hand or rejecting language) do not seem to the point. Mystics feel what they utter is not in vain—language is useful in leading others to the mystical experience and also in verifying whether others have had the prescribed experience (by seeing what they say or *how* they say it). This applies to their assertions about the mystical, too. To alter a Ch'an analogy, in such assertions words are used as more than a finger pointing to the image of the moon reflecting in a pool of water—they try to convey an image of the "moon" itself.

Can something from the everyday world (that is, language) reveal something true about the mystical? To maintain that all claims must be false is to accept the mirror-theory of language. Much about the mystical may not in fact be encodable, but the works of mystics suggest that something is.

But in trying to show that the claim "Everything in the Godhead is one" is as accurate, meaningful, and generally put into words as well as can be expected when dealing with something nonordinary, all that has been accomplished at best is to untangle a few conceptual knots connected with this form of religiosity. Thereby the writings of mystics may be a little more intelligible to the unenlightened. Nothing more substantial toward judging the value or validity of the mystical insight has been attempted. And far from aiding in inducing such an experience, defending the accuracy of some descriptions embeds concepts more firmly as acceptable to the intellect. An antimystical effect is thereby produced. We are still left in the realm of language and, as the Ch'an adage goes, "Wordiness and intellection—the more with them, the further astray we go."[65]

Part IV

Mysticism and Science

Chapter 6

Concerning Joseph Needham on Taoism

Simply put, the objective of this chapter is to show that Joseph Needham in his classic, *Science and Civilisation in China,* distorts the nature both of science and of "philosophical Taoism" (*Tao chia*[a]) as presented in the *Tao te ching*[b] and the *Chuang tzu*[c]. "Taoist" in this chapter will refer solely to the thought of these texts, even though there are other phenomena legitimately labelled "Taoist" and neither text is a consistent whole.[1]

What precisely "science" is is notoriously difficult to determine. But Needham seems to be thinking in terms of a natural (physical and biological) science whose methods have been characterized by another as always changing yet converging in varying degrees around such techniques as observation, generalization, hypothetico-deductive use of assumptions, controlled experimentation, measurement, use of instruments, and mathematical construction.[2]

Basic Objectives and Factual Claims

If one accepts the basic objective of the natural sciences in the West from the Greeks to the present to be intellectual understanding of nature, with technological advantages hovering nearby, it would then be hard to assert that the fundamental intent of the Taoist texts is *scientific*. Closer to the truth (and to more traditional interpretations) would be that the *Tao te ching* is concerned with a way of life conducive to living a natural span of time with as little external and internal interference as possible; and a mystical freedom, a freedom from attachment to life or fear of death and so forth, is the primary goal advocated in the *Chuang tzu*.

Needham, to the contrary, sees scientific and Taoist aims as basically the same. For him, it is "faith in natural science" to feel that all "man can do is to study and describe phenomena" without concern for ultimate beginnings or ends (p. 40)[3] and without reference to spirits or other mythic entities. This he perceives likewise as central to Taoist thought.

But ambiguity in the phrase "to study and describe phenomena" leads to difficulties with such a characterization. Taoists do depict the world without reference to a supernatural realm of gods (except in parables), but to infer that therefore these factual claims are ipso facto scientific is surely wrong. Artists, for instance, do likewise in giving nonscientific (sometimes very unscientific) descriptions of the world. The contrasting Weltanschauungen and ways of life of the Taoist and scientific enterprises will become clearer as the argument progresses. Only that similar claims can arise out of differing contexts, involving different orders of questions, or from divergent visions of the world, is being stressed here. Thus, David Hume advanced claims stating the unreality of an enduring subject which sound very Buddhist and yet do not have that intent: the Buddhist assertion of the impermanence of constructed entities and the lack of enduring selves arises in a soteriological context of radically ending suffering, not in the more limited context of our philosophical questions. The Buddhist and philosophical claims converge only on an abstract level. Such claims cannot be cited to support the assertion that Buddhism and philosophy are the same enterprise.

To apply this observation: Taoists were certainly not ignorant of nature—all societies have some natural knowledge necessary for survival—but their goal was not to further empirical understanding. To say that the absence of God today in scientific theories is a return in the West to a Taoist outlook (p. 581) is the same as saying that Hume is a Buddhist based upon the extremely tenuous grounds that both points of view converge on one item abstracted from their respective contexts. Or to see the remark about the useless tree being the one that attains the greatest size (*CT* 4) as approaching the idea of natural selection fits it into a scheme which distorts it: the point of the illustration more likely is about living a long comfortable life unimpeded by human purposes, not about an evolutionary theory involving the adaptation and development of later generations—"survival of the fittest" (p. 80) applies only in a very different sense from that of the evolutionary. So also Taoists in emphasizing relativity of points of view or the universe's subtlety and immensity "were groping after an Einsteinian world-picture" (p. 543) only in the extended sense of "relativity" embracing Copernicus, Locke, medieval scholastics, and anyone else dealing with the relativity of frameworks—their commonality rests *not* in the area of science, let alone in one particular scientific theory.

Needham commits the same mistake with his comment upon the passage that Heaven and Earth are not humane (*TTC* 5): "No one can understand this unless it is realized that the expulsion of ethical judgments from natural science was an essential step in its development" (p. 49). Rejecting the artificiality of social standards as indicative of reality may overlap with a "scientific world-view" (p. 48), but this does not force all who do so into a scientific mode of thought. The purpose in the Taoists' case is not merely descriptive or explanatory, but is extra-scientific. The Taoist purpose involves values and courses of conduct that scientists need not adopt to remain scientists. To be truly parallel, the content in terms of factual claims must not only be the same, the roles the claims play in the two enterprises must be the same. Such congruence does not exist in this instance.

The *Tao te ching* and the *Chuang tzu* assume as part of their world-view the basic knowledge and interpretation of their day concerning the world, just as any religious text does. For instance, although no treatises before the Han period deal explicitly with the *yin-yang*[d] perspective (a way of viewing experience and the world evolving out of a particular model, in this case, perhaps the relation of light to dark, or male to female), both texts presuppose it (*TTC* 42, *CT* 2, 4, 6, 11, 13, 16, 21, 24, 25, 33).[4] Another passage (*CT* 14) contains questions which scientists would also ask—whether the sky is revolving and the earth standing still, whether they are mechanically arranged, and so forth—while the Taoist reply is couched not in terms of specific testable hypotheses, but of general structures (the six ultimates and five constancies) more metaphysical in nature. Harmonious interconnection and interdependence of the whole of reality are basic.

The various views on the Way (*tao*)[e] appear to be the results of construing what occurs in mystical experiences, both those experiences occurring when the sensory and conceptual apparatus of the mind is in total abeyance, and those sensory experiences in which conceptual categorization is loosened,[5] in the contexts of such cultural concepts. The Way in one of its aspects (non-being (*wu*[f]), the nameless, the vacuous self-so (*tzu jan*[g]), the inexhaustible source of particulars) cannot function as a *scientific* explanation insofar as scientific accounts must account for why one state of affairs occurs and not another, not point out something uniform for all reality regardless of what empirically is the case.[6] But in its other aspect the Way reflects the notion of effortless, harmonious interaction: it is a natural process governing everything "not so much by force as by a kind of natural curvature in space and time" (pp. 36–37). The *Chuang tzu* especially emphasizes the ever-active process of change: the Way is the invariable order and structure underlying transformations, which remains unaltered by whatever mutual interaction between parts occurs (*CT* 1, 6, 7). A decrease in one respect results in an increase in another, and thus the "whole" is not diminished.

From this, some points important for the issue at hand appear: (1) uniformity of the Way, (2) interconnection of events, and (3) regularity in inevitable change. Just as any natural claim about the world is not necessarily scientific, so also just because Taoists presuppose the fundamental world-view of Chinese "common sense," this does not make them scientific. The questions become whether the world-view contains scientific elements and more importantly, what use Taoists make of it. Taoists play off Confucian ideals—as *yin* to Confucian *yang* (pp. 61–63)—and Chuang tzu utilized a sophist, Hui Shih,[h] as the material he worked upon without Taoists becoming Confucians or sophists. The same could occur even if the basic world-view were scientific in some respects.

Consider first such ideas as the uniformity of the Way or the impartiality of Heaven. Leaving aside questions of its philosophical status, the uniformity of space, time, and the relation between events is basic to classical, although not all contemporary submicroscopic, mechanics; only then are lawful predictions in the everyday world possible; its very intelligibility appears dependent upon such a category. The uniformity of the Way is analogous to the uniformity of physical processes. But, as with the earlier example of Hume and the Buddha, the Taoist affirmations of natural causes for the process of change and of the uniformity of change throughout time can only indicate an area of overlapping on an abstract point between two incongruous systems.[7] Needham's maintaining the universality of change and transformation as one of Taoists' "deepest scientific insights" (p. 161) may be the result of his reading in something not there in the texts. For he is mistaken when he alleges Taoist thought parallels the "unity in Nature which is the basic assumption of natural science" (p. 47). A minimal *uniformity* is essential to the sciences (i.e., whenever or wherever conditions x arise, the *y* occurs), not the *unity* Needham mentions. For Taoists more is meant by the term "unity." The oneness of the Way in the *Tao te ching* and such phrases as "all things are one" (*CT* 12) are connected with mystical nonduality. Needham is conflating two ideas here and not attaching enough importance to one aspect of the Way.

But the uniformity compatible with science remains; one must look at the rest of the contexts to see if there is any more related significance. Is the interconnection of the elements of reality necessarily scientific? Here Needham definitely reads too much into the texts. To say that when the *Chuang tzu* (18) speaks of the non-fixity of biological species (e.g., man arising from horses and later returning to the "mysterious workings"), the text "comes very close to a statement of a theory of evolution" (p. 78) misrepresents entirely the framework of the passage. A theory of evolution is advanced as the result, if not of experimentation, of at least observation in the light of a limited range of alternative explanations; Chuang tzu's "circle of beings," on the other hand, is merely one application working out what is dictated by his perspective, not the result of any sustained empirical investigation. It is the difference between factual claims dictated by metaphysics and those claims tested by observation and open to revision. Once again: being *scientific* involves more than being a natural factual claim, which elsewhere could conceivably be incorporated into a scientific scheme. Needham's comment upon the interdependence of the hundreds of bodily parts (*CT* 2) is strange for precisely this reason:

> These words are indeed striking when we think of what is now known about the complex interrelations of stimulators and reactors in living organisms and their development, or the mutual influences of the glands of the endocrine (p. 52).

It is one thing to note the "pure organicism of Taoist thought" (ibid.), here operating on the level of a person, and something quite different to connect it with complex biological theories developed through painstaking research and experimentation. The two perspectives coincide upon the parts of the body being interrelated—but they have in common only this very general point without the type of knowledge, methods employed or basic intents being identical.

The Taoist doctrine of the ebb and flow of the Way should not be seen as a doctrine of evolution. There is an eternal movement from the nameless Way to the "mother" of heaven and earth and then to all creatures and back again (*TTC* 1, 40). But this is not a doctrine of changes among the creatures, as is evolution. It involves an issuing forth from an abiding source and a return to it. Certainly the Darwinian notion of natural selection—a battle of tooth and claw with the fittest surviving—is completely alien to the Taoist emphasis on operating by weakness (*TTC* 40) and noncontention (*TTC* 8). The Taoist symbols of the receptivity of the Way—non-being (*TTC* 40), mother (*TTC* 6, 25), the valley spirit (*TTC* 6), silence and emptiness (*TTC* 4, 25), water (*TTC* 32, 78), the weak and soft conquering the strong (*TTC* 36, 43)—only reinforce this conclusion. The scientific doctrine of evolution and this doctrine of emanation converge only on the abstract level of the idea that things are impermanent. Commonality between science and mysticism can only be artificially created by imposing the concept of evolution upon the Taoist doctrine.

Sometimes the scientific and Taoist claims do not even have a commonality. To maintain that the *Chuang tzu*, in suggesting that the dependence of a shadow upon an object for its motion perhaps indicates the dependence of everything upon something else (*CT* 2), is adumbrating "a principle of non-mechanical causation" (p. 51) is to find a factual claim (causation) that the passage does not contain: dependence is not equivalent to all other types of relationships, let alone the specialized conception of causation. Nor does Chuang tzu necessarily have anything in mind about "biological change" (p. 80) when speaking of owls and horses preferring different environments: the objective of the observation concerns differing "points of view" (discussed below), not adaptation which could be taken as the mechanism giving rise to the differences—this question of *origin of species* Chuang tzu never deals with.

Thus, serious doubts exist concerning the allegedly scientific nature of Taoist interdependence. To take up a third point mentioned earlier, do the repetitions and regularities Taoists see constitute a scientific view of nature as connected systems of events governed by laws? Needham correctly notes that the Chinese world outlook involves an idea of order positively excluding the notion of law (p. 572)—there are no precisely formulated abstract laws of nature (p. 582). Instead affirmed is a world-view of an organic cooperation of all beings as parts of a hierarchy of wholes forming cosmic patterns while obeying the internal dictates of their own nature, not of laws externally imposed (pp. 582–583). The Way despite its profundity (*hsüan*[i]) presents a discernable order rather than randomness: cycles (of the seasons, etc.), returning to the "root"

(*TTC* 40), and reversion (extremes leading to their opposites) at least. These repetitions provide points of stability throughout the process of change. Here science and Taoism converge on an abstract point. The purpose of the Taoist point of view, however, is extra-scientific: people can reply upon the dependable and accept the inevitable—to look upon even the cycle of life and death as not in itself evil, but as a necessary return to the process of arising. The Taoist extra-scientific values relate, not to gaining knowledge of the world, but to living a total way of life. That Needham would speak in this regard of "the calm reckoning of the scientific mind aware of compositeness and prepared to face decomposition" (p. 41) expresses more an idolization of scientists than anything intrinsic to scientific methods: there is a major difference between detecting orderliness to change, and the religious reconciliation of Chuang tzu's idea of transformation.

Not only is the intent nonscientific, there is a fundamentally different stance or orientation towards nature (however it was conceived at the time) than the scientific. It involves participating more than analyzing and remaining as detached as possible. The divergence may be brought out by examining the Taoist antitheoretical point of view, and the contrast between contemplation and scientific observation.

Wisdom and Understanding

The role of theory in science is essential. Science's central goal is conceptual understanding—patterning diverse arrays of experiences within conceptual frameworks[8]—not practical control of the world. Injecting clarity and simple order into what is initially complex is paramount. Thus, Darwin's theory of evolution, although devoid of predictive or retrodictive capabilities, is considered scientific since it supplies a mechanism (natural selection) which makes it seem reasonable to us that what happened ought to have occurred as it did. Theory-construction is not a passive reading off of facts from observation, but is a human product. As Max Planck says of science as a whole: "Science is a created work of art; for new ideas are not generated by deduction, but by a creative imagination."[9] Ian Barbour nicely sums up another point: even scientific concepts (such as mass and acceleration) "are mental constructs used to interpret observation; they are symbols that help us organize experience."[10] Such preformed concepts employed in the context of laws abstract certain aspects of experiences as being the ones most significant for our purposes; these laws in turn are subsumed under explanatory theories. Each step is abstractive, replacing complex experience with constructs—not complete, exact replicas of nature—to achieve particular and limited purposes. The search for the intelligible has led upon occasion to a total disparaging of what is given directly in sense-experience, as in the case of Parmenides.

Explanation in the sciences depends upon the same human element. For instance, to explain heat, reference is necessary to athermal particles (otherwise an infinite regress would occur).[11] Since what is without heat is not given in experience, the role of inference and imagination is obvious. Once freed from speaking only of what can be sensed, phenomena diverse on the surface can be brought into an understanding unified around theoretical entities. The status of such entities is the subject of the realist-instrumentalist debate. One disputant, W. V. O. Quine, stresses the fabricated nature of them, as well as physics and mathematics in general, by calling them irreducible posits introduced for convenience and comparable epistemologically to the gods of Homer.[12] What is deemed "real" depends upon the needs of the conceptual system as a whole.

All human thought involves abstractions. However, Taoists work to decrease the importance attached to these conceptions, while scientists live in a world in which such abstractions are central. Both Taoist texts contain much attacking the production of such fabrications. Certainly Taoists have not postulated multiple, unexperienceable theoretical entities used to unify experiences. We are commended to learn to be "unlearned" (*TTC* 64, 71) and are told that only by "unknowing" can we hope to know the Way (*CT* 24). Knowledge derived from limited frames of reference give rise only to a relativity of points of view: when all are seen as equal, what is long and what is short, what is good and what is evil? The "axis of the Way" indicates that what is, for example, high from one point of view (e.g., the value one attaches to one's own well-being) is low from another (the value we attach to another's well-being). From the point of view of the Way, there is ultimately no high or low since the concepts arise only within limited frameworks. By taking the wider view, all constructs, even "is" and "is not," are seen as not of ultimate significance. What is death from one point of view is a return to the process of change, a birth of sorts, from another. Chuang tzu's famous dream about being a butterfly—upon waking, he could not tell if he had dreamed or now was a butterfly dreaming he was

Chuang tzu (*CT* 2)—illustrates the problem of determining which limited viewpoint is correct.

Needham observes the Taoist attack on knowledge (*TTC* 3, 19, 65), but feels the emphasis upon striving to be without knowledge or desire, to banish wisdom and to discard knowledge is "obviously in apparent contradiction with the interest of the Taoists in natural knowledge already demonstrated" (pp. 86–87). Thus, he concludes that Taoists are not attacking science, but only the Confucian social knowledge of the time. The pertinent line from *Tao te ching* 3 therefore could be paraphrased as (pp. 88–89): "empty their minds (of preconceived social ideas and prejudices) and (thereby) fill their stomachs (with the greater amount of food made available through scientific knowledge)." Taoism becomes not an "anti-rational mysticism" but a "proto-scientific anti-scholasticism" in his eyes (p. 89).[13] The "absolute justification" of this interpretation is the greatest inventions of ancient China such as the uses of water power (ibid.). But as Needham himself realizes (and as will be dealt with later) both texts contain passages strongly condemning technology. If such technology is his most solid support, then perhaps his theory is wrong.

In their attacks upon learning and knowledge, no doubt Confucian learning and rites were prominent in the Taoists' minds. However, something broader is intended by Chuang tzu saying one cannot discuss the ocean with a well frog nor the Way with a scholar (*CT* 17). The doctrines which the scholars meticulously learned and memorized cramped their vision as much as the limited point of view of the frog. Why would not all discursive knowledge (rational knowledge, knowledge of objects, and especially scientific knowledge) fall under such an attack? When Needham comments on one passage (*TTC* 3) that one empties the mind not of "true knowledge" but of prejudices and feudal distinctions thus "keeping memories compatible with sound judgments of Nature" (p. 89), his reference to memories and judgments seems out of keeping with the emphasis upon unknowing. A more traditional and less forced interpretation of the passage would be to say that the Taoist sage-ruler keeps the people free of all learning (cf. *TTC* 65), thereby avoiding any arising of desires, and merely feeds them (with no implied reference to improved technology). To bolster his case, Needham cites an authority on the rise of modern science who contends that experimental science found an ally in religious mysticism with its reaction against the intellectual pride of medieval European orthodox scholastics (p. 90). But another authority on the rise of modern science, Hans

Reichenbach, notes the connection of mysticism with the abandonment of empirical observation,[14] and thus inhibiting technological advances.

If the Taoists do mean abandoning discursive knowledge when advocating discarding knowledge and desires, the following quotation from Needham is certainly totally misdirected:

> . . . what was the main motive of the Taoist philosophers in wishing to engage in the observation of Nature? There can be little doubt that it was in order to gain that peace of mind which comes from having formulated a theory or hypothesis, however provisional, about the terrifying manifestations of the natural world surrounding and penetrating the frail structure of human society (p. 63).

That the tranquility Taoists claim is not routinely claimed by scientists in the West should be sufficient to see that the tranquility could not have come through framing tentatively-held hypotheses or any similar theoretical understanding.

Taoist "true wisdom" contrasts radically with scientific understanding. To be in accord with the always-so (*ch'ang*[j]) is to be illumined (*TTC* 55). But who has found the Mother (the *tao*) knows the sons (all things) (*TTC* 52). This mystical omniscience is not scientific knowledge of the "surface" differentiations but of their common "root" reality. It cannot be accomplished through scientific investigation. In fact, the direct opposite is necessary and thus: the sage knows everything under heaven without going out of doors; he can see the way of heaven without looking out of his windows; in fact, the further he travels the less he knows; therefore, the sage knows without going about and sees all without looking (*TTC* 47). The least forced interpretation of this passage is a mystical one which condemns any scientific investigation of things. The "doors" and "windows" referred to in the passages cited above may refer to the senses and thus reinforce a mystical interpretation. Another passage reinforces it: "True wisdom is different from much learning; much learning means little wisdom" (*TTC* 81).

Learning is contrasted with knowledge of the Way (*TTC* 48, 81). The sage abolishes learning and returns to the simplicity of the "uncarved block" (*TTC* 19, 28, 64, 71). The Taoists' main concern may be with Confucian learning, but their doctrine applies with equal force to any enterprise that increases our differentiations. Therefore, since science must proceed by making distinctions, science, too, interferes with returning to the "uncarved block." This leads to the conclusion that the Taoists would condemn scientific knowledge.

But Needham is correct in noting the importance of conforming to what is natural. The issue is whether discursive knowledge is involved in such action. On this point, Arthur Danto appears right in saying that know-how (a skill) is involved, not knowing-that (discursive knowledge of a state of affairs).[15] Take the illustration of cutting up the ox (*CT* 3; cf. *TTC* 72). Is scientific knowledge of the anatomy of the ox involved as Needham contends (p. 45)? The story supports better precisely the opposite. At first the carver saw the whole carcass; after three years, he saw no more whole animals; later he worked only with his mind, not his eyes, since his spirit no longer needed the control of his senses. Thus, he saw less than the whole picture after three years and eventually arrived at his final skill by not even seeing the parts, that is, the anatomical divisions; he followed the structure immediately before him without applying external knowledge of the nature, location or whatever of the parts of the beast. He responds with a still mind to what is there, not to preconceived notions of what he would find. Only by unknowing such discursive knowledge as anatomy did he achieve his spontaneous skill. Any intellectual understanding would go against the grain. Scientific knowledge is part of the "underbrush" (*CT* 1) filling the mind, cluttering up the person and interfering with what he must do. For another example, consider the swimmer Confucius is portrayed as encountering:

> I go under with the swirls and come out with the eddies, following along the way the water goes and never thinking about myself. That's how I can stay afloat. (*CT* 19)

It is not by studying flow patterns or hydraulics that he survives what seemed to Confucius an unswimmable river, but by forgetting everything, even himself. Even ordinary "knowing how" to swim would involve fighting the currents and would result in drowning.

In light of this, it is hard to see how Needham can maintain the Taoist way of life is even "proto-scientific." He concedes that Taoists distrust reason and logic (p. 579) and that the Way is inscrutable to the theoretical intellect (p. 543). But, since natural science by its very nature extends the scope of reason to encompass as much as possible and necessarily has a theoretical component, Taoism will always be antagonistic to science in this crucial regard. Mystical wisdom involves something always open to experience, not the tentatively-held constructions of science found by experiment and conjecture concerning the structures or order behind appearances.

Contemplation and Scientific Observation

Nor are Taoists protoscientific with respect to observation. To see why this is the case, something basic to scientific observation must be considered. In giving explanations of what occurs in normal sense-experience, science presents pictures of the world in which what is observed is characterized as having features separating (at least heuristically) one "object" from another, and in which persons are seen as spectators—discrete objects among a collection of objects. The whole of scientific observation, measurement, experimentation and so forth makes no sense apart from this framework. The Chinese world-view centers around events and constant, transformative processes rather than distinct entities, as does the classical Western approach. There is nothing unscientific about this difference in models and Needham may be correct in saying that some elements of the structure of the world as modern science knows it were prefigured in *yin-yang* speculation. F. S. C. Northrop contrasts the Greek and Chinese ways of *knowing* nature, though, as follows: the former developed the way of knowing nature by postulation of external entities and by hypotheses accompanied by the appropriate mode of verification (empirical fitting of "facts" to theories) while the latter concentrated upon the immediately apprehended.[16] Needham of course denies this: *yin-yang* and the five agents (*wu hsing*[k]) have the same status as proto-scientific hypotheses as the systems of the pre-Socratics and other Greek schools (p. 579). Northrop's distinction between ways of knowing, although an improvement, does not properly stress that the varying approaches to reality entail different orientations toward perceptions, for one can construe perceptions as indicative of entities "out there," separate from each other and from the observer, or as aspects of an underlying unity.

To see the contrast with the Taoist approach, reference must be made to those passages which point to mystical experiences. The *Tao te ching* declares that by learning one increases day by day while by practicing the Way one decreases (indicating as a limit the total end of conceptual discriminating) (48); that the sage has no extensive knowledge (81); that one should embrace the One (the undifferentiated) (10, 22), attain complete vacuity (*hsü*[l]) and the calmness of realizing the eternal (16); that the sage is ignorant (20), returns to the uncarved block (*p'u,*[m] the undifferentiated state), and reverts to the root (16). These passages clearly imply mystical experiences; others may fall within this group; for instance, those passages about the Way being invisible, inaudible, and without form (14, 35) or about closing the mouth, shutting the doors (perhaps the sense organs), untying the tangles and so on (47, 52, 56) may refer to the necessity of stilling sensory-conceptual activity. Elsewhere the *Tao te ching* does refer to meditative practices: concentrating the breath and cleansing the mirror (of the mind) (10) and attaining utmost emptiness and stillness (15, 16). The illumination needed to know the everlasting (*TTC* 10, 16, 22, 24, 41, 52, 55) also strongly suggests mysticism. In the *Chuang tzu,* the pertinent expressions are "fasting of the mind" (*hsin chai*[n]) (4) and "sitting and forgetting" (*tso wang*[o]) which is explained as: "I smash up my limbs and body, drive out perception and intellect, cast off form and do away with understanding, and make myself identical with the Great Thoroughfare" (6). Chuang tzu also speaks of discarding little and great knowledge to become clear (26), and wandering outside the realm of forms and bodies (5).

The effect of this unknowing on perception in those experiences in which sensation does occur hardly supports a scientific interpretation. Like a switch in Gestalt, emphasis is turned from the differentiations to the core of commonality—the oneness of the Way in everything. Chuang tzu speaks of seeing things as equal (*CT* 2): if one perceives things with attention to differentiating factors, then one's liver and bladder are as different as the states of Ch'u and Yüeh; yet from the point of view of their sameness, the "ten thousand things" (i.e., everything) are one. From this point of view, one can "embrace the ten thousand things and roll them into one" (*CT* 1). Such perception involves a leveling of "this" and "that" (*CT* 2), not becoming attached to any particular feature or aspect—only then does one reach impartiality, the Great Understanding (*CT* 26). The passive contemplative (*kuan*[p]) approach of "mystical perception" is mindful of what occurs. But in tending toward the elimination of the conceptual element of perception, one remains indifferent and leisurely even at the sight of magnificient scenes (*TTC* 26). Contemplatives remain disinterested; differentiating features are not the center of attention, nothing attracts their attention more than anything else and nothing is retained, their minds being empty of the discrete. The mind becomes like a mirror.

With this difference in ways of seeing the world, mystical perception is not merely noting the world as given apart from specific descriptive terms—the "that-ness" of the world apart from the "how-ness." Rather, a substantial change in awareness occurs: approaching the world without differentiating concepts being involved. Nor is such "merging into one" the result of an intellectual process: " . . . to wear out your brain trying to make things into one without realizing that they are all the same—this is called 'three in the morning'." The parable of the monkeys and the nuts fed to them then follows (*CT* 2), the import of which for this question is not to get caught up in the level of labels rather than the level of substance—the keeper fed the monkeys the same number of nuts per day as before, but the monkeys were placated by getting four nuts in the morning (and only three in the evening) rather than three in the morning (and four in the evening) because they were caught up in differentiating factors only. Simplicity as an element in theory-construction is very much a mental enterprise, sometimes involving a great deal of effort to reduce the number of ultimate ontological categories involved. Quite distinct from the scientific approach is letting "your mind wander in simplicity" and blending "your spirit with the vastness" as you "follow along things the way they are" without personal views (*CT* 7). In short, science may unify phenomena under broader and broader theories but it directs attention to more and more differentiations, while Taoism pulls in the opposite direction, even if concepts are not totally eliminated.

Once scientific observation is understood within its context of a wider analytic world-view, it is difficult to agree with Needham about "Taoist protoscientific observation of natural change" (p. 85). The subject matter of the natural sciences is exclusively what only appears when the "uncarved block" (*TTC* 1, 19, 28) is cut—this is what is *empirical* for the sciences. Names appear, indicating for the Taoists the differentiations. Concepts arise in pairs (*TTC* 2): we only call something "good" if we discern something distinct from it, that is, something "bad." Only when the great Way declined did such concepts arise (*TTC* 18). Thus, the Way that can be spoken of is not the real Way (*TTC* 1). The man of superior virtue is not conscious of his virtue (because he has nothing to contrast with it) and thus truly possesses virtue (*TTC* 38). If we react to concepts, we live in a world of discriminations, not in accordance with the great Way. A proscription of names is thus necessary (*TTC* 32, 37), since the use of them is the first step taken in converting nature into what is apprehensible and what is a source of desires.[17] Attention is directed to particulars, and the Way—nameless (*TTC* 1, 32, 37), featureless, silent, formless, unchanging (25), unseen, unheard, uncomprehensible, unnameable (14) origin of all—is lost.

On the other hand, science is necessarily a matter of propositions and hence of such differentiations. Even the most basic concepts are meaningful only in the context of elaborated theories. Observations and the "facts" are subsequently shaped in the light of these concepts. " 'Observations' are always abstractions from our total experience, and they are expressed in terms of conceptual structures."[18] Scientific observation is a reaction to concepts. Preconceived questions and categories direct the scientist's attention to particular aspects of phenomena, for example, isolating what the theory designates as relevant causal factors. Scientists cannot approach nature without a set of preconceptions (albeit revisable ones). These preconceptions force nature into conceptual boxes and guide what areas to investigate, what methods to use, and what will count as an answer (a "fact"). The instruments employed similarly shape research. Infants and brainless photosensitive computers do not make scientific observations—such observing is a theory-laden activity of a particular person with particular interests.[19] It is a mistaken view of science on Needham's part to feel a scientist must be as receptive as a little child (p. 161)—a child, no more than a computer, would have the necessary attentiveness to selected elements and the ability to make sense out of them.

Contemplation, on the other hand, does approach such an ideal of receptivity: "The sage all the time sees and hears no more than an infant sees and hears" (*TTC* 49, Waley's translation). Moss Roberts depicts such contemplation as observing phenomena with innocent sacramental wonder free from names, desire, and purpose thereby leaving things intact.[20] The mind with its vacuity becomes like still water, a mirror reflecting what is there (*CT* 7). This mystical objectivity is not that of science, where objectivity is thought of in terms of experiments repeatable in all relevant aspects for the purpose of intersubjective confirmation by a community educated in a certain discipline. Scientific detachment does not include abandoning interest in particulars; human wishes and purposes are central as long as the analytic element continues.

The contemplative stance is obviously inimical to the attention to preselected aspects (and the often laborious effort) required for any experimentation. Thus, Needham's reason for the failure of Taoists to develop any experimental method or any systemization of observations—because they were so wedded to the empirical that they did not elaborate a logic or adequate corpus of technical terms for the scientific enterprise (p. 161)—does not account for the very different attitude Taoists have towards nature.

The world for Taoists is not set over against a spectator. Instead, the world's structure is more participated in, as with the swimmer surrendering to the swirling water. "The sage leans on the sun and moon, tucks the universe under his arm, merges himself with things . . . " (*CT* 2). With the theoretical/conceptual apparatus loosened, if not entirely eliminated, one participates in the Way, not knowing or understanding it as one would an object under study. The ideal of "clear and distinct" Cartesian ideas is integral to the scientific point of view, but not the Taoist approach. Even a sense of "I" evaporates in the "rolling into one." All perception might be thought to be "immediate experience" in the Taoist sense except that it is taken normally (and always in science) to be experience *of* an object, that is, indirect indications of a world "out there." In a mystical framework having no reference to a subject distinct from an object or to one object distinct from another, such a view of the nature of perception is not possible.

Seeing all things as equal also gives a more prominent position to each element experienced. The paradigm of scientific understanding or explanation of a particular entity or process is the subsumption of it under a general "covering" law permitting prediction. The Way is not a philosophical abstraction of sameness deemphasizing individual differences as a law embedded in the analytic point of view would. For Taoists, the spontaneity and variety of nature is valued: each individual "thing" has its own virtue (*te*[q]) arising from the Way; each element exists and is integral to the harmonious operation of nature. The parable of drilling seven holes in Chaos (*Hun-tun*[r]) to make him like us (thereby killing him) (*CT* 7), and the example of not lengthening a duck's legs or shortening those of a crane's suggest at least each individual's value and the lack of external, uniform standards. Later Chinese art upon which Needham concedes there is Taoist influence deals more with uniqueness than with generalized models, let alone the very abstract and exact scientific drawings of charts or diagrams. Many features of such art (e.g., lack of concern for perspective) reflect other than scientific standards.

Technology Versus Wu Wei[s]

Turning to the practical side of science, that is, turning from the intellectual understanding of the world to applications of this scientific knowledge for human benefit, once again one finds Needham maintaining the same position. Lieh tzu[t] riding the wind, for example, is a half-belief, a wish-fulfillment embodying a distinct flavor of Baconian affirmation of the future powers over nature which might await the investigators of nature (p. 65).

There indeed is a purposive strand in Taoism (especially in the *Tao te ching*) distinct from the contemplative strand. As Herrlee Creel points out, to be without desire in order to gain the things you desire (*TTC* 7, 28, 48, 66, 67) is to cultivate an attitude as a means to power.[21] Taking the weak position to conquer the strong is such a technique of control. From Needham: "By yielding, by not imposing his preconceptions on Nature, he will be able to observe and understand and so to govern and control" (p. 37). But this technique, no matter how effective it may be, is not *scientific* in any strict sense. Nor is it for governing and understanding nature as Needham feels. Nor is it compatible with the contemplative type of *wu wei* (discussed below) which is the major stance of Taoism.[22]

Little needs to be mentioned concerning "religious Taoism" (*tao chiao,*[u] *Hsien Taoism*[v]) since of concern here is Needham's views of "philosophical Taoism." According to Creel, the two traditions were never closely associated.[23] This movement might have been a source of science: the quest for physical immortality is an attempt to fight nature (i.e., death), and thus is scientific or technological in spirit. But Needham is incorrect in saying "From the beginning Taoist thought was captivated by the idea that it was possible to achieve a material immortality" (p. 139) if this is to indicate the intent of the *Tao te ching*: philosophical Taoism aimed at no extension of the normal life-span, but dealt only with how to survive that long by being free of striving and personal desires (cf. *TTC* 7, 24).[24] Technology involves overcoming nature for our advantage; nature is treated as an object to be exploited. Such a stance toward the world is completely contrary to Taoist contemplation.

This brings up the subject of *wu wei* (action free from striving). *Wu wei* is action free of reflection and desire which interfere with the natural and spontaneous activity of the Way. Nature has a pattern that can be followed, and the Way as a practical way of life reflects the Way as structure of the world. By conforming to the

Way, it readily lends its power (*TTC* 28); by being passive, one taps an inexhaustible reserve of power. By not striving against the grain, by avoiding partiality—laden with personal motives—one leads an effortless life without plans or expectations. Aberrations of the Way such as sadness, joy, love, and hate result only from personal motivation and attachment, not from natural occurrences as such. Action is still purposeful (afterall, the carver and the swimmer had objectives), but one is responding spontaneously to the situation at hand—not trying to bend the situation either for one's personal profit, or reacting according to one's preconceived ideas of the nature of reality or of what is good or bad. And yet by doing nothing (through striving), there is nothing that is not done (naturally by the Way) (*TTC* 48, *CT* 7).

Enough was said earlier on scientific observation to raise serious doubts about another of Needham's claims: "To be able to practice *wu wei* implied learning from Nature by observations essentially scientific" (p. 71). Scientific observations are not necessary to practicing *wu wei*; indeed, Taoist observations are the opposite, insofar as they involve what is immediately before the observer without categorizing. In addition, to define "*wu wei*" simply as the opposite (*wu*) of actions contrary to nature (*wei*^{w}), as Needham does, is misleading because all disciplines, including science, of course, feel their actions are in keeping with nature.

All factual claims, including those of science, have implications for how one lives, that is, what courses of action are reasonable (or even conceivable) in the light of what one knows. But technology attempts to improve life by means antithetical to the Taoist intent—by these means, one does not attempt to live as the world "lives," but one sets oneself over against nature.

Needham not surprisingly disagrees. Parts of the second chapter of the *Chuang tzu* represent for him a technological spirit without a background of theoretical science (p. 84). In his view, the carvers, cicada-catchers, swimmers, swordmakers, bellstand-carvers, arrow-makers, and wheelwrights appear as illustrations of technicians (p. 121). The carver and the swimmer cited earlier are cases of the application of the Way to everyday life where scientific skill would have appeared appropriate but is not applied; "technology" in a sense is involved, but not the scientific sort (i.e., connected with the scientific and analytic approach to reality). Taoists advocate going with nature, not utilizing science to twist nature to our advantage. The *Tao te ching* (80) speaks strongly against such technology: in the ideal society, utensils, boats, carriages, and weapons would not be used; writing would be replaced by knotted cords. Needham can look at this chapter solely in terms of the question of social organization (p. 100). Passages preferring the natural—such as the one in the *Chuang tzu* about what is natural for oxen is having four feet, and what is of man is being yoked and having a rope through the nose—also attack such technology.

Also in the *Chuang tzu* (11), a hermit chides a ruler who wants to make use of the Way to make grain grow for nourishment of the people and to direct the operation of the *yin* and the *yang* to secure the comfort of all; the hermit feels the ruler is concerned only with the material basis—his is only a desire to control scattered fragments of things (pp. 98–99). Needham comments that if one bears in mind our knowledge of soil conservation, this tale becomes as profound and as prophetic a passage as Chuang tzu ever wrote. More sense of the passage could be made if one would think in terms of the spiritual intent of Taoism and less in terms of twentieth-century technology: the objective is living in keeping with the Way, not adding material well-being. Here the partiality of Needham's point of view is clearly limiting his understanding.

Even Needham reluctantly concedes that there is a "paradoxical anti-technology complex of Taoists."[25] It would not appear at all paradoxical if he would concede that Taoist thought is not scientific. He offers this in explanation:

> In their anti-technology complex, the Taoists surely represented the popular feeling that whatever machines or inventions might be introduced it would be only for the benefit of the feudal lords; they would either be weighing machines to cheat the peasant out of his rightful proportion, or instruments of torture with which to chastise those of the oppressed who dared to rebel. (p. 125)

But the story of Tzu-kung, the disciple of Confucius, and the old farmer in the *Chuang tzu*[26] does not support this at all. The farmer's staunch refusal to employ a device enabling him to irrigate his field in much less time and with much less energy is because it would introduce him to a competitive way of life disrupting the "pristine purity of his nature;" for in this disquieted state, the Way will not dwell in him. There is no reason not to take this at face value and instead to search for the type of sociological reasons Needham does; nor was this invention a weighing machine or instrument of torture. For the Taoist, it could be said that any artifiical means is a torture; but, needless to say, this is not what

Needham has in mind. Arthur Waley's comments and quotations seem more appropriate:

> We must then "bind the fingers" of the technicians, "smash their arcs and plumb-lines, throw away their compasses and squares." Only then will men learn to rely on their inborn skill, on the "Great Skill that looks like clumsiness."[27]

Conclusion

The above at a minimum is very damaging to Needham's argument. In numerous places he most certainly is wrong and elsewhere his are highly questionable interpretations. His high regard for science as the "true world-view"[28] may have distorted his perception of Taoism: Taoist thought is made scientific since another mode of knowing (the mystical) is not considered legitimate. But a scientific point of view entails more than advancing non-supernatural claims about the world. It involves the aim of the claims and the approach toward the subject matter. That is, the presuppositions and not merely any belief-claims abstracted from different enterprises are central. The seemingly scientific aspects of Taoist thought belong to a matrix of beliefs, questions of meaning, and attitudes radically nonscientific in intent and in approach to reality.[29] Needham does note a numinous, although not mystical, aspect to Taoism because it arose before science and religion were differentiated (p. 47). But these differences in fact make Taoist ways of life adverse to science, and therefore the reason Taoists do not develop the natural sciences is not merely that they distrust reason (p. 579) or that the social ideal of Taoism did not call for science (pp. 582–583), but that the entire enterprises are at variance, right down to the experiences involved.

Part V

Mysticism and Theology

Chapter 7

The Religious Irrelevance of the Ontological Argument

Thirty years ago, Cyril Richardson wrote of the "strange fascination" that Anselm's attempt in his *Proslogion* to demonstrate the existence of a "being greater than which nothing can be conceived" has held.[1] If the number of articles on the subject is any indication, this fascination has not abated. A major difficulty with the ontological argument can be seen even when one assumes that Anselm, Descartes or some contemporary advocate of an ontological argument does in fact *succeed* in demonstrating the existence of such a being. Does the establishment of a "being greater than which nothing can be conceived" have any relevance for the religious believer? This question will be approached from this series of perspectives: "a being," "greater than," "can be conceived," and the nature of a philosophical demonstration. A negative response will be forthcoming in each instance.

The objections usually raised against the religious relevance of the ontological argument fall under the rubric of religious objections to any philosophical argument about religious matters.[2] Such objections include these: that faith in God is based upon an immediate experience, not argumentation, and so the faithful not only do not need philosophical proofs, but also the very attempt to prove God's existence is sinful, since it places the believer outside the immediate presence of God; that, as Pascal said, the "God of the philosophers and the learned" is wholly distinct from the living "God of Abraham, God of Isaac and God of Jacob"; that reasoning itself is an infringement of the secular upon the sacred; and that faith would not be faith if a philosophical proof compelled belief, that is, that a Kierkegaardian "leap of faith" is required. Each of these objections rests upon a recognition of the error of supposing that discussions of the reasonableness of the propositional basis of a faith can be substituted for the living faith itself. In any case, let us assume that the religious criticisms of the general enterprises of natural theology and philosophy of religion can be convincingly met. We can then turn to the being whose existence is demonstrated by the ontological argument.

"A Being . . . "

Is this being of religious significance? That is, is being a "being greater than which nothing can be conceived" either a necessary or sufficient property of a religious conception of God? And does the ontological argument provide a good reason for accepting belief in a religious god (as opposed to, say, a *deus ex machina* introduced to round out a conceptual system)? Anselm obviously felt he was dealing with something of religious importance. But the one essential feature of the god of any traditional form of theism is that the god is the source of the meaning that religious persons see in the world. Does Anselm's being give meaning to the world? Not necessarily, since this does not follow from its definition. It may be the most likely candidate, but Anselm realized that he had to show that this being is the god contemplated in Christian theology (*Proslogion* III). More generally, establishing the existence of this being is relevant to the issue of the existence of a religious god only if some belief-claim entailed by faith in God is involved. The Christian depiction of God, to use Alvin Plantinga's characterization, is of a personal being who has existed eternally, is almighty, perfectly wise, perfectly just, has created the world, and loves his creatures.[3] Can Anselm legitimately conclude his argument (as he did in *Proslogion* III) the way Thomas Aquinas concluded his non-ontological arguments with the phrase "This all men speak of as God"? Such a remark may make sense in connection with the cosmological or teleological arguments, but serious difficulties arise with its use in connection with the ontological argument.

First, is what the ontological argument establishes a *necessary* condition for a religious god? If so, something important has been accomplished. Paul Tillich's view of God, however, constitutes a counter-example: "It is as atheistic to affirm the existence of God as it is to deny it. God is being-itself not *a* being."[4] Thus, being a being is not a necessary property to all Christian conceptions of God. To speak of an infinite being (a being unlimited by other beings), even if possible, would still make God a being. God would be the greatest being, but no matter how great God were, God would still be a being—and thus to Tillich still an idol. Substituting "a reality" for "a being" in the ontological argument will not help: for the argument to proceed, the reality must be objective and particularized—something in some sense comparable to realities with less perfection. The ontological argument's being would still be *one* real thing, not "being itself." Alvin Plantinga and Charles Hartshorne both attack Tillich on this point and ardently support the idea of God as a being.[5] But the fact remains that some Christians find this restriction erroneous: it is the ground of being, not the top member in the list of beings who created the others (*Proslogion* V), which is sacred.

A second assault comes from certain mystical traditions. For example, in one form of traditional Indian religiosity, anything we conceive to be a distinct reality, no matter how exalted, does not exist but is merely a fabrication arising from nescience (Skt., *avidyā*). Other mystics would stress ultimate reality's absolute otherness from beings by referring to it as *non-being* (or claiming it alone is real while all else is ultimately non-being). The being of the ontological argument may be greater than can be conceived (*Proslogion* XV), but it is still a being grounded in our differentiations. We may be led by reasoning to *one* reality as the highest conceivable reality and all else as "unreal" in some sense, or even to the subject as the only reality (although most theists—even theistic mystics—would not want to overcome a basic duality of God and creation). Nevertheless, this will remain an alleged reality corresponding to an *object* of thought—the experience which constitutes reality for Śaṁkara will not be present. According to Śaṁkara, only by superimposing *(adhyāsa)* the idea of a being upon the real can we see ultimate reality *(Brahman)* as an object. Seeing *Brahman* as the all-knowing, all-powerful creator Īśvara *(saguṇa brahman)* is experiencing only the lower form of *Brahman*,[6] not the definitive experience of *Brahman* free of what we attribute to *Brahman*.

Making assertions about God need not reduce God to the status of an object among other objects (Tillich's would not), but the ontological argument does. Supporters of the argument might reply that at least being something, if not an object, "greater than which nothing can be conceived" is necessary to a religious god. Against this, one need only remember that some theists (including process theologians), following J. S. Mill, have advanced the idea of a god endowed only with finite power—obviously not the greatest conceivable property. According to this position, our highest conceivable being does not correspond to how reality actually is. That some religious theists would adhere to such a position is a sufficient counter-example to this condition.

Supporters of the ontological argument might then insist that possessing "necessary existence" (i.e., the existence of the concept itself entails its instantiation), a property involved in one form of the argument, is necessary to a religious god. A remark that is characteristic of this position is provided by J. N. Chubb: "It is revolting to the religious sense to look upon God as a being who might not have been there. Such a thought is immediately dispelled in the contemplation of the majesty and awesomeness of God's being."[7] Charles Hartshorne affirms the same,[8] and J. N. Findlay bases his ontological disproof of God upon the religious sense that in order to be a fit object of worship, God's nonexistence cannot even be conceived.[9] Professor Richardson's position counters this:

> If it should turn out that God's existence can logically be denied and all forms of the ontological argument are false, that would by no means carry as a consequence that there may not be a God who is a fit object of worship. There is no reason why we should so restrict the word "God."[10]

A type of necessity more usually attributed to God is that of being the source necessary for our very existence—that is, if there are any phenomena, then God exists—not that of any logical necessity in the concept "God."

Therefore, there are solid grounds for refusing to admit that the ontological argument has established a necessary condition for a religious conception of God. And even if "necessary existence" were required, it still would not suffice for locating a proper object of religious focus if Paul Henle's argument concerning the possibility of there being many beings existing necessarily (but being otherwise unremarkable) is correct.[11] There could be a veritable horde of these beings populating the universe—and the problem would still remain of finding criteria for determining which one is God. (Also note that it would be rather odd, although not logically inconsistent, to call any one of them "omnipotent," since no being could destroy another necessarily existing being.)

". . . Greater Than Which Nothing . . ."

Can the ontological argument, by other means, supply *sufficient* conditions for there being a religious God? The idea of a "being *greater than which nothing* can be conceived" looks promising, but this notion of a "perfect being" (unsurpassable in any property deemed good or desirable) presents difficulties. At its root, the problem is this: all the ontological argument can establish is the claim that, as Hartshorne states it, "There is a perfect being," or "Perfection exists."[12] And this claim is so abstract that different believers can fill the being with whatever properties they prefer, merely by showing each property to be a perfection. For example, the later sections of Anselm's *Proslogion* present a typical Western medieval conception of God. This is only to be expected, since in the preface Anselm stated his objectives as "to prove (*astruendum*) God really exists . . . and also to prove whatever we believe concerning the Divine Being." Anselm "believes in order to understand," and his understanding of God will have to reflect his beliefs, which were acquired independently of the ontological argument. To take another example, Plantinga feels maximal excellence consists of at least the traditional triad of omniscience, omnipotence, and moral perfection.[13] But why are any of these chosen? Of course, we cannot go from the general formula "There is a perfect being" to specific virtues without additional arguments. But by whose standards are we to judge? Why is omniscience rather than being joyful a central great-making property? Does our tradition and culture condition what we accept as perfections? And since having one perfection does not entail having another, how are we to know which set belongs to God? Consider these problems with some traditional attributes of God:

1. *Personhood.* Whether characteristics of a person are necessarily the highest conceivable virtue can be easily doubted. For example, Buddhists, who deny that anything real is ultimately describable in terms of a self (*ātman*), would find talk of personhood as a perfection totally contrary to the way "things really are" (*yathābhūtaṃ*). Conceptions of non-personal ultimate realities also present difficulties in this regard. Also, one might ask what actually constitutes personhood. Is personhood essentially social (i.e., the product of social interactions)? Is being able to respond to human beings enough? Is feeling emotions necessary to being a person? Is God then perfectly angry? For Chuang tzu, in the Taoist tradition, feelings of sadness, joy, delight, and anger are deviations from the Way (Ch., *tao*), but would Christians find the fact that Chuang tzu also includes love and hate within this group acceptable?[14]

2. *Rewarder of the righteous.* Is the conception of a god who rewards and punishes a higher conception that that of a god who forgives everyone? In other words, is justice or mercy better? Which is

the better expression of love? To take a different tack, is a rewarding and punishing god a more perfect conception than, for example, *karma* which is an impersonal mechanism relating actions and retributions? In a related way, one might ask if a cycle of rebirths is better than having one's everlasting fate determined by one life. What standards neutral to both positions can there be which would enable us to decide which is better?

3. *Creator of the heavens and the earth.* Anselm took being a creator to be central to God (*Proslogion* III, V), but is it self-evident that being the source of something else is a perfection? Might not control of others—or being the source of their existence—be a limitation? In Jainism, it is asked how could the will to create arise in a perfect and complete being? We may also ask, is being concerned with human history a perfection? If God needed us to fulfill a plan to accomplish some other purposes, this would plainly be judged an imperfection by most standards. Perhaps the highest conceivable being is one which is changeless and unconcerned with the world and with people. Aristotle's Unmoved Mover is certainly perfect from one point of view, although this characteristic is not necessarily part of a religious concept of God. Hartshorne finds adaptability better than changelessness and unconditionality, but most mystics would disagree: impermanence or change is imperfect (or unreal).

4. *Morally perfect.* A "being greater than which nothing can be conceived" is not necessarily a moral one. Some mystics see "good" and "bad" as mere labels which we attach to what seems advantageous or harmful to us from our limited point of view.[15] What we deem "evil" is just as essential to the make-up of the world as anything else, and thus just as "good" from a neutral point of view. All self-centered concerns must be overcome to see that this is so. For this group of mystics, that than which nothing greater can be conceived is "beyond good and evil" in the sense that this dichotomy reflects only our limited valuations. To say "God is morally good" is to reduce God by predicating to God what is not applicable apart from our interests. The "irrational" or "immoral" actions and demands of Yahweh in the Old Testament also might be pointed to as examples of the inapplicability to the sacred of our notions of what is good for us.

Values accepted as positive also may be relative to other beliefs and values in a system of belief. The extreme instance of the relativity of values is the ontological demonstration of the devil:[16] what most people would consider most heinous might very well be perfections—that is, might be much more than the "absence of good"—for that perhaps fictional but possible group, the Satan worshipers;

and the highest conceivable being established by the ontological argument thus is the devil.

5. *Omniscience.* The danger of a sophisticated anthropomorphism is very real with regard to the question of knowledge—that is, making the highest conceivable being's knowledge to be more complete, but of the same fundamental nature, as the knowledge possessed by people. Plantinga, for example, feels it is plausible to hold that God knows every true proposition.[17] Does he think God would know every true proposition because it would be good if we knew them? What if this type of knowledge is limited to people alone or only to beings having a linguistic ability? Could God's knowledge be instead mystical wisdom, which does not increase the number of known states of affairs but which involves an insight into the ontological status of all such states of affairs? According to Meister Eckhart, God is neither a being nor intelligent and does not know either "this" or "that." Some mystics play down propositional knowledge to the point of not calling it *knowledge* at all since it either does not reveal the ultimate nature of things or is positively mistaken about it. According to this group, would God necessarily have this propositional knowledge, which is at best of limited value? Or could some entirely other standard obtain? Could it be that the highest conceivable being does not know anything, but is rather the source of our ability to know? For some people, this may well be a higher conception than that of a being who merely registers true statements.

6. *Monotheism.* Because the ranking of all beings must be done according to the standards of specific cultures and religious schemes, coming up with any one set of properties considered proper to God which would be acceptable to all Western and Eastern monotheists might in itself be impossible.[18] But at least each would accept that there is only one god, and that, though there are differences in the particular religious conceptions of this one god, there are not different religious gods. But even the idea of *one* god is not acceptable to all religious people. For example, within the antagonistic relationship of the two Zoroastrian deities, those features which are good according to Zoroastrian beliefs are isolated from those which are bad. Therefore, since there would be an admixture of good and evil qualities, to advocate one god in the name of simplicity would be an imperfection for a Zoroastrian. Some mystical traditions (viz., Sāṁkhya-Yoga) also reject the idea of a fundamental god and remain irreducibly dualistic—any conception committed to fewer ontologically irreducible elements would not reflect how reality is actually constructed.

The important conclusion from this is that the relativism involved in the very notion of the "highest" or "most perfect" keeps us from legitimately concluding that if the ontological argument is sound, at least we know that a religious god exists and that the god is all-powerful, all-knowing, or whatever. Justification for talk about the nature of God will have to be found elsewhere. The question, "Which religious conception of God is established by the ontological argument?" is not applicable because the ontological argument cannot aid in establishing any one. Hartshorne admits as much when he says that the ontological argument can only show that a purely abstract "divine actuality" exists which is to be filled by revelation, experience, or whatever. What the argument does establish is so vague that it permits us to enshrine our current conceptions of what is important by making them necessarily part of the sacred, somewhat as everyone tends to justify their actions by construing them as the will of God. The vehicle for this procedure is the empty concept "perfection." As far as the ontological argument is involved, God becomes merely a mirror of what we currently deem, from our limited perspective, to be best. We create "God" in our own image.

Because there does not appear to be a core of perfections common to the different religious traditions, the only way to avoid this relativism is to establish criteria of perfection acceptable to all religious believers. And this shifts the problem back to the basic problem of relativism: is there a neutral, independent standard of adjudication or are all religious values of equal validity (i.e., is each tradition in the same epistemological position)? That there are a variety of accounts of the sacred does not logically entail a relativism (a pluralism of equally valuable but conflicting belief-systems) or a skepticism (the denial that there are means to determine which of the conflicting belief systems is best). Nevertheless, it would seem difficult to come up with a standard of perfection acceptable to all disputants (e.g., standards for deciding between Hartshorne and Śaṁkara on whether the concrete religious god "contains" the abstract absolute or vice versa) which does not beg the question. On a fundamental level, it is hard to see how one can reject an ultimate commitment to a certain scheme of things without appeal to another, equally ultimate. The contribution made by the ontological argument to this problem is that it entails "a being" and "existence" as perfections. But either condition may be rejected. This would be reason enough to reject the premises (more on this later). Beyond this, the ontological argument can add nothing. Anselm said God is whatever it is better to be than not to be (*Proslogion* V): God is every true good (*Proslogion* XVIII). Still, all specific religious conceptions of god involve sets of specific concepts from a particular culture and era. And any set of perfections can be equally accommodated to the ontological argument. Hartshorne admits that, from an abstract definition such as Anselm's, nothing concrete can be deduced.[19] But he misses the damaging nature of this fact: nothing of a substantial nature can be established by the ontological argument, that is, no religious conception of God or even any one property of God can be established by it. If a reason could be shown for commitment to the idea of "a being" and if one set of properties is determined by other arguments as uniquely perfect for all religious believers, then it could be argued that the ontological argument shows this set is instantiated in reality. But the deep-seated relativism of perfections makes this a formidable task (if it does not preclude the possibility entirely). And until this is done, the ontological argument is left without the field necessary for its operation.

". . . Can Be Conceived . . . "

In addition, there even seems to be relativism among various conceptual schemes as to what is *conceivable*. It is possible that one conceptual scheme will not have the capacity to express consistently an insight which is self-evident in another.[20] We cannot assume all natural languages entail one system of conceivability, since, for example, different metaphysics and mutually contradictory geometries can be stated in English. Close to the issue at hand, the idea of a creator was self-contradictory to Spinoza, but was necessarily true to Leibniz. Or: most but not all philosophers find the very notion of a "necessary being" meaningless. Hartshorne's dipolar theism (an individual being who is both infinite and finite, both the actuality of a concrete being and "bare existence" itself)[21] is self-contradictory from the point of view of classical theism. In the *Proslogion,* Anselm attempts to reconcile many mutually contradictory properties: being compassionate and passionless (VIII), being all-merciful and all-just (IX–X), being everywhere and nowhere in space and time (XIII–XIX). The idea of being the *ground* of personhood or of knowing may not be consistent with being a person or a knower—that is, to explain a property, the *explanans* must not have that property. In general, Anselm will ascribe to the being of the ontological argument any property which he deems best, but the classical conception of God that results is one which Hartshorne repudiates—thus, the ontological argument establishes according to Anselm something it does not establish according to Hartshorne. Thus, to make logical self-consistency (or consistency with the idea of perfection) the criterion for something being conceivable constitutes a problem: what is inconceivable in one scheme may be self-evident in another. Internal consistency and conceivability reflect beliefs and values.

Because what is conceivable is dependent upon the conceptual scheme being employed, the problem is to determine which such scheme and its correlated way of reasoning reflect the way things really are. This runs into the problem of relativism again. In addition, why need any of our conceptual schemes be absolute? We can even question whether our highest conception must be instantiated. But more importantly, the ontological argument may rest upon the questionable assumption that to be real, something must be conceivable to us. Anselm did claim that God is a being greater than can be conceived (*Proslogion* XV), but he also made it clear in his response to Gaunilon[22] that God is conceivable even if he is more than our conceptions convey—he is "a being" and "perfect" even if we do not know all the perfections involved or their true degree. But why should the thoughts of a "people on a second-rate planet attached to a second-rate sun" (to use Whitehead's phrase) have any say in the matter at all? May there not be many beings inconceivable in any of our conceptual schemes, beings which are much greater than we are able to conceive? What then becomes of an argument which deals with a "being greater than which nothing can be conceived"? There may still be such a being, but since what is conceivable depends upon specific conceptual schemes, what is conceivable to us may not be too much of a restriction.

In addition, mystics feel many concepts imply a being and therefore are necessarily wrong—concepts operate by making distinctions, and "ultimate reality" is free of all distinctions (i.e., nondual).[23] The mind constructs representations of the world that make reality graspable, while mysticism directs the mind away from what can be grasped by concepts to the depth of the mystery of reality. That is, ultimate reality is wholly other than what is made intelligible by concepts. In that case, perhaps being conceivable to us—being intelligible to us—is itself a restriction and so Tertullian's "*credo quia incredible est*" represents the proper response to reality.

Another peculiarity of the ontological argument involves the fact that it makes of the awareness of a "being greater than which nothing can be conceived" the product of reasoning and concepts alone. This is odd: we have to struggle to gain any understanding of the simplest empirical phenomenon, but we seem confident about our knowledge of God. Attempts to justify natural theology rely upon its attempt to understand our experiences and the world. But the ontological argument cannot appeal to the experiential—it deals exclusively with our conceptions. However, the Copernican and Einsteinian revolutions also show that highly successful and well-corroborated theories may be fundamentally in error. From the Aristotelian heavens to the Newtonian system of mechanics, the empirical findings of scientific research (in conjunction with new ways of thinking) have overthrown what the intellect advanced as perfect, that is, "self-evident" *a priori* ideas of natural order such as the "natural" Aristotelian circular motion of heavenly bodies. A loss of certainty has also occurred in mathematics: before Lobachevski and Riemann, Euclidean geometry was taken to be *a priori* true of reality. Concepts even when tied to experience often lead to conceptual problems. When we restrict our attention to our constructs alone, as in the ontological argument, another problem arises: we come to worship what we project from our own mind. One of C. S. Peirce's comments on such a procedure is worth noting: "The a priori method, practiced by rationalists like Plato and Descartes, is often no more than a rationalization of what is pleasing to the system-building, rationalizing mind of the introspective philosopher, impervious to fresh evidence."[24] What we accept becomes what is agreeable to our previous beliefs, just as the Aristotelians produced arguments against Galileo which seemed self-evident to them.

In light of this, we should be cautious about treating our concepts with such ease that we talk with confidence and authority about the highest conceivable being with only our constructs as a basis. It may well be *hubris* to pontificate on the nature of God and ultimate matters in such circumstances. Caution and modesty in metaphysics rather than dogmas may be warranted. Chuang tzu may very well be correct in saying that any talk of a creator is only reasoning from our ignorance.[25] Herodotus' remark that if horses and lions had hands, they would form their gods after themselves should be taken seriously when we attempt to rely solely upon our ability to conceive. In the case of the ontological argument, the emptiness of the concept "perfection" only aids in enshrining our own conceptions.

The Function and Nature of Philosophical Proofs

All of the above criticism raises serious doubts as to the religious value of the ontological argument. A religious defense of the argument may be attempted in various ways. The most usual line of defense is to see the argument as strengthening one's faith. Two remarks characteristic of this approach are John Hick's claim that if such a being is not worthy of worship then clearly none ever could be,[26] and Norman Malcolm's claim that the ontological argument has the religious value of removing some philosophical scruples that stand in the way of faith.[27] For Plantinga, the ontological argument is not a logical demonstration that removes all grounds from doubt or produces absolute knowledge of God; instead, the ontological argument aids in establishing the claim that theists are rational or justified in their religious belief. However, this approach cannot succeed. The problem again is that the being established by the argument is empty of content and thus there is no guarantee that a religious being is involved at all. The argument establishes that a being *x* exists, but what still remains to be shown is that *x* is necessarily or sufficiently religious. At best, by selecting the proper perfections, one can use the ontological argument to reaffirm—in a question-begging fashion—one's current faith.

This problem with the ontological argument is not the general problem of whether concepts can prove anything about reality. Rather, since the ontological argument is removed from any religious experience or scripture, and from other philosophical arguments, the possibility of its having any substance is removed. Philosophical arguments which attempt to establish the existence or reasonableness of a religious entity may be legitimate. It could even be argued that in the light of different revelations and different understandings of the status of various religious experiences, such arguments are required: if one has experienced God, one still needs to know that the experience was not delusory, and so on. In this way, reasoning may be inherent in religious thought. But none of this changes the status of the ontological argument. Nor can the ontological argument be faulted for not establishing every property of a religious conception of God—no one argument could reasonably be expected to. It is also trivially true that establishing the ontological argument's "being" is not establishing God: one must show that the concept "God" coincides with "a being greater than which nothing can be conceived."[28] But the problem with the ontological argument is more severe: at best, its being is an empty shell that can be filled with whatever substance one prefers. Hence, the argument is incapable of adding anything to our knowledge; it cannot increase our understanding by revealing a new property, nor add any certainty to one's beliefs. Because of this, it cannot figure in an informal argument (as opposed to a logical deduction) to show that a particular faith is "beyond a reasonable doubt" by using it in conjunction with a cluster of other arguments each mutually supporting each other. Other arguments may be substantial, and reason may be able to establish God's existence, but because the being whose existence is demonstrated by the ontological argument is hollow, it cannot strengthen the reasonableness of any one religious conception in the slightest.

If the ontological argument cannot aid in establishing even the plausibility of one conception of God, it has been suggested that any such formal proof should be viewed as merely articulating one's belief-commitments.[29] For Hartshorne: "The value of a formal proof is not that it establishes its conclusion for every man, no matter what his assumptions and attitudes, but that it establishes a logical price for rejecting a certain conclusion."[30] The ontological argument may reveal the logical implications for denying the existence of "a being greater than which nothing can be conceived," or contradictions between our assumptions. But then it would only *clarify* our situation; it would have no evidential or persuasive force. We would still need to decide which premises, if any, to accept or renounce. "Necessary existence," "a being," "perfection," and "*esse qua esse bonum est*" are either explicit premises or entailed belief-claims that could be renounced. To renounce one or more would be to reject the argument. However, in the case of the ontological argument, even if we decided to accept this belief-framework and permitted the argument to proceed, the conclusion is still so abstract as to be empty.

Because of its inability to support any conception, the ontological argument also cannot aid in overcoming doubts within a faith—Anselm's "faith seeking understanding" will not be satisfied. The argument cannot provide any understanding not there previously. It merely justifies a belief from within a circle of faith, and therefore is circular.

Arguments in general do not normally convert.[31] Even for science, the role of persuasion versus that of reason in theory-choice is debated in philosophy.[32] To reply to another possible use of the ontological argument: the conviction involved in religious faith is more than the mere acceptance of belief-claims, and is not compelled by such acceptance.[33] Even if arguments have importance in this area, the ontological argument would have little power because of its abstract nature.

A religious defender of the ontological argument may try to claim that it could induce a religious experience within those who understand it. Study of the ontological argument may prepare the mind for such an experience. Indeed, the argument appears originally to have come to Anselm in an unusual insight-experience in an altered state of consciousness. Additional appeal to Anselm can be made: the preface and first chapter of the *Proslogion* refer to forgetting the troubles of the world and turning to God, and to arousing the mind for the contemplation of God. Needless to say, the understanding of the ontological argument has long since left such a setting in most discussions of it. More to the point, though, is that in the face of the above criticism, the most that can be aroused is only a deeper conviction of one's own previous image of God, not a fresh religious experience. In itself, the argument may be awe-inspiring to a logician, but would this response be a *religious* experience in the sense of involving a traditional god or involving a commitment of faith? Given the argument above, we must answer "no." Of course, one could reply that Anselm discovered a new object open to a religious response. But this is not what Anselm claimed to have done, and even if it were true that Anselm discovered such an object, it would have to be admitted that, unlike any other religious god, this one began as an inference unfounded in any sense of presence. Its only reality is a mental product; and the experience of it is only a rational inference, not a sense of presence, power, and ultimate reality.

As if this were not enough, consider one last focus of criticism: What exactly is meant by, and what actually is accomplished by, a *demonstration* such as the one the ontological argument provides for a "being greater than which nothing can be conceived"? To demonstrate, or prove, something does not mean merely to produce an argument which is formally valid, that is, one where the conclusion is logically deducible from the premises; in addition, the premises must be acceptable. Such an argument would provide an absolutely certain foundation to belief. With regard to the ontological argument, questions especially have been raised concerning the premise, "The concept 'a being greater than which nothing can be conceived' is itself coherent." Objections could also be raised to other premises, for example, "Existence *in re* is better than existence *in intellectu* only." But many follow Malcolm in asserting that the ontological argument succeeds if and only if the central claim is true. Hartshorne, for example, states that he never held that the conclusion was established for all philosophers no matter what their assumptions—what argument in philosophy can do such a thing, he asks—but only that if one accepts the premise "The existence of God is consistently conceivable," then one is obliged to accept the conclusion; the ontological argument itself cannot accomplish this and so he concludes that it is not an adequate defense of theism.[34]

Hartshorne's insistence on what the ontological argument does and does not do reveals much about a philosophical demonstration. Some of J. N. Findlay's comments offer another informative insight. After presenting an ontological disproof of God, he concedes in a reply to criticism that "there can be nothing really 'clinching' in philosophy: 'proofs' and 'disproofs' hold only for those who adopt certain premises, who are willing to follow certain rules of argument and who use their terms in certain definite ways."[35] He hopes his argument will hold water for those who share a "contemporary outlook," "instead of claiming (absurdly) that it would hold for all persons, whatever they might assume, and however they might choose to use their terms."[36] He goes so far as to remark: " . . . my argument also *doesn't* hold for those who regard the Ontological Proof (or some other *a priori* proof) as a valid argument."[37] Later, Findlay himself switched positions on the ontological argument by changing his "attitude to a single premise,"[38] that is by taking the disputed premise to be true rather than false.

We find ourselves in a very odd situation. Two persons can hold opposite opinions on one premise and can proceed to construct an *a priori* argument that establishes the existence of a "being greater than which nothing can be conceived" or to hold that the concept is incoherent. Is this the end of the matter? Does whether or not the being exists depend upon whether we choose to use the term? Of course we assume one alternative is right and one is wrong, but how do we tell which? Hartshorne admits that scarcely anything of importance is axiomatic for everyone in our culture, and that giving axiomatic status to a claim is a relative and more or less subjective matter.[39] In science, even if there is no logically deductive decision-process, consensus does occur (perhaps because of commitments to values transcending specific theories which all scientists share). But it appears impossible to obtain universal agreement upon any metaphysical claims about the world. There cannot be found any neutral canons of justification for determining whether the concept "a being greater than which nothing can be conceived" is coherent or not. In the end, we can elect to employ the concept, but we are equally free to declare the concept incoherent. No arguments could be advanced which would compel anyone to abandon either position. Findlay's simple "change in attitude" becomes paradigmatic of the situation we are all in with regard to the acceptability of the ontological argument. Obviously this greatly dilutes any power the argument might have. It cannot fail, since someone can always be found who accepts the premises and ways of reasoning required, while the opposite position remains just as unassailable. More than simply not being "clinching," the argument is neutralized.

Some would argue that the ontological argument and other arguments concerning God need not prove God's existence, but need merely show that belief in God is reasonable.[40] Is the disputed premise then reasonable? Plantinga thinks "there is nothing *contrary to reason* or *irrational* in accepting this premise."[41] But then again he finds the following argument sound:[42]

> Either God exists or 7 + 5 = 14
>
> It is false that 7 + 5 = 14
>
> Therefore God exists.

He readily concedes most people would not accept this—only those with a previous commitment to God's existence would accept the first premise. And the problem is that many would not accept the concept in the ontological argument either. How can Plantinga show that accepting the necessary premise is any more reasonable than the above syllogism? We are at a standoff once again. Just as there is relativism as to what is a perfection and even as to what is conceivable, so also what for one person is a convincing reason for accepting the premise may not be a reason at all for another person. What is deemed reasonable depends upon how one sees the world, that is, how we see the world as fundamentally constructed bears directly on what we accept as in line with reason. Some religious beliefs involve fundamental world-views, and so shape what is accepted as fact and thereby what is reasonable. Hartshorne sees the choice between accepting "Deity exists" and accepting "Deity does not exist" as a choice between "two metaphysics, two competitors for the task of elucidating what we can and cannot mean by any of our basic conceptions. They concern, not 'what are the facts?', but 'what is it to be a fact?' "[43] With such a deep-seated and important divergence here, impartiality is impossible and, consequently, what is reasonable will be relative. Nothing in these matters can be proven "beyond a reasonable doubt" for everyone, because what is reasonable varies. Ways of reasoning and questions of the rationality of less fundamental beliefs will enter the picture only after the fundamental choices have been made. Arguments can be constructed within the assumed belief-framework to support one's religious faith, but they may not impress a person holding an alternate position.

Are there criteria independent of specific visions of the world which, if not providing grounds for adjudicating between these visions, would at least help in determining whether any one such vision is in a broad sense rationally acceptable? Two possible candidates are the need to account for all of our own experiences, and the need for coherence between all our beliefs. Thus, ideally, all our beliefs would be open to some form of criticism, and whims or prejudices would not have complete control. The final justification for the rationality of any one belief may be the total network of our belief-system and how we lead our lives; perhaps only this could convince someone to look at the world differently.

But obviously this is not sufficient to establish one vision. Questions such as "How central a role in how we see the world should scientific theories or mystical experiences play?" will have no unanimous answer. And, in general, the question as to how we blend together elements from science, nonordinary experiences or whatever into a useable conceptual framework—with the process of mutual shaping operating between the basic framework itself and the more specific elements—will give rise to a variety of irreconcilable answers. Because there is no neutral procedure for determining our basic convictions, the necessary fundamental choices remain nonrational. In this area, Augustine appears correct: we must believe in order to understand. And Nicholas of Cusa: faith is the beginning of understanding. Every "science" presupposes some first principles apprehended by faith alone. This being the case, Richardson's comment on "visions of life" such as the one underlying any use of the ontological argument is appropriate:

> Perhaps the Christian apologetic, therefore, should be more concerned with "de-proving" than with proving, with showing that all visions of life rest on faith or unfaith; on decisions in which there

> is no logical certainty, but only the leap into a boundless mystery. No position is privileged; *all* are open to challenge and to doubt.[44]

The leap may not be totally blind since the choice must be reasonable—at least to the chooser.

Conclusion

But the necessity of choice does remain and the ontological argument will be of no assistance, far from inescapably demonstrating that God exists as conceived within any full-blooded theism. The deduction within the argument succeeds only after the controversial premise has been accepted for reasons other than those offered by the argument itself. In effect, the ontological argument enters the picture only after we are convinced of the entailed conclusions on independent grounds. And, adding this to the problems concerning identifying the ontological argument's being with a specific religious conception of God, the argument is reduced to no more than an exercise in formal logic or speculative metaphysics of perhaps some academic interest. Nothing inimical to religious faith is established, but the ontological argument remains definitely incapable of offering comfort to religious believers.

Part VI

Mysticism and Psychology

Chapter 8

Concerning Carl Jung on Asian Religious Traditions

Carl Jung's writings on various Eastern religious traditions have been extremely influential in both the West and East, but a central question needs to be raised: Do the psychological concepts he employs to understand these religious traditions adequately convey their content? In attempting to answer this question, paradigmatic examples will be selected from his works to deal with one issue: the way in which his analytical psychology affects his understanding of these traditions. As such, this is as much a study of the problems of understanding other religious traditions as it is a critique of Jung's specific efforts in this regard.

Translation and Understanding

An illuminating way to get into the problem is to look at two instances of the "translations" Jung provides for religious claims. Jung constructs a line from the *Tibetan Book of the Great Liberation* thus: ". . . the Trikāya is the All-Enlightened Mind itself."[1] He deals with it in this manner: "Put into psychological language, the above sentence could be paraphrased thus: The unconscious is the root of all oneness *(dharmakāya),* the matrix of all archetypes or structural patterns *(sambhogakāya),* and the *conditio sine qua non* of the phenomenal world *(nirmāṇakāya)*" (11: 495).[2] The gods, he adds, are the archetypal thought-forms belonging to the *sambhogakāya*. The other example concerns the *Tibetan Book of the Dead:*

> the *Sidpa* state . . . is characterized by the fierce wind of karma, which whirls the dead man along until he comes to the 'womb-door'. In other words, the *Sidpa* permits of no going back, because

> it is sealed off against the *Chönyid* state by an intense driving downwards, towards the animal sphere of instinct and physical rebirth. That is to say, anyone who penetrates into the unconscious with purely biological assumptions will become stuck in the instinctual sphere and be unable to advance beyond it, for he will be pulled back again and again into physical existence (11: 516).

These paraphrases strike anyone studying the texts from other than a Jungian perspective as very odd. Following the Yogācāra account of the three bodies *(trikāya)* of the Buddha, the *dharmakāya* is "absolute reality," the *sambhogakāya* ("body of enjoyment") is seen by bodhisattvas and appears in different places, and the *nirmāṇakāya,* seen by ordinary people, is likened to a body conjured up by a magician. *Prima facie* nothing concerning the unconscious or its make-up is referred to. So also nothing on the surface of the *Book of the Dead* would lead us to think that it is discussing the unconscious or biological assumptions.

Importantly, Jung is not claiming to be giving psychological *explanations* of what these texts are saying, that is, specifying the psychological conditions under which people would make such claims. Nor can the above paraphrases be construed as exhibiting merely the psychological aspects of the concepts involved. Rather Jung claims to know and to appreciate the value of, say, the *Book of the Dead* and to be interested in seeing "whether any of the psychological facts known to us have parallels in or at least border upon the sphere of Eastern thought" (11: 494). This attitude permits him to use such phrases as "put into psychological language," or "that is to say," or "as we should express it in our own language," or "corresponds" when shifting from the Eastern expressions to his psychological terminology. He is so certain of their equivalence that throughout his writings phrases such as "obviously," and "without doubt" occur in making those shifts.

Even ignoring the issue of commensurability, for a translation of concepts to be legitimate, the conceptual schemes of the religious traditions and of Jung's analytical psychology must be similar, or, at a minimum, the concepts involved must fulfil similar roles in different schemes. Thus, it may perhaps be legitimate to use the phrase "Christian mantra" to refer to the Jesus-prayer of the Eastern Orthodox Church, even though Christians do not have a similar term, because of the similarities in purpose of mantras and of this prayer.

And Jung claims his psychology and the Asian religious traditions are similar in purpose: the "great Eastern philosophers" are seen to be "symbolical psychologists" (13: 50). Elsewhere he does admit that the purpose of yoga is distinct from that of psychotherapy and that there is no "psychology" in the strict Western sense in the East (11: 475). But the "metaphysics" clothing Eastern thought is irrelevant (13: 50), and "for our most modest psychological purposes we must abandon the colorful metaphysical language of the East" (9.1: 358). Can the "metaphysical" language be ignored, however, without distorting the intention of the Eastern thinkers? For example, was it the intention of the Buddha to transform gods into ideas (that is, "visible thoughts based upon the reality of the instincts") as Jung contends (10: 525, 529)? And if so, was this the sum total of the Buddha's way of life or even central to it? We would certainly not be led to such a conclusion without previously having accepted Jung's system. Jung ignores all other dimensions of these religious ways of life and ignores their stated intention—that of a radical ending to suffering.

Jung himself first encountered Eastern religious traditions only after having constructed a comprehensive psychological system into which he could fit the "data." Indian and Chinese thought did not provide any fresh influences for his work. He merely took it as reconfirming what he already believed. The key concept for understanding his treatment of Asian religions is stated in *Psychology and Religion* (and elsewhere): "Not only does the psyche exist, it is existence itself" (11: 12). In connecting psychological and ontological categories in this manner, correlations can be made which follow naturally from this perspective. Thus, categories fundamental to two different systems, the unconscious and the *dharmakāya,* are correlated. More generally, gods are correlated with the psychological facts which wield the greatest power within a system (11: 81).

But whatever the legitimacy of these particular claims, Jung's procedure truncates the Eastern concepts by eliminating the ontological dimension, and this leads to highly questionable results. For example, in the claim that the "psychological equivalent of this dismemberment [in the *Chönyid* state] is psychic dissociation" (11: 520) correlates two clearly distinct phenomena: one psychological in nature allegedly occurring during a lifetime, and one allegedly occurring in the intermediate state between rebirths. This is not the same as noting that there is an element in the process of rebirth as described in the *Book of the Dead* which is Freudian in appearance while noting also the differences (the Tibetan account of conception versus the Freudian account of early life) (11: 515–16). Even interpreting the text as providing a biological foundation to Freud's theory would not obviate the differences in conceptual frameworks.

Instead, Jung is claiming that the Buddhist claim is about a psychological state in this life. This distorts the intention of the Eastern texts by bringing in concepts as parallels which are essentially foreign in intent. Of course, conceptual schemes are by their nature selective (since each deals with only certain problems), but in simplifying they still may be useful.[3] The difficulty here is not the issue of whether Jung successfully brackets metaphysical issues (rather than psychologically reducing religious ways of life). Rather Jung's error is to substitute his *theoretical* constructs as parallels or equivalents to religious concepts.

To see this error, it must first be emphasized that his constructs are theoretical. Jung claims to advance no metaphysical statements (11: 476, 543), but he does concede that the archetypes are posited entities (9.1: 384): these "primordial images" are never directly perceived (hence they are theoretical), but are partially perceived in concrete symbols. They are theoretical posits advanced by Jung as inherited dispositions to explain the occurrence of various symbols throughout history in culturally unrelated parts of the world. The archetypes per se are the ordering patterns structuring and conditioning the human psyche. The concept of the unconscious itself is also needed to explain observed facts (11: 40) but by definition it is not open to direct empirical examination. He even delves into describing the nature of the archetypes: they are "psychoid," shaping mind and matter. All of this indicates that his system has a framework of speculative, metaphysical assumptions, contrary to what he says.

This reveals something of the rather complex nature of his system. What is important here is that he sets up his explanatory/theoretical system in parallel with Eastern religious traditions. That is, his concepts are not offered to explain these religious concepts, but to be *equivalent* concepts for the Eastern ones. This will surely be an unsuccessful procedure. Highly elaborated theoretical constructs are unlikely to parallel concepts from another conceptual scheme.[4] The only reason we have to believe, say, that the *sambhogakāya* has anything to do with his complex theoretical concept of archetypes is that Jung's system dictates that it should. This may in principle be possible, but an argument would have to be formulated to make such equivalencies plausible. Jung does not do this, but merely proceeds to point out what he sees as parallels. His interpretative scheme has a place for every feature that is relevant to his concerns, but this only means that the theory-laden translations distort consistently. Nothing could in principle falsify his position and consequently no matter how much he studies Asian traditions, he would have no reason to change it. Jung would only see his concepts exemplified more and more, just as "solar mythologists" of an earlier era saw references to natural phenomena being misinterpreted no matter how much they studied.

No translation or paraphrase would be legitimate if only the psychological aspects of a total phenomenon are being incorporated. Jung's correlations, therefore, are flawed in ascribing his theory to the Asian religious traditions. This situation can be readily seen in his discussions of the nature of the "enlightened mind" (discussed below). According to Jung, Asians believe in self-liberation (11: 482). This ignores those traditions in India and East Asia which are based upon salvation by the power of others. But let us concentrate on those traditions which rest upon enlightenment by means of one's own action. Common to these mystical traditions is the aim of transforming ourselves by directing attention away from the habitual ego-centric cravings which normally guide our actions. Meditation and other methods center around either "concentration" techniques, which still the sensory and conceptual activity of the mind, and/or "pure awareness" techniques which abolish the normal conceptual restrictions upon sensory stimuli. Within Theravāda Buddhism this distinction is between *samatha*-cultivation and *vipassanā*-cultivation.

In all of Jung's psychological characterizations of Eastern religious traditions, there is an absence of the ontological dimension of the mystical. For instance, in Advaita Vedānta, the mystical is the ground of all reality—indeed, it is the total substance of all that we experience. For many Asian mystical traditions, the "person" is an assembly of interacting parts that has no ultimate reality. The true reality—the "knower of knowing"—is the timeless ground of all subjective and objective reality. Jung's concern with the conscious and various unconscious parts of the mind simply is irrelevant to the central and ultimate concerns of mystics.

Enlightenment and the Unconscious

Jung's treatment of this transcendence of normal self-awareness relies exclusively upon his concept of the unconscious. "The East bases itself upon psychic reality, that is, upon the psyche as the main and unique condition of existence" (11: 481). "The psyche is therefore all-important, it is the all-pervading Breath, the Buddha-essence; it is the Buddha-mind, the One, the Dharmakāya. All existence emanates from it, and all separate forms dissolve back into it" (11: 482). Whether all these religious concepts are equivalent may be challenged, but Jung recognizes only one concept as equivalent to each. This psyche "which in Indian philosophy is called the 'higher' consciousness, corresponds to what we in the West call the 'unconscious' " (9.1: 282–3). *Samādhi* (concentration of the mind, including concentration free of any object) "so far as we know is equivalent to a state of unconsciousness" (9.1: 287). More exactly, the collective unconscious (the layer of the unconscious common to all persons regardless of culture and personal differences) is the equivalent of *buddhi,* the enlightened mind.[5] In fact, he equates consciousness with *avidyā*, "nescience" (11: 485); elsewhere he inconsistently equates *avidyā* with unconsciousness (12: 96).[6] All extraversion in contradistinction to the "self-liberating power of the introvertive mind" (11: 484) is "depreciated as illusory desirousness." This is the essence of suffering (11: 481). An Indian "in as much as he is really Indian" does not "really think" but only perceives the results of an unconscious function (10: 527). "It is safe to assume that what the East calls 'mind' has more to do with our 'unconscious' than with mind as we understand it, which is more or less identical with consciousness" (11: 484). Even the assertion in the *Tibetan Book of the Great Liberation* that "the 'Mind has no existence' obviously refers to the peculiar 'potentiality' of the unconscious" (11: 501). However, the enlightenment-experience (e.g., *nirvikapla samādhi*) as described by mystics is a pure and still *consciousness* free of any object, including any sense of ego. This self-knowledge is like a radiating beam of light free of any illuminated object. Nothing in the depiction of these experiences suggests Jung's detailed depiction of the multiple differentiations within the unconscious. And nothing in Jung's analytical psychology can accommodate such a state of consciousness free of an ego. The enlightenment-experience is likened to awaking from a dream, while Jung's theories deal with the content of the dream.

The basic problem here is that Jung "cannot imagine a conscious mental state that does not relate to a subject, that is, to an ego," although he concedes the idea of consciousness without an ego is conceivable for the East (11: 484).[7] As long as there is awareness, there must be someone who is aware; and the only alternative, an ego-less mental state, is for him the unconscious (11: 484). In short, mystical consciousness, according to Jung, "can only be the unconscious to us" (11: 484). Similarly, "universal consciousness is logically identical to unconsciousness (9.1: 287). He has to say that either we are within normal self-consciousness or we are within the unconscious in his complicated sense—no other alternatives are open for him. Thus, he says of the Taoist Chuang tzu: "If you have insight, says Chuang-tzu, 'you use your inner eye, your inner ear, to pierce to the heart of things, and have no need of intellectual knowledge.' This is obviously an allusion to the all-knowledge of the unconscious, and to the presence in the microcosm of macrocosmic events."[8] Since his theory dictates that the ego cannot be completely transcended, Jung must interpret this mystical experience as an experience of unconsciousness, not as the contentless and cognitive experience that mystics claim it to be.

Without the restriction of Jung's conceptual system, no one would view the various types of enlightened states as involving an unconscious in his involved and complex sense at all. He notes that the enlightened mind is described as undescribable, unknowable: "This is certainly true of the unconscious and a further proof that the Mind is the Eastern equivalent of our concept of the unconscious, more particularly of the collective unconscious" (11: 502). Another section of the *Tibetan Book of the Great Liberation* "shows very clearly that the One Mind is the unconscious, since it is characterized as 'eternal, unknown, not visible, not recognized' " (11: 496). He next notes that the text goes on to display positive features which are in keeping with Eastern experience, attributes such as "ever clear, ever existing, radiant, unobscured." But these positive features differentiate the two concepts in an important way: the type of enlightened mind he is describing is characterized as conscious, nondual and void of any content. In his notion of the *unconscious,* the unconscious is populated by at least a few distinct archetypes, a feature which cannot but cause us to differentiate the two concepts. The collective unconsciousness has the detailed structure of theoretical posits, while the mystical is free of all structure and is directly experienced. He dismisses the sense of "mystical oneness" by claiming it is a "contamination of the contents of the unconscious" (11: 491). But since the nonduality of the enlightened mind is so central, and, since nothing related to his theoretical concept of archetypes is stressed, this maneuver is forced.[9] Descriptions of the *samādhi*-state portray it more like a beam of light illuminating no object at all (no content of consciousness) than as having all mental content blur together into a single object. The emphasis is on the beam of light (the consciousness), not any object. No amount of reasoning by way of what the two concepts have in common (for example, the sense of reality in mystical experiences and the fundamental ontological importance Jung attaches to the unconscious, or the timelessness of the archetypal patterns and the lack of a sense of time in mystical experiences) will vitiate the central and vital differences.

Perhaps the most crucial point at which the concepts of "enlightened mind" and "collective unconscious" diverge is that the former is in some sense a *conscious* state of mind. The state of *samādhi* is a state of awareness without self-awareness or any other "content," a state which (as mentioned previously) Jung cannot conceive. For those religious traditions which do not emphasize *samādhi,* enlightenment is also conscious. Thus, for the Theravāda Buddhists, enlightenment comes outside the trances *(jhānas/dhyānas)* with the insight that the world is impermament, its elements are each without a self, and the world inevitably leads to suffering. And it may be added that even if the enlightened mind could be characterized as not a conscious state of mind, Jung would still have to present arguments before he could conclude that his complex conception of an unconscious with personal and collective layers, and so forth, is involved. In short, they cannot be the same.

Mystical Enlightenment and Individuation

If the various types of enlightenment have nothing to do with the collective unconscious, perhaps Jung's psychotherapeutic goal, that is, individuation, does. Individuation is "the process by which a person becomes a psychological 'in-dividual,' that is, a separate, indivisible unity or 'whole' " (9.1: 275). According to Jung, the goal of modern psychotherapy is to bring up into consciousness fragments from the unconscious which are then built into the conscious life; a form of psychic existence then results which corresponds better to the whole of the individual's personality and so abolishes fruitless conflicts between one's consciousness and unconscious (11: 552). For Jung then it is impossible to abolish the conscious ego, and so the objective of therapy is to bring about a balance between, or integration of, the conscious and unconscious. Concern for the ego is replaced with concern for the self, the totality of mental existence.

Jung realizes that at least some Eastern traditions do not have individuation as their goal. Hence, for example:

> Yoga has quite definite conceptions concerning what is to be achieved, and does everything to reach this anticipated goal. But with us, our intellectualism, rationalism, and our doctrine of free will are such dangerous psychic forces that, whenever possible, psychotherapy must avoid setting itself such goals.[10]

Yoga aims at shifting the psychological center of personality from the ego to the impersonal non-ego (9.1: 358; elsewhere he says the goal of all Eastern religious practices is the same as that of Western mysticism, that is, to shift the center of gravity from the ego to the (unconscious) self; 11: 581). Both the West and East are one-sided: the West is preoccupied with the conscious part of a person and the East with the unconscious (11: 493). Therefore, individuation is needed by both. The East withdraws too much into the unconscious (11: 497): the methods of the Buddhist Pāli canon and the *Yoga-sūtras* do induce a "remarkable extension of consciousness" which "is all very beautiful, but scarcely to be recommended anywhere north of the Tropic of Cancer" (9.1: 288). (Tibet might present a problem for him.) We in the West can study yoga, Jung says, but we ought not to apply it because of the difference in *ethos* (extravertive versus introvertive) (11: 534; cf. 13: 7): "in the West, nothing ought to be forced on the unconscious" and "no insight is gained by repressing and controlling the unconscious, and least of all by imitating methods which have grown up under totally different psychological conditions" (11: 537). The West may produce its own yoga, but it will be based upon a Christian foundation, not a blending of East and West or a transplanting of Eastern techniques and principles (11: 483, 554, 568). Jung contrasts the science-based "Western mind" grounded in the conscious mind with the "Eastern mind" grounded in the unconscious. However, the West already has, as part of its own long established mystical traditions, a long history of developing meditational techniques. Jung's broad and outdated generalizations do not do justice to any of the cultures involved.

The Sāṁkhya-Yoga system itself is certainly not amenable to Jung's framework. All the mental structures of interest to psychology are part of nature *(prakṛti),* not the true conscious observer, the self *(puruṣa).* This involves an absolute dualism, not a polarization of "Universal Being" as Jung claims (11: 500). The objective of the yogin's practice is to isolate the self from nature, not integrate the conscious and unconscious parts of the self. To accomplish this, the "personality" constituted by nature is dismantled. What is normally unconscious is brought into awareness. The purpose of yoga is not, as Jung says, to discipline the *kleśas,* but to destroy these defilements of the mind, thereby purifying consciousness.[11] In this mystical system, what Jung considers the mind is actually part of nature—it belongs to the clutter from which the luminous self is to be freed. As part of the process toward enlightenment, the yogins clear their minds of all unconscious elements. Jung's process of individuation, on the other hand, involves only the reconciliation of the forces within nature.

Mysticism and Psychotherapy

Concerning China, however, Jung comes to a different conclusion. There the individuation-process is the basis of "Eastern therapeutic systems" (9.1: 341; 13:11, 13–14).[12] To see whether or not it is legitimate to conclude that the goal of modern Western therapies—assuming all such therapies have *one* similar goal—and of some Eastern religious traditions is the same, let us turn from the work of Jung himself and consider the views of others within psychology, psychiatry, and history of religions on the issue. Five possible relationships between psychotherapy and the religious traditions under consideration are apparent:

Identity of goals. Jung has support in his contention concerning some East Asian thought from Erich Fromm on Zen Buddhism. It is not, however, totally independent corroboration since Fromm's knowledge of Zen derives almost exclusively from the work of D. T. Suzuki who was, in turn, influenced in his exposition by Jung. For Fromm, the state of "well-being" occurs when we are open, responsive, awake and "empty (in the Zen sense)," having dropped the ego and having given up greed and self-will; awakening is the derepression of the unconscious (the unconscious being the whole individual, not just what corresponds to society).[13] Others (e.g., Abraham Maslow) also see the goal of both mysticism and psychotherapy as the same—becoming less self-centered and more centered on the cosmos. Such a position sees the realization of enlightenment as the maximal goal of psychotherapy or as containing all the benefits of it. With enlightenment, all the problems dealt with in psychotherapy have evaporated, even if this is not the intended goal of the religious traditions. So also practicing even elementary meditational techniques aids in attaining psychological health. And conversely with the attainment of psychological health by means of a therapy, we are enlightened.

Others outside psychology, for example, Joseph Campbell, Richard Wilhelm, Heinrich Zimmer, W. Y. Evans-Wentz, R. C. Zaehner, and D. T. Suzuki, find Jung congenial. This may be because they find all people from different cultures ultimately to be one,[14] and consequently consider that when systems from different cultures deal with the mind, they must ultimately be saying the same thing. Or they may have found in Jung's concepts what they think is a ready-made, convenient system for translating and assimilating foreign ideas. But because each system speaks of "self-knowledge" broadly construed, it does not imply that each view of the nature of the "self" is the same. The Asian and European concepts may be similar only on a very general level. For example, the idea of an "unconscious" might be taken over from Jung's writings when all that is really being denoted is merely something more than ordinary consciousness—not everything the term denotes for Jung. Even Suzuki, while accepting such Jungian constructs as the "collective unconscious," asserts that there is a layer of the unconscious—the "cosmic unconscious" where we are "consciously unconscious" or "unconsciously conscious"—that Jung cannot deal with in his framework.[15] Similarly Wilhelm in using "*animus*" and "*anima*" for "*hun*" and "*p'o*" respectively still ends up giving an exclusively Chinese content to these concepts.

But whatever the reasons and possible divergencies in meaning, it must be noted that Jung is not without supporters who find his concepts useful.

Enlightenment as preparation for psychological health. A second position is that enlightenment and psychological well-being are not identical, but that the former prepares us for the quest to attain the latter, or psychological health is a by-product of the spiritual quest. A modification of this position is that elementary meditative techniques can at least be utilized to break through encrusted habits, thereby permitting the rebuilding of the mental life necessary for psychological health. That is, meditation can be employed as a means regardless of the goal.

Psychological health as prerequisite for mystical enlightenment. The third possible relationship reverses the order. That is, achieving psychological well-being is a necessary precondition for undertaking the quest for enlightenment. Only by replacing psychological fragmentariness with an ordered wholeness—a sense of *self*—are we in a position to pursue the more arduous task. We need to know our position within the realm of nescience before we can move out of it; if we are confused, the meditative exercises will not help. Psychological health may also lessen the dangers involved in meditation. This latter task, however, is not one of building upon the sense of self, but instead one of abolishing it. As a Buddhist monk says, "one must strengthen the ego before one can get rid of it."[16] Or as Abraham Maslow observes "precisely those persons who have the clearest and strongest identity are exactly the ones who are most able to transcend the ego or the self and to become selfless."[17] How much strengthening is actually required (since no special effort is required to be in the realm of nescience), and whether psychological health as a goal limits the enlightenment-enterprise are matters of debate.

Differing goals. The fourth and fifth positions cover the other end of the spectrum: that psychotherapeutic and Eastern religious goals are not at all related, and perhaps may conflict. Eastern religions and Western therapies deal with mental processes and hope to bring about a transformation of the person resulting in mental "health," but there the commonality ends. In the words of Edward Conze, they "differ profoundly in their theoretical assumptions about the structure of the mind and the purpose of human existence, and in the methods which they prescribe for the attainment of mental health."[18] Specification of a mentally healthy state will vary with these differences as to the nature of the mind, that is, with differences as to which mental abilities ought to be considered central. According to holders of this position, Jung's remarks about yoga and psychotherapy should be extended to all the Eastern meditative traditions.

What is important about contemporary psychotherapy from this point of view is, as Conze again notes, that it is a product of modern civilization which aids in a greater adaptation to the conditions of our society, thereby keeping us going within it.[19] Psychotherapy is for those who are out of step with society and wish to be in step. In other words, psychotherapy is designed to bring about the personal adjustment and effectiveness within society of those who are out of step with it. Berger's and Luckmann's assessment of therapies could be cited here for support: therapy is a means of creating symmetry between social and personal norms, a means of social control by which "deviants" are kept within institutionalized definitions of reality.[20]

Robert Ornstein brings out the difference of this process from the nature of the Eastern religious traditions: psychotherapists are trained to deal almost exclusively with human dysfunction, not to develop and understand extended modes of consciousness (along with the alleged *knowledge* they provide).[21] The intention of the various Eastern traditions under consideration is a salvation which involves the suspension of our ordinary self-awareness. Psychotherapeutic health is for Jung and others *self*-centered, becoming a separate individual by balancing the conscious and unconscious. In the Eastern traditions, "the ordinary self is not to be continually massaged, pandered to, affirmed, or even 'observed', but merely set aside as an unreliable judge of events outside its province."[22] Our well-being is attained not by unifying a personality-structure or by satisfactorily functioning within a society, but by overcoming any preoccupation with the needs and desires of an alleged entity called the "individual self." When we return from these practices, we may or may not be well-adjusted to society, but any practices entailing the loss of self-consciousness, of seeing oneself as a separate distinct entity, will necessarily differ from practices reinforcing personality as central. At best, the ends of mysticism and psychotherapy will be complementary, reconciling worldly and transcendent needs.

From this point of view, the psychological "self" is at best a reduction of the reality involved in the subject. At worst, this "self" is a creation with no reality behind it. We waste energy in trying to maintain a sense of a unified "self" rather than opening ourselves to the mystical. Psychotherapy expands the identity of the "self," while mysticism lessens any such sense. In the words of Jacob Needleman, the therapeutic task is to build a stable personality, while the contemplative path shows us how the energy we put into maintaining a consistent identity diverts us from a larger kind of wholeness.[23] Psychological phenomena are part of a fragmentary shadow-world that is to be overcome. Mystical practices may lead to a selflessness that will appear to psychotherapists to be an unhealthy lack of self-respect or assertiveness. Psychotherapy may open a person to be filled by a culture, but mysticism allegedly opens a person to ultimate reality. From this point of view, psychotherapy and mysticism must diverge in theories of mental health and therefore in their goals.

Conflicting goals. The fourth positions slides easily into the fifth: that the goals of psychotherapy and of Asian religions are antagonistic—what are our real concerns from the one point of view are illusory from the other. Either self-awareness or mystical awareness is illusory in the sense that the only reality to it derives from mis-reading some experiences. If suffering arises from being out of step with reality, then what we deem necessary to restore mental health will depend upon how we conceive reality. Here any grand differences between "Western and Eastern world-views" are not as significant as differences in values: whether reality is found within socially-approved conceptions or by practices designed to transcend these conceptions. In such a situation, the goals of Eastern and Western practices cannot but conflict: the Eastern guidance is towards transforming our world-view; the Western guidance is towards making us more comfortable and useful within whatever society in which we live (whether Eastern or Western) with its accustomed and misguided world-view.[24] Psychotherapy in making us "normal" removes the set of mental anxieties with which it is designed to deal; but in putting us at ease, the urge for attaining a goal other than social integration is killed off. From the point of view of the spiritual disciplines, rather than working through the problems to the root cause (a misconception of reality), we settle for functioning normally within society. Thereby we become more entrenched in the erroneous, self-centered perspective of reality—we see reality in terms of concepts which do not in fact apply, and suffering inevitably follows. Psychotherapy at best solves problems the way morphine does: it eases the pain without healing the cause. Rather than helping us "awaken," it keeps us "asleep" by making us more comfortable.

The essentially linguistic/conceptual methods employed within psychotherapy, the absolute importance of the therapist's personality as a model for the "patient," and the interconnection between therapeutic objectives and cultural values all tend towards cutting down the possibility within psychotherapy of developing the nonordinary states of consciousness which are deemed necessary for enlightenment. Of course, from the point of view of psychotherapy, we are not being re-imprisoned by such techniques within a concept of an illusory self, but are being aided in our contact with reality; attaching importance to self-less states is the mystic's error.

Conclusion

Most of the people writing on the relation of Western psychotherapy and Eastern religiosity would endorse either the position differentiating the goals involved or the more extreme position. This suggests that Jung's remarks about yoga are more appropriate than his remarks about Chinese thought and individuation, if we are going to risk generalizing about "Eastern therapeutic systems." Certainly to the extent that his concept of individuation is tied to his theoretical assumptions concerning the unconscious, the goals are not "translations" of each other even with respect to the Chinese traditions at which he looks.

From this examination of Jung's writings and the work of others on the relationship of Eastern and Western mental disciplines, it must be concluded that Jung's application of his analytical psychology to Asian thought has resulted in a distortion of the latter. Anyone studying these traditions without a previous commitment to Jungian thought and aware of the problems involved in such a comparison will agree that Jung's commentaries do not illuminate Asian thought but only reveal the nature of Jung's own psychological system.

Part VII

Mysticism and Ethics

Chapter 9

Must Enlightened Mystics Be Moral?

Two basic positions relating mysticism and morality oppose each other. One is that there is an unresolvable tension between the two: the inward orientation of mystical practices leads to a total disregard of all worldly affairs. No action affects the unchanging ultimate realities, and so no act is important. A conflict thus develops between the realms of morality and of spiritual freedom—morality as much as immorality is seen as the product of ignorance. Like the enlightened prisoner returning to Plato's cave, enlightened mystics do not deem the values of our shadow world to be of ultimate significance.

The opposite position is that only mystics are truly compassionate and moral. Only mystical experiences permit us to escape our normal self-centeredness, thereby freeing an outflow of love: the lack of personal attachments enables the mystic to be deeply concerned with all people. Further, only with the proper selfless motivation can we truly help another person; otherwise, we would only be imposing our own selfish desires upon others. Connected with this is the claim that we need to know how reality is actually constructed and what is in fact good for other people in order truly to help and to be effective. And only enlightened mystics have the correct knowledge. The rest of us are operating, albeit unknowingly, out of ignorance and greed.

To show that the actual situation is more complex than either of these positions indicates, specific examples from classical mystical traditions which cover a range of possible enlightened actions will be discussed. A preliminary step to this is to discuss basic terminology.

Basic Terminology

Morality

Morality involves how we ought to deal with other persons rather than with personal development. David Little and Sumner Twiss list the conditions for an action-guide (any rule constraining and directing our actions and attitudes) to qualify as moral: (1) The action-guide is intelligible to the holder; (2) It is generalizable, that is, extendable to all people outside one's own group; (3) It is considered supreme and justifiable; minimally, the action-guide has *prima facie* priority and needs no further nonmoral justification; and (4) it is other-regarding: some consideration of the effects of one's actions upon the welfare of others is involved.[1] One presupposition is that the actor is free to choose different courses of action. Most mystical traditions make this assumption—concepts such as *karman* are not deterministic but instead permit the control and predictability necessary for making genuine choices (at least for the unenlightened).[2] Whether specific enlightened mystical policies for action are moral sometimes involves a criterion (for example, generalizability beyond orthodox Hindus in the case of the *Bhagavadgītā*) or presuppositions (for example, whether there are "persons" in the case of Buddhism). The most usual issue will involve *motivation:* to be moral, we must act for the other person's own sake regardless of whether our own welfare is enhanced. Pure altruism or supererogatory acts of sacrifice for the benefit of others are not necessary, but to be moral we must not accord ourselves highly privileged positions. Regard for others becomes a principle for action, even if ultimately concern for others is also self-serving. On the other hand, taking others' interests into account is not necessarily seeing from the impinged-upon party's point of view: what the enlightened mystics consider the others' real interests to be will be grounded in what the mystics see as the true nature of reality—not what we or the other persons involved take to be real. Any other-regarding action would be comparable to releasing Plato's prisoners from their confinement.

Mystical Ways of Life

Mysticism consists of a way of life (which involves a set of values, action-guides, and implicit beliefs about the fundamental construction of reality) connected to "an interior or introvertive quest, culminating in certain interior experiences which are not described in terms of sense-experience or mental images, etc."[3] The objective of correcting the way we live requires overcoming a basic misconception of reality: we think reality is a collection of independently existing parts that can be manipulated to satisfy our independently existing self. Since reality is not constructed so as to satisfy our personal desires, attachments become the source of suffering. Thus, what need correcting are our knowledge of reality and the self-centered desires.

"Morality" may be a Western concept; but a way of life may still be characterized as moral, even if that way of life does not have a category for this aspect of a way of life. A mystical way of life is moral when its action-guides are other-regarding, generalizable, and so on. A distinction must be made between any enlightenment experience and the resulting enlightened state: after this experience, sensory and conceptual content is present in the mind, although the content may be restructured by the newly acquired knowledge of the true nature of reality (as seen by that mystic). In this state, differentiations occur, as indicated by the mystics' ability to use language. The possibility of other-regardingness also is present.

Mystical traditions have developed different sets of practices for removing attachments and for realizing the correct view of reality, thereby enabling us to align our lives in accord with the way reality truly is. Employed in conjunction with other exercises, guides for actions impinging on others provide an outlet for enacting a nonself-centered way of life. Mystical traditions have long lists of action-guides for those devoted full-time to cultivating enlightenment (for example, the Vinaya of Buddhism); for the laity, there are usually some basic rules (for example, do not kill or steal) and a general *ethos* or "style of doing things" (for example, nonviolence, *agapē,* self-control, joy rather than "fear and trembling," optimism, or world-denial) which gives a general orientation even if it does not determine one course of action in any actual, complex situation. Such action-guides are enjoined upon all unenlightened persons as a first step in a quest for enlightenment because this selflessness is a necessary base for the rest of the cultivation—only the enlightened might be "beyond good and evil."

Moral action-guides are usually an integral part of mystical traditions' path to enlightenment (since such actions lessen a sense of self-centeredness). How morality on such paths would relate to the mystic's enlightened state is not clear. If morality is an integral part of the unenlightened life, must it be part of the enlightened life? Or does the mystic in enlightenment transcend morality? That is, is morality merely a tool on the unenlightened path that loses its significance after enlightenment? Is morality part of the temporal and not the eternal? Mystics in different traditions address these issues differently, as will become apparent below. Actions and attitudes are deemed "good" or "bad" depending upon whether they are advantageous or not in the quest for enlightenment: unless religious or other values override, enlightenment is the determining criterion for values. Only a nonmoral sense of "good" (in the way that, for example, a pen may be good) is involved during the quest for enlightenment. The mystic's action-guide may nevertheless also be moral. That the action-guides are moral cannot be established by the claim that they lead to enlightenment—only whether they are other-regarding and so forth matters for this. Mystics are concerned with "virtues" in the classical sense and with the right way to live: more specifically, the "goodness" of the motive (with regard to enlightenment), not the moral "rightness" of an act, is important.[4] There may be a complete discontinuity between moral and mystical norms. In addition, any other-regarding behavior may have to be abrogated at least temporarily for enlightenment to occur. Thus, the issue remains of how moral values relate to mystical ways of life, both on the path to enlightenment and in the enlightened state. Translating such terms as "*dharma*" and "*śīla*" as "morality" does not resolve the problem. Whether mystical and moral values converge is a matter for empirical study, not definition.

The goal of the mystical quest is not to attain isolated mystical experiences which may have no lasting effect upon the person but *enlightenment* (knowledge of the fundamental truths of the nature of reality and a life in accordance with them). This involves an inner transformation of the whole person, not merely a change of belief or experiences (although either of these may touch off the transformation). In enlightenment, a framework of belief-claims is internalized: one no longer merely accepts intellectually the idea that, say, all is impermanent: one *sees* that it is true of everything. This may involve no change in the belief-claims themselves nor any change in behavior if one had been adjusting one's life in accordance with this knowledge. But dispositions are transformed: one is no longer motivated even subtly by greed or by anything dependent upon misguided belief or the incomplete application of the belief framework. Even this change may be minute if one had been practicing within a tradition for many years. Enlightenment also brings a peace or joy of living in the present. There is a freedom similar to that of those who accept their impending death or who have millennial expectations: there are no desires, no needs, nothing to lose, no self-image to maintain—and usually no feeling of a need to *do* anything. This may lead to being undisturbed by the suffering of others. This, in turn, leads to the issue of whether the enlightened can be concerned with the welfare of others.

Actions in Enlightened States

Spontaneity and Even-mindedness

In the enlightened state, actions motivated by selfishness are rendered impossible. Conduct changes only if there is a radical shift in values and beliefs. Otherwise, the motivation for action is all that changes. After perhaps years of strenuous work, spontaneity is now acquired. With an inner stillness free of personal objectives, one moves through the world responding immediately to what is at hand without attachments and without deliberation: the present moment rather than desires connected to the future is the only concern. There is the effortlessness of simply "being" rather than consciously "doing."[5] No conscious following of rules is involved. Trying to follow rules (or even any awareness of rules or a sense of self) mediates between reality and the inner motivation: with such an awareness, one would still be trying to force reality to comply with one's wishes. One acts free from the personal will and free from the tentativeness resulting from the mind reflecting on what we ought to do.

The lack of deliberation does not imply that the enlightened do not have the knowledge and values of a particular way of life. Rather, in enlightenment a framework of belief is completely "internalized" (that is, the beliefs come to govern one's dispositions) since immediately responding to "what is there" depends in part upon what is deemed real (for example, whether "persons" are deemed real). As Peter Berger says of anyone completely socialized, he "can conduct himself 'spontaneously', because the firmly internalized cognitive and emotive structures make it unnecessary or even impossible for him to reflect upon alternative possibilities of conduct."[6] The self-centered habits (Skt. *saṁskāras*) previously propelling actions have evaporated. The spontaneity of the enlightened state—the responding to a situation without a future goal in mind—may make the very idea of "motivations" such as love or compassion seem inappropriate. But the motive internalized by the enlightened may be other-regarding and thus moral. No conscious deliberations are made, but the enlightened ability is like the skilled know-how of the Taoist butcher cutting up an ox:[7] the mind may appear to mirror only what is there, but beliefs and intentions to accomplish a specific end are present. In this way, enlightenment involves wisdom (internalization of beliefs and values and the ability to apply them), rather than merely an incremental increase in factual knowledge.

The enlightened state also involves a disinterestedness or even-mindedness (Skt. *upekṣā*). This detachment from self-interest relates both to emotional responses and to behavior: with regard to the former, one is like-minded in success and failure, in joy and suffering, since one is not motivated by selfish love or hate; with regard to behavior, it means an impartiality extending in some traditions even to animals.[8] It is a pure form of utilitarianism in that regard. There are no preferences or attachments; nothing is valued for oneself more than something else; whatever comes one's way is accepted without liking or disliking. Nothing in experience attracts or repels. No person is emotionally more valuable than another to the enlightened: one is impartial to all. This does not mean that the enlightened, if they are other-regarding, treat every sentient being in exactly the same way rather than act appropriately to their needs. Nor need they be unable to predict the outcome of their action or be indifferent to its impact or future consequences. Rather, the enlightened merely are free from personal desires, including any attachment to possible personal reward or punishment for their actions.

The word "desire" is often used ambiguously. It may refer to (1) the purpose or intention for an action, or (2) the emotional motivation for an action or the attachment to an action. In the enlightened state, mystics are free of all desires in the second sense, but not in the first sense. In short, enlightened mystics may still have purposeful actions, even if they have no personal "desires" in one sense of the word.

Thus, this disinterestedness need not lead to indifference (that is, uninterest) since it relates only to the lack of personal gain. There is no incompatibility between even-mindedness and compassion in Buddhism: the latter relates to our treatment of others and the former to our response to the flux of any events with regard to ourselves. That is, other-regardingness is something other than disinterestedness, and thus the disinterested mystic may have internalized a commitment to be other-regarding. It could even be argued that such disinterestedness is necessary for true other-regardingness.

Beyond Good and Evil

But while being other-regarding can be incorporated into an enlightened state by way of the internalized set of values, it need not: the enlightened mystic may not be "evil" in the sense of harming others for personal gain since all selfish motivations are ended, but he or she may be simply indifferent. A sage need not be a saint. The emphasis is shifted to the action itself—*how* it is carried out (that is, selflessly) rather than *what* is done—with the result being insignificant to the actor, although not necessarily insignificant to others. The enlightened are beyond the rules and sanctions governing the unenlightened within the mystical quest. But being "beyond good and evil" must be understood properly. The enlightened cannot do anything they will because they have no sense of a personal will. The enlightened have internalized a set of factual beliefs which permits no *self-centered* option to occur—they cannot commit an immoral act, that is, an act overwhelmingly self-regarding rather than other-regarding.

But because the enlightened are not restricted by any rules, they may opt for different courses of action. Although no actions are selfishly motivated, basic choices still remain to be made for the enlightened way of life. That the enlightened must still choose is indicated by the Buddha deciding to teach others the way to enlightenment rather than to become a solitary Buddha (*pratyekabuddha*). Choices are also restricted to certain options by the beliefs and values of the enlightened. In the Theravādin account of the Buddha's enlightenment, his choice is moral.[9] He showed a genuine concern for others and also satisfied the other requirements of morality. Morality is possible because the "quietism" of any nonsensory and nonconceptual enlightenment-experience (and perhaps of part of the training) need not entail a lack of action or a moral quietism (indifference to worldly matters) in the enlightened state. Being absolutely selfless also permits other-regardingness and so forth.[10] Nor would a lack of conscious decisions in the enlightened way of life regarding good and evil rule out being other-regarding if that is part of the internalized values. One does not "love and do as you will," as Augustine says, since no self-centered "will" or conscience is present. Instead, helping others becomes a reflex-action or a skill developed within the chosen way of life.

Nevertheless, despite the fact that selfish options are impossible, detachment does not compel any course of action. Non-other-regardingness, in the form of indifference or inaction, can be opted for without disrupting the enlightened state of mind. The solitary

Buddhas and potentially any enlightened Theravādin follower so opt. In addition, enlightened Jaina monks, who opt not to harm any creatures (and thus do not act at all and consequently starve to death), are passively other-regarding but are not positively helping others. Their choice is *nonmoral* in the sense of being determined by values or considerations other than moral and selfish ones. The action may be judged in terms of behavior or result alone as selfish, but the motivation is neither other-regarding nor self-regarding. Even in interacting with other persons the enlightened need not be other-regarding: the importance is upon the nonselfish motive—the actual actions may be coldly noncaring. Attention is paid to the performance of an action but not necessarily to its selection. There may be emotionless killing or other acts disregarding persons and their individuality.[11]

This reveals the sense in which the enlightened are "beyond good and evil." Seng ts'an, the Third Patriarch of Ch'an Buddhism, once extolled his listeners "Be not concerned with right and wrong—the conflict between right and wrong is the sickness of the mind." That is, moral value judgments of "good" and "bad" are the products of the unenlightened mind (in particular, of the personal will). Such reflections would interpose a sense of individuality (of the actor and the impinged-upon parties) not possible in the enlightened state. Thus, the enlightened are beyond good and evil in the sense that they are not concerned with such categories, even if they have internalized an exclusively other-regarding concern. Indeed, in the enlightened state, mystics, if they have internalized an other-regarding concern in their enlightenment, cannot choose but to act morally. This raises the philosophical issue of whether persons can be characterized as "moral" if they cannot possibly perform otherwise. (That is, if one has no freedom of choice, can one be commended if one happens always to act morally?) The morally perfect might paradoxically be said to be beyond such a category.

Examples

To illustrate these points and to show the different relations between inner cultivation of the mystical sort and outer action, examples from six classical traditions will be given. They have been chosen because they cover the range of possible categories created by the two types of values (moral and nonmoral) and the two types of outward responses (action and inaction). Moral values can be grouped broadly, and somewhat arbitrarily, as "this-worldly" (concerned with the material well-being of someone in this life) and "other-worldly." Thus, five categories emerge: this-worldly moral action (represented by Christianity), other-worldly moral action (Mahāyāna Buddhism), this-worldly nonmoral action (Taoism), other-worldly nonmoral action (*Bhagavadgītā*), and inaction (Advaita Vedānta). Tantrism is discussed briefly to illustrate immoral conduct on the path to enlightenment. Each tradition has differences within it; each evolved over time; and since these examples are from writings, they are the results of advocacy and idealization. But they still represent the different possible categories.

Medieval Christianity: Giving a Cup of Soup

More so than actions in the other traditions to be discussed, medieval Christian mystics advocate this-worldly action. And it also fulfills the criteria of morality. Two factual beliefs of importance for this action are that, despite suffering and the need for nonattachment ("inward poverty"), the world is good (since God is good, so is his creation) and that individuality is real. This permits other-regarding concern for the physical well-being of persons. The values of these mystics reflect those of traditional Christianity arising out of the basic commandments to love God and to love one's neighbor as oneself.[12] For these mystics, the love of God converges with love of neighbor, the "contemplative" life with the "active." In this regard, Jan van Ruysbroeck and most other mystics condemned the libertine and antinomian Free Spirits who in their state of "perfection" felt incapable of sin—everything was attributed to God—and so were free of remorse or consideration for others in whatever they did.[13] Any mystics for whom the mystical life did not involve a moral dimension were similarly condemned for spiritual gluttony.

Variations exist within any tradition, but some remarks by Meister Eckhart represent this tradition, at least in this regard. Eckhart could accept the identity of the is-ness (*Istigkeit*) of all things and still feel concern about problems on the differentiated "creaturehood" level:

> We ought to get over amusing ourselves with such raptures for the sake of that better love, and to accomplish through loving service what men most need spiritually, socially, or physically. As I have often said, if a person were in such a rapturous state as St. Paul

> once entered, and he knew of a sick man who wanted a cup of soup, it would be far better to withdraw from the rapture for love's sake and serve him who is in need.
>
> . . . [N]o person in this life may reach the point at which he can be excused from outward service. Even if he is given to a life of contemplation, still he cannot refrain from going out and taking an active part in life. . . . I say that the contemplative person should indeed avoid even the thought of deeds to be done during the period of his contemplation, but afterwards he should get busy.
>
> If . . . the outward life interferes with the inner, then follow the inner; but if the two can go together, that is best of all and then man is working together with God.[14]

Eckhart emphasizes detachment (*Abegescheidenheit*), which is higher than love because God gives himself over to the disinterested.[15] This involves desiring nothing, neither loving nor hating the world or persons, but letting things be (*Gelassenheit*) without grasping or self-assertion. In this nonassertive mode of action, one completely "forgets" oneself. It would be impossible for persons living in God's love to do evil "even if God commanded it" because they seek their own advantage in nothing but act solely for loving-kindness.[16] The soul "dwells in a condition beyond the necessity of virtues: where goodness as a whole comes natural to it"—the soul has "transcended all necessity for virtues: they are now intrinsic in her."[17] With Christian virtues internalized, God acts and the soul is passive, "simply *being* to the full in actionless action."[18] This unites the "contemplative" and "active" lives: one can act while maintaining an inner calm. By removing desires, one learns to act without losing the interior silence. Nothing is done for hope of heaven, fear of hell, or any other personal desires. There is no self-will, not even to conform to God's will. One lets go even of God in order to let God be God. In the enlightened state, one lives without a why (*sunder Warumbe*), without a purpose. If one asks why you are doing something, the only possible reply is "I do it because I do it"[19]—no other motive operates. The Christian values internalized in the enlightened way of life are not exclusively this-worldly, but they do involve an other-regarding component, and thus the advocated way of life is moral.

Mahāyāna Buddhism: Insight and Compassion

The Mahāyāna *bodhisattvas* from the beginning of their careers differ from the Hīnayāna worthies (*arhants*) in their goal (attaining the omniscience of a Buddha rather than merely escaping the cycle of rebirths) and in the centrality of compassion (*karuṇā*) towards all sentient beings. These concerns are summarized in the formulas "I surrender my all to promote the welfare of others and to attain complete and perfect wisdom," and "However innumerable being are, I vow to save them." Insight (*prajñā*) and compassion become twin foci informing the belief- and action-components of a way of life. The compassion relates to alleviating any suffering but most importantly to stilling the rebirths of all beings (and thus to a complete end of their suffering). The *bodhisattvas* of the Prajñā-pāramitā tradition, who are enlightened (that is, have perfected insight), see that all phenomena are like dreams and mirages: entities arise dependent upon other things and are void of any self-existence (*svabhāva*), just as there is no water in mirages. The world, in other words, is not constituted by separate, independently existing, "real" elements. The enlightened *bodhisattvas* still have sensations and find language useful—they merely do not project ontologically their experiential distinctions into fabricated entities. They no longer have the self-centered desires which propel the cycle of rebirths but opt to remain in the realm of suffering to help others and to attain Buddhahood. It is the *bodhisattva's* "skillful means" (*upāyakauśala*) tied to insight which now permits this and which becomes the channel through which insight is implemented through word and deed for compassionate action adjusted to the need and capacity of each sentient being. With their rebirths no longer determined by their actions, they can choose the most helpful rebirths. Prior to enlightenment, all desires, including desires for enlightenment and to help others, are tainted by the lack of enlightening knowledge. After enlightenment, *bodhisattvas* help beings materially but they concentrate upon demonstrating the Buddhist doctrine—the most helpful type of giving in light of Buddhist ultimate values and beliefs—to all beings even-mindedly.

Is the *bodhisattva's* concern other-regarding? With the internalization involved in enlightenment, their compassion and insight become one.[20] No distinction can be made between their own welfare or purpose and that of others.[21] In such circumstances, it becomes difficult to attach meaning to the phrase "totally other-regarding." But genuine other-regardingness is one component: even though the attainment of Buddhahood directly depends upon the motivation of compassion, concern for others is internalized in the enlightened state. Thus the *bodhisattvas*' motive is moral.

A second problem is that the *bodhisattvas* with their insight perfected see no *object* while being compassionate. Can one be genuinely other-regarding if one sees no giver, recipient, gift, act of giving, or reward? Similarly, perfected love (*maitrī*) is directed to nonpersonal events or no object at all. How can the paradox of seeing no beings and yet not abandoning them be resolved? To cite a text: "Countless beings should I lead to Nirvana [the end of rebirth] and yet there are none who lead to Nirvana, or who should be led to it."[22] But this means only that there are no independent, permanent entities existing through their own self-existence: there is something not totally unreal which arises conditionally and which can be directed to the end of suffering. The suffering is there even if there are no self-contained centers of suffering.[23] There may be no "beings," but something is there towards which compassion is deemed possible and appropriate. Thus *bodhisattvas* can internalize other-regardingness without a sense of independent existence.

The claim that surface-appearances are deceptive also permitted the later Mahāyāna idea that the end (stilling the process of rebirth) justifies any means. That is, the skilled means used to end the suffering of others could involve a *bodhisattva* in violating any norm of the standard Buddhist code of conduct (while still living free from any consequences). This "holy cunning" could involve adopting objectionable modes of livelihood, lying, stealing (to deprive robbers and kings of ill-gotten gains which would lead them to their ruin), having sex with an unmarried woman (to prevent her from harboring thoughts of hatred and ill-will), and even killing a person who intends to murder a Buddhist monk or his own parents.[24] Such actions may redefine *bodhisattvas* as exemplars of virtue, but the concern is still moral: they are willing to do anything to help others and are as concerned with the perpetrators as with their victims. The Buddhist code of conduct is taken to be less absolute when the concern shifts from merely helping oneself (as with the Theravādins) to a genuine interest in others. In addition, since technically there are no "beings," the precepts against killing and so on are inoperative: guiding what really exists may be best accomplished by other means. Skillful lying (that is, telling what the *bodhisattva* knows is not true to lead the listener to enlightenment) may be better than a rigid adherence to truth. The important point here is only that skillful means are other-regarding.

Upaniṣads and Advaita Vedānta: Knowledge and Indifference

The Upaniṣads and Śaṁkara's Advaita Vedānta contrast radically with Eckhart and Mahāyāna Buddhism on these points. The early Upaniṣads may not be mystical but instead metaphysically speculative in nature; they also are not uniform in their doctrines. But the general view is that the fundamental reality of the world (*brahman/ātman*) is the only reality (according to the nondualist interpretation) or is the ground of all phenomena that are real (according to the qualified nondualist interpretation). The goal is to realize that the reality in us (*ātman*) is identical to the reality of everything (*brahman*). This is a process of knowledge since "who knows thus . . . becomes" (*ya evaṃ veda . . . bhavati*) what one knows. The later Upaniṣads require proper conduct to attain the enlightening knowledge (*Kaṭha Up*. I.2.24); but this is not discussed in the earlier texts. In the earlier Upaniṣads, "who knows thus" is beyond harm, beyond the sanction of any repercussions from actions, and so can do anything. The ground of the world is beyond pleasure and pain, untouched by evil, and unconcerned with the things of the world (*Chāndogya Up*. VIII.4.1; *Īśa Up*. VIII; *Muṇḍaka Up*. III.1.1; *Kaṭha Up*. I.2.14)—and since one who knows thus becomes thus, the enlightened is in exactly the same situation. The unenlightened become good or bad by good or bad deeds (*Bṛhadāraṇyaka Up*. IV.4.5), but the knower of *brahman* can behave any way (*Bṛhad. Up*. III.5.1). The enlightened can commit any deed—steal, procur abortions, kill their mother or father—and not be harmed (*Kauṣītakī Up*. III.1; cf. *Bṛhad. Up*. V.14.8; *Chānd. Up*. IV.14.3; *Chānd. Up*. V.10.9–10). Their motives for these or any action, however, are not clear since the enlightened either have no desires (*Bṛhad. Up*. IV.4.12) or obtain all desires (*Chānd. Up*. VII.26.2, VIII.12.6).

This situation leads to indifference. Charity and noninjury (*ahiṃsā*) are for the unenlightened (*Bṛhad. Up*. VI.2.16; *Chānd. Up*. III.17.4; *Chānd. Up*. V.10.3–6). The ground of reality is beyond the concerns of the world, and thus the enlightened are not tormented by what they have done or have not done (*Bṛhad. Up*. IV.4.22–23; *Taittirīya Up*. II.9.1). The unborn reality (*ātman*) is beyond the sanctions of *karma* and so does not increase by good deeds nor decrease by bad ones (*Bṛhad. Up*. IV.4.22). Franklin Edgerton felt that noninjury is logically deducible from the Upaniṣadic doctrine of identity because one identifies oneself with other selves: that is, one would harm oneself if one harms others.[25] But the one self which we all are is not the socially-constructed individual self with which we normally identify—it is in fact the unharmable, unchanging ultimate reality. That we are *identical* with this one reality—rather than being interacting parts of a very large whole—cannot easily support compassion. Nothing we do affects this reality—nothing phenomenal reaches it. Edgerton must contend with the claim that who understands realizes that no one slays or is slain: the true self is never born nor does it die (*Kaṭha Up.* I.2.18–19). One could not kill the true self even if one wanted to. Thus, within such a factual framework, one cannot but practice "noninjury" no matter what one does. No actions are better than others, and so indifference is the only reasonable reaction.

Śaṁkara takes the option most damaging to a moral point of view: *brahman* alone is real—all else is unreal. Social duties and rules known through the Scripture are binding prior to the realization of our identity with *brahman* (*Brahmasūtrabhāṣya* III.1.25, II.1.14). But there are no obligations for those who have the enlightening knowledge (*BSB* II.3.48; *Bhagavadgītābhāṣya* IV.10, XVIII.48). Nor can moral action bring about enlightenment. Showing a genuine concern for any individual reveals the lack of enlightening knowledge. In fact, *all* actions are the result of ignorance (*Upadeśāsahāsrī* X.15). Enlightenment thus results in the end of all activity (*BSB* IV.1.14). All actions are based on products of ignorance—the distinctions between actor and action, and between action and result (*BSB* I.1.4). Action results from misidentifying the true reality with objects (the body or the mind) (*Upad.* X.14)—the true self does not act, and seeing this extinguishes good and bad works. Where does this leave those "liberated in life" (*jīvanmukta*)? With enlightenment, ignorance is replaced by knowledge; but in the enlightened state discriminations still occur (although the true nature of these discriminations is then known). Thus, actions are possible (but cf. *BSB* III.4.20). According to Śaṁkara, the enlightened cannot act as they like (*BSB* III.4.26), but should act for the good of others, even though they need not do anything (*BGB* III.24, III.28). The enlightened quietly go about doing the orthodox duties internalized prior to enlightenment, passing their lives unknown (*BSB* III.4.50). Later, Advaitins advocated a code of conduct which was conventional from an orthodox Indian point of view, and in the last two centuries this tradition has been heavily influenced by Western values. But to be consistent with the factual beliefs of the enlightened point of view, for the enlightened no action is any better than any other. No choices matter. The fruits from past actions (*prārabdha karma*) simply must work themselves out and then the body dies (*BSB* IV.1.15).

Indifference to "other people" is all that can be justified within the Advaitin framework: there are no "other people" or other reality which we could help or whose interests need to be considered. All reality is absolutely one, not merely parts of one whole, and beyond the reach of action. Nothing one does can affect this reality. Other-regardingness is rendered impossible because there is no "other" to regard, and thus morality is impossible. All the distinctions we make are only part of a dream and not grounded in reality. No action is any better than any other. And concern for others or self-centered actions are equally pointless. There are no individuals to lead anywhere since we are always identical to Brahman. All individuality has the status of characters in dreams. Nothing in the "dream" realm is of significance, and hence what does any action matter to the enlightened? To the extent it is possible, inaction is the response.

Bhagavad-Gītā: Duty and Disinterested Action

The disinterested action (*niṣkāmakarman*) of the enlightened in the *Bhagavadgītā* shifts attention to our social role. Central to the god Kṛṣṇa's teaching to the warrior Arjuna is that the true self does not act (V.8, III.27)—only matter is active (IX.33). To realize this is to realize that no one really slays and no one is really slain (II.19–21)—the true self (*puruṣa*) is unaffectable. By seeing the nature of action properly, one is out of the cycle of rebirths (IV.9; cf. XV.20). Attention is thereby transferred entirely to the mental attitude, the action itself being unimportant (III.1): one's attention should be focused upon the action alone, not its fruits (II.47). Kṛṣṇa views the results of action (for example, it is the fruit of these warriors' past actions that they should die in this battle, Arjuna being only Kṛṣṇa's agent). Our only concern is with how we perform our actions. What causes suffering is not the action itself—for we must always work while we are alive—but being attached to the fruits of these actions, that is, having a sense of mineness or I-ness which causes desires and longings for particular outcomes to occur (II.71). Since only matter acts, the true self has nothing to do with the realm of activity—in particular, the self cannot be identified with, or possess, anything in the realm of activity. Rebirth is overcome by even-mindedness (V.19): holding pleasure and pain, gain and loss, victory and defeat alike (II.38,IV.22), looking equally upon a Brahmin, a dog, and an outcaste (VI.18), with a lump of clay and one of gold being the same to the enlightened (VI.8), the enlightened can act without personal repercussions (IV.2, 14; VI.21, 22).

With the proper knowledge, one can perform disinterestedly (the *karmayoga*) and perform the action required by one's duty as a sacrifice to the Lord (the *bhaktiyoga*) (III.9). The duty (*dharma*) which regulates one's deeds depends upon such factors as one's age.

In principle, there is a confluence of one's class duties (*varṇadharma*) with the duties of one's own nature (*svadharma*). Conflicts between universal duties (*sādhāraṇadharmas,* such as truthfulness and noninjury) and class duties (such as killing in war) are resolved in favor of the latter.[26] Thus, there is no greater good for a warrior than a battle required by duty (II.31). The basic choice becomes whether to fulfill one's duties or to strive against them, which we are free to do (XVIII.63). Duty governs the realm of activity; only a misidentification of the self with matter gives rise to the false sense of self that causes one to strive against one's duty. Thus, Arjuna's important choice is not between two types of action—fighting or not fighting—but whether to have personal concerns. Ironically, it is in one's self interest to act disinterestedly but according to one's nature.[27] Acting according to one's nature (that is, fulfilling one's true duties) also aids in the maintenance of the welfare of the world (III.20–25), just as for Kṛṣṇa nothing has to be done and yet he acts because otherwise people would perish (III.24).[28] Thus, the *Bhagavadgītā* affirms actions and unites freedom (*mokṣa*) with duty (*dharma*) in the enlightened life. Unlike in the Upaniṣads, the enlightened are not beyond duty.

Service to others thus converges with enlightenment in this way of life. But is choosing to perform disinterestedly one's duties moral? Class duties may be generalizable norms (although this is not obvious since there are no duties for anyone except orthodox Hindus, that is, *dharma* may only denote in-group norms). But is the choice at all other-regarding? Arjuna's initial dilemma of whether to fight is motivated by a concern for the potential victims. He reasons that the war will cause the destruction of the family laws and through a chain of consequences lead to many persons ending up in hell (I.38–44). Kṛṣṇa replies that Arjuna's grief is based upon mistaken beliefs resulting from not seeing things as they truly are—most importantly, not seeing the unaffectability of the eternal self. But Arjuna's new motivation is not other-regarding. Either he is concerned with his own enlightenment or he is focused upon Kṛṣṇa alone—Arjuna is not responsible for, nor concerned with, the consequences of action. Arjuna accepts his role as a warrior, but he is not responsible for his assigned role—he is merely Kṛṣṇa's agent, and Kṛṣṇa is responsible for the results of Arjuna's actions. He is fulfilling his duty, but for duty's sake: he is thereby maintaining society, but that is not his concern. That is, Arjuna's actions may be helpful to others, but his motive is not moral.

Arjuna's enlightened actions are the same as his unenlightened ones (if now accomplished more effortlessly, since he is focused upon the actions themselves and not their consequences). The war goes on: Arjuna's selflessness results in "killing" others. But even if he were to slay all the worlds, he slays nothing (XVIII.17). As with the Upaniṣadic and Advaitin frameworks, one cannot but practice non-injury (*ahiṃsa,*) since the true self cannot be affected by any actions. What appears to us to be killing cannot emotionally affect the person who sees things correctly, since he realizes no killing is actually involved. Thus, noninjury is due as much to ignorance as injury, and seeing one as better is likewise tied to our ignorance. With no sense of personal responsibility and with a "holy indifference," Arjuna can spontaneously and automatically kill "with a semblance of a smile," as the *Mahābhārata* says. Ironically, Arjuna kills the warriors for their own good, as he remains focused upon Kṛṣṇa. Kṛṣṇa may or may not be moral, but Arjuna is no more moral or immoral than a tool.

Philosophical Taoism: Spontaneity and Governing

Philosophical Taoism (*tao chia*) can profitably be seen as a reaction to the ritual rules (*li*) and hierarchies of social relationships which govern all interpersonal actions and in effect define what it is to be human for the Confucian tradition. Learning related to these rules is the central task of Confucianism. This contrasts with Taoist un-learning to let the Way (*tao*) governing reality to operate unimpeded by personal and social desires. If we act free of all striving (*wu wei*), then the Way will act spontaneously and effortlessly. Our actions are non-contentious and non-interfering, letting things follow their natural course. Thus, both the *Tao te ching* (chapter 48) and the *Chuang tzu* (chapter 7) say "do nothing (through personal striving) and everything will be done (naturally by the Way)." To accomplish this, we must discard knowledge and return to the "uncarved block" present before our nature was carved up by social rules and other distinctions. Our actions will then be free of the deliberations present in activity that is goal-driven and follows preconceived plans. We become empty of a sense of self and consequently harmonize with the natural course of the Way. The totality of our inner character, quality and power (*te*) is aligned with the Way. Thereby, we live a long life free from strife.

Is this position moral? It could be argued that the forgetting of distinctions is the internalization of a set of values: only when we can no longer distinguish "good" from "bad" will we be truly good (*TTC* 19). Ideas of "morality" arose only when the Way declined (*TTC* 18), that is, when all people were truly good, nothing existed to contrast with goodness and so no concepts existed to designate "good" (cf. *TTC* 2). But problems arise concerning the values internalized. For at least the strand of philosophical Taoism concerning personal cultivation, Herrlee Creel is correct in saying:

> Morally, Taoist philosophy is completely indifferent. All things are relative. "Right" and "wrong" are just words we may apply to the same thing, depending upon which partial viewpoint we see it from. . . . From the transcendent standpoint of the *tao* all such things are irrelevant. To advocate such Confucian virtues as benevolence [*jên*] and righteousness [*i*] is not merely foolish, but likely to do harm.[29]

For this Taoism, individual personal cultivation (or, better, uncultivation), not other-impinging actions, is central; other-regardingness thus cannot enter the picture. The sage is concerned with life in this world but is nonmoral.

Antonio Cua disagrees: Taoists differ in attitude toward carrying out rituals, but they do not condemn the Confucian rituals as such,[30] and, assuming Confucians are other-regarding, the Taoists thus could be other-regarding. But Chuang Tzu's famous response to the death of his wife (beating on a tub and singing)[31] reveals a totally negative judgment of the artificiality of Confucian ritual requirements. Similarly, the Taoist claim that heaven and earth are not humane (*jên*) (*TTC* 5) runs directly counter to Confucian emphasis on humaneness. The entire thrust of Taoism is towards fewer and fewer rules, less social cultivation, and so forth in order to allow the pure spontaneity of the Way to flow, which benefits all (cf. *TTC* 34, 62, 77, 81). Cua realizes that the Confucian and Taoist attitudes cannot be maintained concurrently.[32] But this is because they are incompatible in principle; to speak of them as complements rather than contradictories reflects later Chinese thought, but it goes against the spirit of philosophical Taoism.

The verdict of a lack of moral concern applies to "contemplative" Taoism addressed to people in general that is most prominent in the *Chuang tzu*. But the "purposive" Taoism addressed to rulers and expressed mainly in the *Tao te ching* may differ in this regard.[33] The latter text describes the art of governing and of defensive fighting (*TTC* 30, 31, 65, 68, 69, 76) by taking the negative side to overcome one's opponents (for example, 27, 43). The Taoist sage-ruler, like the Way, is free of human values (*TTC* 5) but does not abandon people and in fact achieves great deeds (*TTC* 23, 27, 63).

Such actions involves purposiveness rather than letting things be. Is it other-regarding? The importance of governing would allow this possibility (in contrast to Chuang Tzu who does not want his mind disturbed with thoughts of governing).[34] Some passages suggest other-regardingness and describe an ideal society governed without interference (*TTC* 27, 37, 80, 81; cf. *CT* 25). To restore harmony to human relations, an inner transformation away from artificiality (*wei*) to action free from striving (*wu wei*) is required, starting with the sage-ruler. The sage-ruler works to remove learning and desire from the people (*TTC* 3, 19, 65) so that they live aligned with the simplicity of the Way. This involves minimal interference with others. Ultimately, the sage-ruler's role becomes strictly passive, as the people transform themselves (*TTC* 37, 57, 59, 75). With the people not contending, the spontaneity of the Way then prevails (*TTC* 46) on the social level. Thereby, the ruler "governs" free from coercion through the power of the Way (*TTC* 29, 30, 32, 34). Thus, the sage-ruler does nothing and yet everything is accomplished (by the Way) (*TTC* 37, 48, 57, 63). Social harmony comes about naturally through such noncoercive and nonauthoritarian leadership. This has the effect of transforming society in a manner considered positive by Taoists, but these passages are too brief and enigmatic to determine definitely whether this is other-regarding in intent. It must be remembered that Taoists value the long life that is attained by aligning oneself with the Way (*TTC* 30). Thus, the passages concerning governing may primarily reflect how a ruler can achieve that goal for himself. The consequences of attaining that goal are that other people also become aligned with the Way and therefore are also helped. But this raises the possibility that the sage-ruler's personal cultivation and long life is the primary intent behind the actions depicted in these passages, not helping others.

Tantrism: Turning Poison Into Medicine

Finally, "left-handed" Tantrism warrants mention, not for the enlightened state, but for its inversion of the rules governing the means to enlightenment. That is, the morally interesting aspect here is not that "to the pure [i.e., the enlightened] everything is pure" but that the Tantric adepts utilize desires to advance their careers.[35] The passions are poisons used to counteract poisons—something dangerous in itself becomes, to those who know, a way to release from rebirth. Ridding oneself of passion by means of more passion involves indulging (in elaborate rituals) in everything deemed negative in non-Tantric Indian religiosity—eating meat, drinking alcohol, sexual intercourse, even murder. What is "evil" becomes "good." The motive is freedom, not hedonistic enjoyment of the materials used in the rituals. This is considered the quick means to enlightenment (nondiscrimination of what the unenlightened take to be separately existing entities).

Tantrism may be reacting to the standard codes of conduct: not eating meat and so forth could become sources of attachments and thus obstacles. Separating absolutely the "pure" from the "impure" becomes a dualism (discrimination) keeping us from responding spontaneously—even the rule not to harm others if obeyed rigidly would tend to absolutize the realm of illusion. What is wrong with stealing or killing if all is ultimately valueless? Seen in this way, Tantrism is not a degeneration of Buddhist or orthodox Indian traditions, but is merely the proper response to something that may tend to absolutize the realm of ignorance: each new set of values and doctrines gives a new source of attachment, and Tantrism is merely pushing back the boundary of attachment.[36] Rules of unenlightened social conduct (including any moral norms) are obstacles that must be overcome. Must not all the conventions of the unenlightened be rejected? Tantrics differ from the *bodhisattvas* discussed earlier by their actions in the unenlightened state and by the lack of concern for any impinged upon parties not voluntarily taking part in the rituals (although compassion does play a role in the way of life as a whole). It is an instance of a selfish means to a spiritual end—and the end cannot be considered moral if it leads to helping persons to harm impinged-upon parties who have not consented to the rituals.

Comparative Issues

Lack of Unanimity Between Enlightened Ways of Life

The variety of enlightened action must show that not all mysticism is the same, even assuming a common core of mystical experiences: enlightened mystics do not concur on one set of values or on one course of actions toward others. The courses of action in fact conflict, not merely differ. This-worldly concerns are prominent only in Christianity and Taoism. Advaitins find a total lack of action as the meaningful response to enlightenment. Compassion is what Arjuna felt toward others only in the unenlightened state (*BG* I.28).

Most people everywhere may follow basically the same code of conduct. There may be universal rules of conduct necessary for the existence of any society; such fundamental rules would be the same for all peoples at all times. But when we turn to the highly disciplined lives of mystics, any cultural universals (for example, injunctions against killing "without justification" or stealing or for truthfulness) become so abstract as to be insignificant, if not meaningless. The value systems may be incommensurable in that there are no agreed standards of correctness or procedure to resolve differences. Thus, the factual beliefs of the Upaniṣads and *Bhagavadgītā* make it impossible to *kill* anything real (and the latter justifies what appears to the unenlightened to be killing), thereby rendering inoperative an injunction against killing. Some traditions would permit killing for the victim's own good. On the other hand, Jainas, who emphasize actions themselves rather than knowledge and dispositions, condemn killing any sentient being (human or otherwise) as unjustified.[37] Thus, there are no universal rules in this area. Similarly, valuations of the world, history, life, and even having a body differ from tradition to tradition. Incorporating a fundamental norm of other-regardingness or love is far from universal. All that is common are detachment and selflessness, not particular, more operational values. Sensitivity to the contexts of the different action-guides reveals the differences.

Lack of Social Action

Another point that stands out is the general lack of social action in any of the classical mystical traditions—that is, the lack of mystics cooperating in groups to bring about changes (political, economic, or otherwise) in a society as a whole, or of any sense of the interaction of groups of persons as groups. Gandhi is an example of the modern mystic for whom social action is central. But for the classical mystics, even when this-worldly concerns predominate, there is little sharing of power or responsibility. Prior to enlightenment, most mystics may be concerned primarily with their own salvation; but after enlightenment even mystics who have internalized other-regardingness express their other-regardingness usually in terms of the immediate interaction of one person with one person. This may result from what has been described as the "hardness of ancient ethics," that is, the belief in traditional cultures that we cannot truly help anyone but ourselves. But also central to this is that the suffering mystics concentrate upon is more related to the fact *that* we exist, not to *what* we are socially. Everything is essentially good or equally unreal. From within the enlightened viewpoint, social concerns appear meaningless, revealing only our lack of knowledge. Other-regardingness would then be better manifested in helping the person immediately before us (especially in leading the unenlightened to the correct point of view) rather than in rearranging structures or fragments of an artificial world. The focus of attention is upon the changeless. There is nothing important to change except each person's knowledge and dispositions.

Not all of these traditions have the asocial character of Advaita or the antinomian effect of Tantrism. If the enlightened interact with others, there often are one-to-many relations such as one person teaching a crowd. For the *Bhagavadgītā,* fulfilling one's social role is the ideal, even if it may appear to be harming society (as with the war in the *Mahābhārata*): there is no conflict between social expectation and enlightened spontaneity. So, too, purposive Taoism has the ideal of a sage-ruler. In many cultures and eras, religious leaders were also political leaders, reflecting a unity of "church" and "state" within one order. Most mystical traditions (including Advaita) also developed monastic communities to aid in the process of enlightenment, in addition to wandering monks who sever all ties to family and perhaps to society. In Christianity, this-worldly concerns have manifested themselves in one-to-many relations of a social nature, as with Bernard of Clairvaux vigorously advocating the crusades, or the reformers of religious orders. For such concerns, meditation is a way to orient oneself by seeing the true nature of the world and to recharge oneself for action. But for those traditions which do not consider our world as real or good, social involvement is rare. For instance, for a *bodhisattva,* since society is ultimately unimportant, action with regard to an epidemic may only be to inform us that there is no independently existing entity called "sickness."[38] No such action is self-centered, but actions harming society may result. Likewise, the emphasis on social roles in the *Bhagavadgītā* does not change the fact that society is merely a stage for action, not the ultimate focus of attention.

Only such one-to-one responses as adjusting the teachings to each individual are considered ultimately effective. Even political acts, such as the Tibetan monk killing a king, are ostensibly motivated only by concern for the immediate recipients (here, concern for the king's and his victims' future welfare).[39] When a radical inner transformation is required to end suffering, aiding one person at a time to change himself or herself may be the best that can be done. Devoting energy to altering laws or social structures would be wasted.[40] Legislation or reward and punishment on a society wide scale would be an external attempt to dominate and manipulate others against their will, even if it is for their own good, rather than to persuade through one's own character and actions as with the Taoist sage-ruler (*TTC* 57). Such force would be ineffective or even harmful. Behavior may change but not the dispositions and hence not the person. Laws are rules of conduct imposed by society as a whole that manipulate conduct under threat of sanctions, not rules voluntarily chosen and adhered to by certain individuals. Thus, laws are severely limited in their ability to change dispositions, unlike codes of conduct within freely chosen ways of life.

The only change on a social scale deemed desirable is a change in the world-view and disposition of each person individually. It is not that mystics are concerned with nature rather than society since usually no such split of "natural" and "social" orders is made; rather, the concern is with the "being-ness" of anything instead of the surface differentiations. Changing laws without changing the inner nature of people would mean that self-centered desires would still persist; such desires would cause us to attempt to circumvent any laws for our own advantage. Because people inherently have the capacity for enlightenment, no special institutions are needed. A reform of social structures is insufficient, and the inner transformation makes any new social institutions unnecessary. For example, wars will be ended only by an inner transformation ending greed within people, not by altering social conditions. Any society or political-economic situation, however harsh, provides the necessary conditions for enlightenment. In addition, successfully to alter society as a whole would require mystics to enroll the unenlightened with their consideration of their own interests from their unenlightened point of view (perhaps under the guise of God's will). Enlightened mystics may be incapable of such compromise.[41]

Nor is there any sense of *progress* in any political or social sense in the writings of mystics. For the classical mystics, any idea that the social arena is the place to improve our situation shows that we are basically misguided. Such social indifference has the effect of tolerance and of supporting the status quo, or of advocating only conservative reform in a period of radical reform.[42] For Christian mystics, judgments on established powers and revolutionary activities are penultimate at best.[43] In China, the Confucians were usually the reformers; the philosophical Taoists merely adapted themselves to any conditions. Any reform means wanting to alter the sensory realm; but for mystics everything phenomenal remains the same—only our knowledge and disposition for action need to be changed. The inner nature is more important than the outward situation. Mystics' solutions to the problems of living focus upon the former.

The this-worldly concern of the medieval Christian mystics is usually expressed in one-to-one activities, not in reforming society. Typical of this tradition is Eckhart's interiorization of Biblical images that could be taken as advocating social activism. For example, the cleansing of the temple becomes a symbolic statement of Jesus entering the soul of the individual; Eckhart's sermon on the passage discusses emptying oneself for the mystical experience, not economics or society.[44] The Kingdom of God is within us, not among us;[45] it becomes an inner state free of a sense of self for each person individually. Justice (righteousness) becomes the state of feeling impartially the same about everything that happens—nothing is desired from God nor does one go beyond oneself to get anything.[46] It "is a sign of inward infirmity that any person should be glad or sad about the passing things of the world."[47] Social concerns would fall within the category of the "merely terrestrial and transient" to be avoided in favor of love for the "eternal realities"[48] neutral to all outward matters.

Enlightened mystics of course may influence social reformers.[49] But it is doubtful that this is their intention. Matthew Fox suggests that Eckhart's listeners may have interpreted his phrase "I pray God to rid me of God" in terms of ridding themselves of any God supporting an unjust situation.[50] Nevertheless, the context of the remark makes it clear that Eckhart wants to be rid of the concept "God" in order that God may enter us inwardly[51]—the mind must be emptied of all sensory and conceptual content, even of ideas of God. It is the "breakthrough" to the Godhead (*Gottheit*) beyond God, not "works" among persons, that Eckhart is discussing. Eckhart is concerned with "an inner poverty" (in which the "poor" wills and knows nothing), not external poverty. It is a matter of unknowledge (*Unwissen*), that is, de-learning and emptying oneself to become receptive to an infusion of mystical knowledge, not a matter of what one possesses. Similarly, his claim that we are all "aristocrats" might have influenced Anabaptists or other reformers, but Eckhart makes it clear that "within us is the aristocrat."[52] "All people are equally noble with regard to their nature"[53]—it is a matter of our "being" and our knowledge, not our external status, and therefore no social change is required or advocated. Our nobility exists regardless of what we do to our outward circumstances. Nothing in principle could affect it; and to seek anything temporal or work for a "why" runs counter to the necessary insight.[54] This was Eckhart's response to the materialism of his day. Interpreting Eckhart's teaching as a call for social reform is comparable to altering and externalizing his advice that we ought to strip the soul bare (of all sensory and conceptual content) for God by walking around naked.

This understanding of all social activity shapes the mystical *ethos*. For mystics, society is an aggregate of individuals held together by a series of individual transactions. Society as a whole can be advanced spiritually only through the spiritual advancement of each person, one person at a time. There is no sense of any social duty as an ultimate value or of society as an ultimate reality even in the *Bhagavadgītā*. The belief entailed by this is that our true nature is not to be found in our social relations. Any physical welfare and even the survival which society provides are not ultimate mystical values. Still society need not be destroyed if one is disinterested, although the enlightened may appear out of step with society (or effortlessly in step with it). And such figures as the Buddha have had profound sociopolitical effects on their cultures even if their intent was to help only those who came to them for spiritual guidance. Modern concerns for social justice and ecology could only become parts of a mystical tradition if it could be shown that such concerns are in the same category as the concern for maintaining the health of the body required by the mystical quest.

Factual Claims, Values, and Mystical Experiences

The variety of enlightened action also suggests that mystics' values are not derived in any simple manner from the mystical experiences themselves. To that extent, Agehananda Bharati is correct in asserting that mystical experiences are morally neutral.[55] Isolated mystical experiences need not change a person—after the experience, one may remain evil, antisocial, selfish, and self-indulgent.[56] Mystics may even be dangerous to society.[57] Values often are the same for the unenlightened and the enlightened within a cultural or religious tradition, and such values vary between traditions as they reflect different concerns and beliefs. But mystical experiences do become part of the experiential background out of which values and world-views arise; they expand the field of one's experiences and thus may figure in a change of beliefs about the nature of reality and of one's values.[58] Mystical experiences, especially spontaneous ones, need not transform a life, but often they do; they are then given central significance in a way of life. If one has been practicing the techniques developed by a mystical tradition for cultivating mystical experiences, one will be internalizing the beliefs and values of that tradition. If the transformation of enlightenment occurs, the mystic no longer has the beliefs enabling him or her to act self-centeredly. But this selflessness is given expression in various ways depending upon other beliefs and values derived from the cultural environment—beliefs and values which in turn may have been shaped by mystical experiences. Thus, a mystical experience is a factor in the total context. It, no more than any one other factor, can be completely discounted (or given exclusive weight) only at great risk.

Since having a mystical experience compels no one set of values or course of action, the problems of mysticism and morality shift away from mystical experiences in insolation to the whole of mystical ways of life. A way of life involves a faith in the nature of reality. Faith does not consist merely of adherence to a set of tentatively-held beliefs, but one's faith does entail certain belief-claims that can be abstracted from a way of life. Ways of life are not always successfully integrated, that is, a person's belief-claims are not always consistent and one does not always act consistently upon one's belief-claims. The basic relationship between factual claims and values within a traditional way of life is that the underlying beliefs about the structure of reality (the world-view) are such that the most general values (the *ethos*) are appropriate.[59] The Indian concept of *dharma* and the Taoist *tao* are instances of concepts unifying factual and normative components into one order, thereby grounding the values in the very structure of reality. Thus, one can live in accordance with reality. But accepting belief-claims will not select one of several courses of action: no enlightened "ought" can be deduced from an enlightened "is."[60] For example, accepting the view that all reality is one interactive whole and therefore all persons are interactive parts of one organic whole does not necessitate love or morality—we could still manipulate the other parts of the whole for our personal gain. There also still may be good reasons to eliminate harmful parts of the whole.[61] For example, just as one may cut off a cancerous limb to save the body, so society may feel justified in killing persons considered harmful to the whole. In addition, commitment to underlying values of a tradition also does not dictate one specific course of action—situations are complex enough that no simple decision-procedure based upon general values exists for deciding how to act.

Nevertheless, religious actions do depend upon how the world is thought to be constructed: options are opened up (for example, killing someone for his or her own good, if belief in a future existence is entailed by a way of life) or foreclosed. What is "reasonable" in general and how one can best help others depends upon such beliefs as one's expectations at death and what is deemed real. Some values and courses of action are common to different traditions, despite differences in world-views. That is, there are different justifications for the same values, and thus no one-to-one relationship between beliefs and values. This is so even though holders of beliefs may believe that their beliefs as to what is reasonable dictate certain values. This also raises problems with the notion that one set of values is inherent in reality, and that we can align ourselves with that set. This, in turn, suggests that mystical experiences of any reality do not provide all substantive values for a way of life, and that, therefore, such values come at least in part from other sources.

Do the factual beliefs or values in mystical ways of life entail or rule out morality? Most discussions of this point equate "mysticism" with "mystical experience" as if one conceptual system or set of values were produced by one mystical experience. Some philosophers argue simplistically that the lack of selves either requires other-regardingness (since there are no selves to be selfish about or to manipulate) or precludes other-regardingness (since there are no selves to help or be concerned about). Walter Stace argues that mysticism is the source of morality: it breaks down barriers of self-centeredness, and thus permits (and justifies) other-regardingness.[62] Mysticism may be the origin of this sense of other-regardiness, but not all mystical traditions involve a sense of love for the other parts of one interacting whole (for example, the enlightened Advaitin's world-view and indifference). Thus, mysticism is not sufficient for altruism. Nor is mysticism necessary, since all other-regardingness does not require an absolute abolition of self-centeredness. The unenlightened, with a sense of separate entities, can be motivated by other-regardingness for these other entities.

The opposite position—that mysticism precludes morality—is defended by Arthur Danto.[63] Certain factual claims constitute the application-conditions for imperatives.[64] For example, if Theravāda Buddhists did not take belief in rebirth seriously, their goal (the radical end to all suffering) could be accomplished by means of suicide—their elaborate way of life would not be necessary. With regard to morality in general, we must be committed to free choice and a reality toward which other-regardingness is possible. To that extent, morality is dependent upon a certain construction of aspects of reality; without such belief-commitments, morality is not falsified but rendered inoperative or groundless.

Danto argues that mysticism dissolves the factual beliefs that make other-regardingness possible. Morality does presuppose the separation of the actor and the other persons whose interests are taken into account when the actor decides how to act. But if those mystical *experiences* in which all conceptual and sensory content is obliterated are distinguished from the subsequent *state* of enlightenment in which conceptual and sensory discrimination return, then nothing necessitates Danto's conclusion. In the enlightened state, mystics are again in a position where it is possible to have other-regarding considerations. Factual beliefs and values of an interpretative system are internalized. Decisions such as how best to help others are made by the enlightened. And in the Christian and Mahāyāna Buddhist enlightened ways of life, mystical and moral values do converge (along with the satisfaction of morality's presuppositions). Certainly the nonduality of the mystical experience does not demand only one interpretation (for example, Jainas and Sāṁkhya-Yogins accept a plurality of real and unchanging selves). Only belief-commitments such as those of an enlightened Advaitin would be incompatible with morality: if all reality is really only one, there are no agents whose interests can be taken into consideration.

In short, even if the mystical experiences informing ways of life could in principle be isolated from other contributing elements, still it is the total ways of life which involve other-regardingness or not.

Conclusion

The attempt here has been to discuss and illustrate the basic relation between mysticism and morality. The basic conclusion is that mystical selflessness may be manifested morally in an enlightened way of life but it need not be—there is a variety of enlightened values and actions. But whether morality should be valued as supreme or even as a positive attribute in a way of life was not examined—moral value may not be the only consideration of the worth of a deed. Similarly, whether any doctrine connected to the mystical ways of life is true has not been dealt with at all. Wayne Proudfoot finds the social character of the self to be the most comprehensive view and moral claims (which conflict with mystical claims under one interpretation of mystical experiences) to be invulnerable and authoritative; mystical identification with the whole (one interpretation of mystical experiences) is thus an abstraction.[65] Certain mystics would of course disagree. And whether there are any objective means of determining the nature of a human being in this matter seems doubtful. Mysticism may be an attempt to escape the human condition, or, for at least some one mystical way of life, may be a reawakening to its ultimate significance.

Chapter Ten

Theravāda Buddhism and Morality

Is Theravāda Buddhism a moral way of life? Contemporary scholars discuss this question surprisingly little. Many scholars assume that the enlightened Buddha was amoral without any discussion of the point. Indeed, that the Buddha is "beyond good and evil" has become somewhat of a cliché. On the other hand, many other scholars implicitly assume that all religions are moral, or speak of a people's code of conduct as their "ethics" and thereby uncritically presuppose that the code is moral. They do not see that whether the way of life is "moral" in the customary sense of the term is an issue. In the case of Theravāda Buddhism, most scholars assume that because this way of life advocates not killing or stealing, it is obviously moral. The term denoting its code of conduct, "*sīla*,"[1] is rendered "morality" or "moral conduct" and the issue does not appear.

Some scholars simplistically conclude that the Buddhist "no self" doctrine dictates moral concern as a consequence.[2] That is, there is no self for the actor to act selfishly about, and therefore the actor must be moral. Such a position misses the obvious: if there are no selves, then there are no *other* selves whose interests the actor can take into account, and therefore the actor cannot be moral either. In short, if there is no self for a person to be selfish about, then there are also no other selves for him or her to be concerned with.[3] Nonmorality would be the result of the "no self" doctrine, if metaphysics determine values in any simple manner.

Instead of such simplistic approaches, this chapter will examine the Buddhist doctrines, goals, values, and the commended action-guides as exhibited in the Buddha's discourses (*suttā*) and in the early history of the Buddhist Order of monks and nuns (*saṅgha*). To a lesser extent, the actions of contemporary Buddhists will also be discussed. Since the early scriptural texts will provide the central data, this account is idealized to a degree—not all Buddhists govern their lives exclusively by such normative ideals. There are Theravāda Buddhists who practice the condemned livelihoods (such as butchers), and there have been wars in Theravāda Buddhist countries. As the anthropologist Melford Spiro notes concerning the Burmese, "Buddhists differ very little from people in general" and "do not subscribe to all the doctrines of normative Buddhism."[4]

However, the conclusions of this study of the normative ideals of the Theravāda Buddhism are that (1) the goals and motives for actions recommended to the unenlightened are selfish (and hence not moral); and (2) although the enlightened Buddhists cannot be motivated by selfish concerns, the enlightened are left with options of either a moral or nonmoral course of action. Therefore, the ideal Theravāda way of life is not fundamentally moral.

Background Issues

Morality and Religious Ways of Life

A necessary preliminary point is to specify exactly what counts as being moral. The concept "morality" connotes something more than any set of rules guiding actions—we may speak of Hitler's ethics, but from that we do not conclude that Hitler was moral. Moral rules prescribe how we ought to act towards others and what considerations we ought to have. More specifically, morality involves actions between people ("other-impinging" action) and also a concern for other people's welfare ("other-regarding" concern). As will become apparent, why we do what we do (i.e., motive), and not the resulting acts alone, is central both to morality and to the Theravāda code of conduct.

David Little and Sumner B. Twiss, Jr., detail the necessary conditions for an "action-guide" (any rule or prescription directing our actions and attitudes) to qualify as being moral.[5] First, the action-guide must be intelligible to the actor. Second, it must be generalizable in the sense that it extends to all people, not merely to the actor's own group. Third, the action-guide is considered supreme and justifiable. This means that, minimally, it has *prima facie* priority and needs no further (nonmoral) justification—we do what is moral simply because we ought to, not to attain some other goal.[6] And last, the action-guide is other-regarding: it concerns those actions impinging upon others and has some consideration of the effect of those actions on the welfare of others. That is, for an act to be moral, the actor must consider the impinged-upon party's welfare for that party's own sake. The actor can, in addition, also be concerned with his or her own welfare—the motive need not be purely altruistic for an act to be moral. But if the motive for one's actions is primarily one's own welfare, with concern for others being clearly secondary, the action is not moral even if the action has the incidental effect of helping another.

People can be judged by both their motives to act and their actions. If one's motive is moral, we are considered moral. Morality must result in action, but a moral motive is essential. If motives other than a genuine concern for the welfare of the impinged-upon parties predominates, then we are either nonmoral (if our actions do not directly harm others) or immoral (if they do). Moral and nonmoral actions may be the same.[7] Similarly, harmful actions cannot be judged solely in terms of the act itself or its results. Accidents and moral action's unintended results are not considered immoral. Only acts committed through greed or when some other selfish motivation predominates and which harm others are considered immoral.

To determine if a religious code of conduct is adhered to out of concern for the impact of actions on the welfare of others, the code must be viewed within its context of a religious way of life. A religious way of life consists of (1) an "ultimate concern," (2) a set of actions and action-guides for dealing with the ultimate concern, and (3) a view of the fundamental construction of reality that makes the former two components applicable and even reasonable.[8] Thereby, one's source of meaning is grounded in the very structure of reality. A way of life can be considered moral if its action-guides are moral. But not all religious ways of life need to be moral, as Soren Kierkegaard's discussion in *Fear and Trembling* of Abraham's "suspension of the ethical" indicates.

The Theravāda Buddhist Way of Life

The nature of the Buddhist action-guides can only be understood in their setting within the prescribed Theravāda ideal way of life. This way of life is centered around a religious concern. For Theravāda Buddhists, the religious concern—indeed, the only concern (M 1.22)—is radically to end *suffering* (*dukkha*). Suffering is the lack of satisfaction that is inherent in the cycle of rebirths (*saṃsāra*). The Buddhist Doctrine (*dhamma*) sets out (1) the application-conditions in the form of factual claims whereby a course of action ending all suffering is possible, and (2) the prescriptions accomplishing this goal.

According to the Theravāda analysis, our suffering results from misperceiving the nature of the world: we slice the world up into distinct entities and attempt to manipulate the rest of the world for the advantage of what we take to be our separate self (*attan*). But since the world is not so constructed, inevitably we suffer again and again. Because the world and our experience can provide no permanent satisfaction, we inevitably suffer. The Buddhist path is designed to provide a way out of this realm of suffering. The sole purpose of the doctrine of "dependent arising" (*paṭiccasamuppāda*) and the analysis of what we take to be a person into five aggregates (*khandhā*) is to create within the listener a perspective whereby experiences can be viewed without recourse to what Buddhists consider *idola mentis* (the sense of "I," "mine," and any other forms of permanence). Such mental creations become the occasions for craving and grasping.

The craving (*taṇhā*) engendered by our erroneous perspective perpetuates the cycle of rebirths. This cycle can be ended only by re-orienting our perspective, thereby changing our dispositions and actions—much like seeing that a rope, which was taken to be a snake, is really a rope renders baseless any concern for the snake. According to the Buddhists, our nescience (*avijjā*) is the mistaken view of the world and our experience that there is permanence in what is intrinsically impermanent, pleasure in what can only bring suffering, the fair in what is repulsive, and a self in what is without self (*anattā*) (A 2.52).

Thus, there is no "self" according to this world-view. However, this does not mean that there is no reality for teachers to direct towards enlightenment. It merely means that there is no permanent center to what we conventionally call the "person." Instead, there are connected streams of the impermanent and conditioned elements (*dhammā*) in cycles of rebirths which can be ended. These constitute the ultimate components of our experienced world. Thus, terms such as "self" and "rebirth" are only conventions which, to be accurate, would have to be restated in terms of *dhammā*. (Thus, saying the enlightened Buddha was not reborn means that a stream of *dhammā* terminated.) This in turn means that the terms "selfish" and "other-regarding" also must be reformulated to reflect accurately the Buddhist world-view. But each term functions well as conventions, and the issue of whether Theravāda Buddhism is a moral way of life can be addressed with these terms.[9]

The illusion that there is a permanent self is merely epistemological. Once the prescribed point of view is internalized, we see what formerly were taken to be "persons" only as collections of selfless elements (Dhp 279). A "person" is no longer a "who" but a "what"—a collection of things. What is murder under such an analysis? Is murder even conceivable when there is no *person* to murder or to be a murderer? Āryadeva, a Mādhyamika Buddhist, argued precisely that while dying from a stab wound.[10]

When we see each of the five aggregates constituting ourselves "as it really is" (*yathābhūtaṃ*) we see correctly (S 3.170–176). "Right views" (*sammadiṭṭhi*) are the vision of things as they are in light of impermanence, selflessness, and the inevitability of suffering (D 2.311). By viewing our experiences in the prescribed manner (i.e., persons and objects as no more than the rising and falling flux of substanceless elements), we overcome the habitual ego-centric attitude giving rise to acts and to craving which, as depicted in the doctrine of dependent arising, starts a new cycle of rebirths. Without nescience, the fluxes of the mind (*āsavā*) stop, motivations due to nescience no longer operate, craving ends, the process of rebirth ends, and "the stopping of becoming is *nibbāna*" (S 2.117).

Kamma and *nibbāna* are contrasting ideas in this way of life. According to Theravāda Buddhists, *kamma* (Skt., *karma*, "deed") is equated with the motive (*cetanā*) behind acts done through body, speech, and mind (A 3.207, 3.415). Karmic effects (*vipāka*) shaping dispositions (*saṃskārā*) occur only when the three unwholesome (*akusala*) roots are operating: greed (*lobha*), hatred (*dosa*), and delusion (*moha*) (M 1.47). Acts per se are neutral in terms of consequences in this life and future rebirths. That is, acts not committed to satisfy a desire cannot perpetuate the cycle of rebirths. Thus, an unintentional killing is karmically neutral.[11] In this way, intentions and motives become central in the Theravāda value scheme, not acts per se.

Nibbāna results from the insight (*paññā*) into the impermanent nature of reality. That is, to end the motives perpetuating the cycles of rebirth, we need to see things as they really are. Thereby "I am" conceit is uprooted (S 3.83–84.) With the cognitive basis of unenlightened action destroyed, the intention to act based upon that error ends. Thereby, craving is ended, and the cycle of rebirths is terminated. Thus, *nibbāna* is simply the state in which the "fires" of greed, hatred, and delusion that motivate unenlightened actions are extinguished (A 1.38; S 3.251).

The necessary insight is only a switch in how we see the world, but such a switch cannot be the product of any karmic act or accumulation of merit. Or as the Theravāda say, *nibbāna* is "unconditioned" (*asaṅkhata*) (Mlp 268–271). That is, no accumulation of merit or anything else we create by our unenlightened acts can force the total transformation of a person that is required to end suffering.

Thus, the enlightened began the path with the desire (*chanda*) for enlightenment but end the quest free of all desires. A person enlightened during his or her last life[12] then acts with no self-interested dispositions. Whether the dispositions which replace the unenlightened dispositions are moral will be a central issue below.

Unenlightened Buddhists' Actions

Various distinctions are important to any evaluation of Theravāda Buddhism for the issue of morality. First, the central distinction is between the unenlightened followers (whether in the laity [*upasaka*] or in the Order) and the enlightened. For the unenlightened, two goals are possible: the more mundane goal of merely attaining a more pleasurable rebirth in a world of the gods (*deva-loka*), or the ultimate escape from suffering, *nibbāna*.[13] Spiro's distinction between "kammatic Buddhism" and "nibbanic Buddhism" brings out this distinction between ordinary followers and those seriously on the path to enlightenment.[14] Acquiring merit (*puññā*) is most central to the former goal, while cultivating the "wholesome" (*kusala*) also leads to the latter. The issue of whether unenlightened Buddhist action-guides are moral will ultimately turn on whether being other-regarding is central or even compatible with either of these ways of life.

The Moral Status of Buddhist Action-Guides (*Sīla*)

The religious component of a way of life in principle should inform all of one's actions and beliefs. But the action-guides most relevant for the issue of morality are those embodied in the code of conduct (*sīla*), the basic precepts that in principle are adopted by all lay and ordained Buddhists. These regulate basic other-impinging action. This code commends abstention from (1) directly or indirectly taking the life of any human or other sentient being (including abortion, VP 3.83), (2) directly or indirectly taking what is not freely given, (3) adultery, homosexuality, and certain other sexual practices (for monks and nuns, all sexual activity is to be abstained from), (4) false, malicious, harsh, or frivolous speech, and (5) consuming any intoxicants.[15] Monks and nuns, more rigorous lay persons, and all of the laity on special days hold various combinations of more precepts, but this basic code of conduct will suffice for evaluating the moral status of Buddhist action-guides.

These action-guides are made intelligible to their holders by the texts and teachings of the monks and nuns. They also are generalizable to include conduct toward, and by, non-Buddhists. But the other two requirements for action-guides to be moral (being supreme in their own right and being other-regarding) do not appear to be met by the Buddhist action-guides. The principal issue is: does concern for the impact of their actions upon the welfare of others figure centrally in why unenlightened Buddhists adhere to this code of conduct?

To answer this question, one needs to see the place of this code of conduct within the Theravāda way of life. The precepts are rules of training voluntarily adopted because of their role in achieving a goal. The code covers the first division of the "eightfold path" to enlightenment (A 1.229–2.39): right speech, action, and livelihood, that is, the various means by which the prescribed analysis of reality being internalized has a practical outlet. Developed in conjunction with the mental exercises (right effort, mindfulness, and concentration) for inculcating the correct view of reality, the practice of *sīla* aids in rectifying our views and intentions. By not killing or stealing, and so forth, Buddhists begin to weaken greed and consequently to weaken the sense of a self whose interests need to be enhanced. Put conversely, any self-advancement feeds self-centeredness, and thus basic to any further training is not appropriating people and objects according to our own interests. The precepts give concrete recommendations for enacting this attitude. Hence, this irony: only by renouncing what appears to be to our advantage (killing and stealing, and so forth, to increase the well-being of the "self") is our real welfare advanced. That is, only by foregoing self-advancement (for our unenlightened desires) do we serve ourselves.

Precisely because of its role in this quest for enlightenment, this code of conduct is not moral. Only self-development is of concern to its practitioners. The effects upon others are of concern only to the extent that they adversely affect the practitioner's own mental equilibrium. That is, only the effect of an action on the practitioner's own request for enlightenment is of central concern to the Theravāda practitioners—the action-guides are thus not other-regarding and therefore not moral. Winston King's observations on contemporary Burmese Theravāda Buddhists reflect this conclusion:

> To kill another being is "bad," *not* because it destroys another living being or disrupts social order, but because it may destroy the peace of mind of the killer and cause his rebirth in one of the hells. . . . Evil is evil, bad dispositions are bad, not because of their social effects, but because they disturb and moil the perfect purity and peace of their subject's mind. And a muddled mind cannot achieve Nibbana.[16]

Killing may disturb the killer's mind because of the suffering of the victims, but choosing a course of action ends with consideration only of the effect upon the killer. Non-killing and other basic action-guides may be necessary to maintain society and may maximize the welfare of all sentient beings, but in the Theravāda Buddhist soteriological way of life, the killer's suffering is the only relevant concern. If it were the case (which it is not) that killing and stealing could help in the Theravāda spiritual advancement, the Theravāda could recommend it. Concern for the victim may not be totally absent from a particular practitioner's motivation, but it is clear that under the Theravāda normative ideal the focus of attention is only the practitioner's own advancement: practitioners let nothing destroy the calmness of mind necessary for their own enlightenment.

Other precepts utilized in addition to the initial five (not eating after midday, etc.) more clearly indicate that the positive intent of the negatively stated rules lies solely within the realm of self-advancement, not with possible effects upon others. This code is adopted because it is profitable to the practitioners. The only sanction involved is just the enhancement or detriment of one's own well-being as determined by the natural laws governing *kamma*: by following the five precepts, we are better off in this life, are reborn in a better state, and so forth (D 2.86).

The Theravāda position is summarized in two verses from the *Dhammapada*: "Let no one neglect his own welfare for the sake of another's however great" (v. 166) and "To avoid all evil (*pāpa*), to cultivate the wholesome (*kusala*), and to purify one's own mind—this is the teaching of the Buddhas" (v. 183). *Pāpa* produces demerit (*apuññā*) leading to bad rebirths; *kusala* is the opposite of what is unprofitable or unhealthy, that is, what produces merit for the practitioner or what also can lead to enlightenment.

Only a nonmoral sense of "good" or "bad" is appropriate in describing these action-guides, similar to the sense of describing a pen as a "good pen." A Theravāda Buddhist subscribes to the *sīla* because it is profitable for the practitioner—just as one follows the advice "do not stick your hand in a fire" for one's own good for nonmoral reasons. Actions are "wholesome" or "skillful" (*kusala*) if and only if they lead the practitioner toward enlightenment. The course of conduct leading to enlightenment is considered supreme and justifiable solely because of this: what is good is what leads to *nibbāna* (i.e., those actions which weaken the sense of "I" and craving), and what is bad is what hinders the quest. No other criterion is deemed relevant—there are no crimes against humanity nor sins against God, but only errors that are unproductive or harmful for oneself. In particular, the action-guides are not supreme and justifiable for moral reasons as required for a code of conduct to be considered "moral."

Just as no actions may be prompted by purely altruistic motives (although this will be questioned later), so also no selfish actions may be totally selfish. But the only consideration the Theravāda Buddhist who is following the normative ideal sees as important is the practitioner's own welfare. Because moral considerations do not enter the decision-making process, we must conclude that for Buddhists on the path to enlightenment, this way of life is not moral. It is motivated by selfish concerns, and thus is nonmoral insofar as no impinged-upon parties are harmed.

Possible Counter-Examples

Since the Theravāda tradition has survived thousands of years and its basic texts developed over hundred of years, the tradition as a whole is not always consistent. Some practices and some passages in the canon appear *prima facie* to conflict with this conclusion. For example, there is the Theravāda "Golden Rule" (although negatively stated): refrain from doing to others what you do not want done to you (S 5.354). Another such passage says that in helping oneself, one helps others and vice versa (S 5.169). Another says that if an action is harmful to oneself, others, or both, do not do it (M 1.416; cf. A 4.134–135). Or monks are constantly intent on accomplishing their own good as well as others' (A 4.125; S 2.29). So also the canon says that by mindfulness (*sati*) we protect ourselves and thereby protect others. The parable of the acrobats supporting each other in accomplishing their objective is another illustration of these passages. In addition, Theravāda Buddhists are typically described as in general gentle and self-sacrificing.

But, again, the issue for morality in each case is whether concern for others' welfare is a motive which enters into the process of deciding how to act. If we are looking out for others' welfare only as a means to advance our own welfare (so that benefits occur for others only incidentally), we are not being moral. The motive for action, not the incidental effects, is central. To modify a Kantian example, consider a bank teller being meticulously honest in his transactions rather than pocketing some of the money only out of concern of losing his job or being sent to jail. He would like to steal, but he fears being caught. The welfare of the customers is assured, but is his action other-regarding? No, his motive is not moral, and the benefit to others is merely a side effect. The same holds with the ideal Theravāda way of life: the practitioner's own welfare is the operative consideration. The benefits to others mentioned in these few passages are only incidental. The operative concern is made clear by the vast majority of the relevant Theravāda texts and practices.

Perhaps a fitting illustration of the motive in this way of life is to relate the sad context from which arose the frequently cited precept of the Buddha "Whoever wishes to care for me, let him look after the sick ones" (VP 1.302). This was not a general recommendation for medical care of all sentient beings, for medicine is a condemned way of livelihood (D 1.12). Rather, this was spoken to the monks concerning certain ill monks. These latter monks had been ignored, being allowed to lie in their cells in their own filth. In one instance, where a sick monk's situation became too bad, he was carried out of the monastery and dumped by the side of the road. The Buddha had to make a special rule to alter this way of the monks' caring for their fellow monks. Each monk's concern extended to himself and to the Buddha (whose teaching was of direct importance), but no further. Their action toward the sick monks can only be considered immoral.

The Buddha's Teaching to the Laity

Adherence to the Theravāda code has an adverse effect on Theravāda Buddhists' social concerns. The radical end of suffering can only be accomplished on an individual basis: one can "purify" oneself only; no one can purify another (Dhp 165). Under the Theravāda world-view and value system, each person is responsible for his or her own condition in the world as a natural product of past conduct determined by the laws governing *kamma*. Similarly, the doctrine of *kamma* dictates that each person is responsible for doing whatever is necessary to improve his or her condition in this life or in future rebirths. Each person is on his or her own in the only sense considered important in the Theravāda way of life.[17] The only societal progress is, therefore, through the individual progress of each of the society's members.[18] Social harmony, justice, or any other ideal less than the *summum bonum* is seen as not being of value and so not worth devoting energy to. No fundamental improvement other than re-direction of a person towards *nibbāna* (or at least a better rebirth) is possible in this realm of impermanence and suffering.

Although the Buddha's Doctrine has only one flavor—liberation (A 4.203)—there are instances of the Buddha advising the laity on matters unrelated to the radical end of suffering. An example recorded in the Theravāda canon is the Discourse to Sigāla (D 3.173–184; cf. A 3.29–30 and A 4.56–58) in which the Buddha gives a householder advice on how to use his wealth to maintain his business, saving for an emergency, how to deal with his servants and slaves, and so forth.

Scholars have questioned the authenticity of these relatively few passages since the trite recital of bourgeois values is totally out of character with the rest of the canon and the basic goal central to the Buddha's teaching. But such discourses may be authentic; they merely reflect a different *ethos* for those followers who are not seriously set upon the path to *nibbāna*. At best, for them the Buddha could say to save their money and be diligent. But such passages cannot seriously be taken as relevant to the normative ideals of the tradition.[19]

The Theravāda texts outline four bases for social harmony: giving, kindly and beneficial words, helpful acts, and impartiality (A 2.32, 4.218; D 3.152). But providing social services for others is seen in general as a positive impediment to the practitioner's quest to end suffering. Spiro notes that the vast majority of Burmese monks consider social service an obstacle to the quest for their own salvation.[20] The Buddha recommended avoiding some socially commendable livelihoods, such as being a physician (D 1.12; D 1.67–69), as interfering with the practitioner's own quest for enlightenment.

There are instances reported in the Theravāda canon of the Buddha advising rulers or describing the effect rulers may have on their kingdom (e. g., A 2.85). And the presence of these Buddhists may have an indirect but positive effect on society at large in some societies. However, social reform was not the *intention* of the Buddha's teaching. Trevor Ling is mistaken in representing a reorganization of society as one of the Theravāda Buddhist objectives (along with a reorganization of each person's inner and outer life to end suffering radically). No "strongly developed sense of a need for a Buddhist state"[21] in the Buddhist canonical texts is even indirectly implied. As Richard Gombrich points out, the Buddha in these discourses was not seriously interested in politics but in the kings' own self-development and liberation.[22] In the words of Winston King, concerns with political struggles are "the very quintessence of samsāric delusion and its un-Buddhistic pursuit."[23]

More generally, the Buddha was not a social reformer but was concerned with reforming the individual.[24] For example, he did not teach against social inequality because it was irrelevant to individuals attaining *nibbāna*. Again in the words of Winston King: "The Buddhist mandate is not to 'save' the world by 'reforming' it but to enable the individual 'self' to overcome it from within—for the world order is fundamentally unsaveable."[25] In the third century of the Christian era, arguably an exception did arise—Emperor Asoka. But a more accurate comment for the tradition as a whole comes from Edward Conze: "To reform the outside world is regarded as a waste of time. Once we have reformed our own minds, nothing can harm us any longer."[26]

Within the Buddhist Order, there are no orthodox Indian classes and women have an almost equal status with men. The Buddhist laity reflects these reforms to a degree, but no effort was made to reform the social norms of the world at large. Nor could the Order, a society of "beggars" producing no material goods, be a model for reforming society as a whole. Laws and edicts could be a tool for transforming individuals' behavior (and thus indirectly perhaps their motives), but the Buddhist canon makes no suggestions of doing this. The precepts are the freely adopted restrictions of a religious way of life, not restrictions imposed by others upon a practitioner.

No matter how social persons are in some respects, from the point of view of the Theravāda normative ideal, society is merely an aggregate of individuals, with only what is profitable within the series of transactions between individuals being of interest. Any benefits for society in general would be no more than a secondary byproduct from looking out for one's own interests. Getting out of the social realm is in principle always the objective of all actions.

Giving (*Dāna*)

The self-interest central to the unenlightened Theravāda *ethos* becomes more apparent by looking at three other activities usually cited as being moral: giving (*dāna*), the "transfer of merit" (*patti*), and the "sublime attitudes" (*brahmavihārā*).

Giving is important for gaining the merit (*puññā*) that is beneficial in a "worldly" manner for this life and necessary for a better rebirth. More propitious rebirths for the long course leading to enlightenment are possible by giving material aid and spreading the Doctrine (although no accumulation of it will effect the total transformation needed for attaining *nibbāna*).[27] Thus, giving has been especially popular among the laity. It also added a positive practice to supplement the abstentions of the *sīla*.

Giving may reveal a freedom from attachment to our possessions, or even our body and life.[28] But the central consideration is the accumulation of karmic merit for the practitioner (Dhp 118). Our normal expectation is that giving should produce merit only if it is done out of real concern for the welfare of the recipient regardless of the consequences for the donor.[29] But the Theravāda value system dictates otherwise. The *Aṅguttara Nikāya* (4.60–63; cf. 3.39–41, 4.236, D 3.258) delineates seven motives for giving, the lowest being expectation of rebirth in a heavenly *deva*-world. Other motives include thinking "It is good to give" and following custom. The two highest motives are giving alms to calm the giver's mind and to adorn the giver's mind. Each, including the first, leads to a heaven. But more importantly for the issue at hand, none of the recognized motives are other-regarding: only self-centered benefits are mentioned.[30]

Among contemporary Burmese Buddhists, Spiro finds giving not to be selfless but to have a soteriological end for the giver.[31] The amount of merit acquired depends upon what is given, how it is given, and especially upon the sanctity of the *recipient*. Thus, such socially worthy concerns as supporting widows and orphans or building hospitals are slighted in favor of giving to monks engaged in attaining enlightenment, regardless of their material needs. In effect, Buddhist "begging" becomes an exchange system: the monks get food and other material support, and the giver receives the teaching and gets merit for giving. Since widows and orphans do not have as much merit to offer, they are of no value to the givers. (The poor's worldly situation is seen as being the result of their own past actions and only improvable by themselves.) Even the monks themselves can be ignored: any goods given to a monk who is actually impious are still seen as expressions of reverence, not for the monk himself, but for the robe and the Order (and so merit still accrues).[32]

Spiro also notes an irony in this arrangement: the more a monk renounces material goods, the more worthy he is and therefore the more material goods he is given.[33] This produces absurd results. One instance he cites is of an austere monk who abandoned his monastery to take up residence in a cave. For the great merit to be acquired by giving to such a clearly worthy monk, the faithful constructed three new monasteries for him next to the one he abandoned. "There are now four uninhabited monasteries in this monk's monastic compound, for of course he will live in none of them. Indeed, it is precisely because he will not live in them that they were built."[34] Concern for his spiritual or material welfare, or that of anyone but the givers themselves, could not be a consideration in such giving.

The Order, since it preserves the Doctrine and teaches the laity, has itself also been a supreme object of giving. Thus, this Order of "beggars" has become a wealthy institution. Since the Buddha himself is the best object of merit, major donations are made to images and symbols of the Buddha.

In short, this practice of giving has the effect of using other people as merely occasions for the giver's merit-gaining—obviously not a moral approach to others. In the words of Spiro, "*Dāna* [giving], to be sure, has beneficial consequences for its recipient, but it is motivated primarily by the self-interest of the donor."[35]

"Transfer of Merit" (*Patti*)

Another Buddhist practice often cited as an example of selfless giving is the "transfer of merit" (*patti*), that is, the dedication of one's accumulated merit to the welfare of another person. The act of dedication does no harm to its practitioner. In fact, the act increases merit for the practitioner since the act of dedication is itself a "good" (i.e., advantageous) deed. Similarly, rejoicing in the merit of another (*pattānumodanā*) produces greater merit for the rejoicer than the original merit-producing act did for the doer.[36]

This practice was not part of early Buddhism, and there is no denying the impossibility of reconciling the transfer of merit with fundamental belief-claims of Theravāda Buddhism. This practice represents, in the words of Spiro, a blatant "inconsistency with the entire structure of Buddhism."[37] Some try to reconcile it with the full responsibility of individuals for their own progress by claiming that the donors only *wish* that other people could reap the benefits of their actions (hence the phrase "dedication" of merit) or that the donees *empathize* in the donor's merit.[38] Any actual transfer of merit from one person to another would conflict directly with the absoluteness of individual responsibility caused by *kamma*. The practice may have become popular, Spiro thinks, because the "faithful are incapable of following the inexorability of the karmic doctrine to its logical conclusion."[39] Thus, a practice entered the tradition that may be contrary to the doctrine of the Buddha.

Whether that is true or not, under this practice, acquiring merit itself, not any moral actions warranting it, again become the focus of action. The act may be done only to show the practitioner's detachment from merit or some other motive unrelated to benevolence.[40] But Spiro provides instances of merit-transfer that are motivated exclusively by self-interest, that is, by the fact that the *donor* gains merit by the intention to help others.[41]

Concern for merit-making for oneself, not a concern for others' welfare, is central. In this way, even such an apparently generous practice as the "transfer of merit" becomes absorbed into the self-interest characterizing the rest of unenlightened Theravāda practice. Spiro mentions this practice as an instance of the larger "paradox of a virtue (generosity) coming to exhibit the same properties as the vice it was intended to combat (selfishness)."[42]

The "Sublime Attitudes" (*Brahmavihārā*)

Another apparently other-regarding aspect of Theravāda Buddhist meditation is the practice of the "sublime attitudes" (*brahmavihārā*): benevolence (*mettā*), compassion (*karuṇā*), sympathetic joy (*mudīta*), and even-mindedness (*upekkhā*). Each is "radiated" out in all directions to all sentient beings. These are preliminary meditative exercises, not the insight-meditation (*vipassanā-bhāvanā*) essential to the quest for enlightenment. But the sublime attitudes may lead to rebirth in the highest *deva*-world (D 2.251; M 2.76; A 2.129). These practices may also have an effect on other sentient beings; the Buddha, for example, supposedly stopped a charging elephant by radiating benevolence. Winston King sees these "radiations" as the Buddhist solution to social ills.[43]

However, the practitioner's own mind-cultivation, not effects upon others, is once again the center of attention. The expressed intention of these exercises is to overcome the practitioner's particular untoward mental states: benevolence is to be practiced by the ill-willed, compassion by those with evil thoughts, sympathetic joy by those who dislike others, and even-mindedness by those who lust. That the meditator is the central concern, and not any possible benefit to the object of meditation, is evidenced by the fact that meditators are cautioned not to cultivate benevolence (love) toward the opposite sex because this leads to lust.[44] These practices break down the meditator's sense of separation from other beings, but the purpose is not other-regarding.

In addition, these meditations are not preparation for other-regarding activity. Each practice consists of *wishes* rather than any necessary commitment to *action*.[45] For example, in the words of Harvey Aronson, who considers these attitudes to be moral, "[c]ompassion consists only of wishing that others be free from suffering."[46] But mere identification with the suffering of another by means of compassion is not moral action. Thinking "We should help the homeless" is not action to help them. The sublime attitudes are concerned only with the practitioner's own inner detachment. Even-mindedness is "complete evenness of mind in perceiving others' happiness or suffering."[47] Such an attitude towards criminals and their victims may lead to indifference and inaction. There is no moral impulse in such an attitude. As Conze says of the practice of the sublime attitudes in general, "on reaching its perfection the social attitude . . . seems to becomes distinctly asocial."[48]

The sublime attitudes shift positive feelings that the meditator has towards people close to him or her to all sentient beings. But in the movement from emotional attachment to calmness, each person is reduced to "a formless depersonalized 'someone' " towards whom compassion is to be radiated.[49] King concludes that despite the personal terms utilized in the practice, the practice is impersonal: "Thus these seemingly ethical and personal attitudes, in the process of their universalization, have almost totally lost their ethical-personal quality. . . ."[50] The practices are reduced merely to a matter of attitudes, and "persons" are reduced to objects toward which no moral concern is exhibited.

But these practices do weaken the meditator's entrenched and mistaken view of distinct entities that should be valued differently. The practitioner of these meditations, as with the other Theravāda practices, is the only beneficiary of concern. It breaks down a sense of self. Any indirect benefit to others is incidental. Indeed, Aronson must admit that the objects of the sublime attitudes are not affected, but the mind of the meditator is protected.[51] This practice is no more other-regarding than any other meditative technique unattached to other actions motivated by moral concerns.

Moral Enlightened Buddhist Action

The conclusion from the above discussion is that, for Buddhists on the path to enlightenment, the advocated way of life is not other-regarding. In fact, selfishness is in principle the motivating concern for this way of life, and hence this way of life is not moral. Such Buddhists are not necessarily hurtful or negative in their actions towards others (i.e., immoral)—indeed their actions may even be incidentally beneficial—but there is an indifference to the welfare of others for their own sake.

The status of *enlightened* Buddhists' actions fares differently. The "nibbanized" (*nibbuto*) person seeks nothing and thus is free. All greed and hatred are terminated since these emotions rest upon the mistaken belief that there is a distinct self whose interests take priority. With the end of all attachments generated by the mistaken perception, suffering ends, that is, the class of desires that could be satisfied has evaporated.

Nibbāna and Morality

Is there anything about such a state of a person that rules it out as being moral? Two possible objections are Arthur Danto's. He argues that the mystical point of view is monistic (thereby allowing no room for moral reflection) and that morality is part of a world considered illusory and therefore is valueless.[52]

Both of these objections can be met. First, during the trances (*jhānā*) there is no mental space differentiating oneself from others, and thus there is no mental space available for moral or any other reflection. But the enlightened state, *nibbāna,* is not of that nature: enlightenment comes with an insight into the nature of reality made while the sensory and conceptual activity of the mind is operating. In the state after such an insight-experience has occurred, reflection and the consideration of alternatives are possible. This is evidenced by the Buddha's ability to use language. Also his ability to adjust his teachings according to the capacity of his listeners (A 1.10) suggests that he was not an automatic machine spewing out at random words and phrases memorized before his enlightenment. This means that there is also the mental space necessary for moral reflection.

A variation on this objection is that the Theravāda "no self" doctrine either prohibits or requires morality. This was dealt with earlier. Buddhists never deny that there is something in the world—they assert only that there is nothing permanent in what we normally take to be persons and things. No "beings" exist which have feelings (*vedanā*) or discrimination (*viññāna*), but there are the feelings and acts of discrimination within "streams of consciousness" (continuous, constantly changing chains of elements) which can be directed towards enlightenment. Even Ling who denies that Buddhism is a religion of personal salvation (because of the "no self" doctrine) realizes this.[53] The Buddha in his enlightened state felt there was something "out there" for which compassion was appropriate, even if there were no "persons" in the sense of permanent, distinct entities. The sentience (desire and interest), thought (conception and valuation), and agency (decision and agency) of each person are there making morality possible,[54] although, from the Buddhist perspective, separate and enduring "centers" of sentience, thought, and agency are not.

The second type of objection (that the world is an illusion and, since morality is only part of the world, morality is therefore valueless) can also be met. Buddhist concerns involve what their religious perspective defines as the *real* interests of persons, not what these people from their unenlightened point of view consider their interests to be. Little and Twiss consider "this-worldly" welfare (such as physical survival, bodily and psychological health, and security from arbitrary violence) as the only legitimate moral concerns; "real" welfare (here, attaining *nibbāna*) is a religious, not a moral, end.[55] But why physical or social concerns must be the only morally legitimate ones is not at all clear—unless one normatively ties the whole concept of morality to particular culturally-accepted ideals (e.g., physical health and survival). Even with a religious goal valued above this-worldly concerns, it may still be asked whether the action-guides of the enlightened Buddhists are generalizable, other-regarding, and so forth. In other words, it may be asked whether they fulfill all the requirements of morality even if the label "morality" does not apply.[56]

Is there anything about Buddhist real interests which would keep them from being incorporated into a moral way of life? What we consider the real interests of a person will be determined partially by how we see the world. In the case of the Theravāda worldview, the factual beliefs of (1) rebirth, (2) *kamma,* (3) possible escape from rebirth and *kamma,* and (4) that no one can save another, accompanied by the valuation of escape from rebirth as the supremely justified goal, shape what we should do to aid others. Thus, teaching (i.e., showing and explaining the path to others) is the highest deed we can do for another. In such a context, the physical survival of one particular slice of the cycle of rebirths is relatively insignificant. From within the Buddhist perspective, our this-worldly concerns are comparable to the concerns of the prisoners in Plato's cave. Once we leave the cave and see things as they really are, many if not all such concerns will seem unimportant. But the possibility of concern for others is not necessarily ruled out, and there is no reason to view the new concerns as necessarily not other-regarding.

The interaction of values and factual beliefs in the choice of one's actions can be illustrated by yet another irony: killing someone for his or her own (real) good. Alex Wayman, speaking of a passage from Asaṅga, a Yogācāra Buddhist, remarks:

> If a Bodhisattva sees a bandit about to kill many men or to commit some other crime leading to immediate damnation, he thinks that were he to kill the bandit he himself would go to hell but save the bandit from a worse fate; and so out of compassion for all concerned except himself does the deed which horrifies him. The theological conclusion is that in this he commits no fault, but instead gains much merit. Such a case occurred in Tibet with the assassination of the king Glaṅ dar ma.[57]

The assassination occurred because the Tibetan king was harming himself karmically by persecuting Buddhists. Without belief in a cycle of rebirths and in the effectiveness of *kamma,* we could not consider killing people for their own good. The monk who committed the murder was in fact reborn in a *deva*-world for his willingness to violate—solely for the sake of others—the precept against killing. Note that when one's own salvation is the central concern, as with the Theravāda, the idea of violating the precepts for another would not occur. Killing became justified in the Mahāyāna when concern for others for their own sake entered into consideration, and when protecting the Buddhist Doctrine was given a higher priority to holding the precepts. The closest the Theravāda come to justifying killing involves a somewhat similar situation but slanted toward concern with the *killer's own* karmic fate. The *Mahāvaṃsa* relates how king Duṭṭagāminī of Sri Lanka undertook a war to spread Buddhism throughout the land and, once victorious, grieved over all the killing. The Arahants assured him that he had been responsible for only the death of one and one half people (i.e., one Buddhist and one person who kept the five precepts but had not taken the "triple refuge"); there was nothing negative in killing the nonbelievers. And in fact, since the war was undertaken for a good cause (a Buddhist "holy war" fought for the sake of the Buddhist Doctrine), the killing and other acts of harming were justified and no demerit at was produced.[58] Therefore, the king would not suffer because of his deeds. Propagating the Doctrine might have been attempted altruistically or only for the sake of the merit—and the king's concern only for the consequences for himself, not for the victims of a war conducted for a religion of non-hatred, would tend to favor the latter (or some other selfish) motive.

Another type of objection to the possibility that enlightened Buddhist conduct is moral is that the enlightened person is "beyond good and evil" and so is not interested in the welfare of others. An enlightened Buddhist is beyond the sanction of *kamma,* freed from merit and demerit (Dhp 39). Therefore, no course of action is binding. The enlightened is beyond all desires, including the desire to help others. The personal intention (*cetanā*) that is *kamma* has been replaced by an even-mindedness which, it is argued, is equivalent to indifference. In reply, Karl Potter's comment on non-attachment (Skt., *vairāgya*) is appropriate: giving up actions prompted by personal desires and overcoming desires connected to our actions mean that we no longer anticipate an action's result only in the sense that we are not personally attached to the outcome (the success or failure, the pleasure or pain), not that we cannot predict its outcome.[59] He contrasts renunciation of the fruit of action with its opposite—resignation—which is blind to the outcome of deeds. In short, disinterest in the effect of an action upon the actor does not mean uninterest in the action's result or in its effect upon others.

Thus, personal non-attachment need not involve an indifference to the needs and concerns of others. It is a difference in the attitude toward how we actually execute our actions, not mindless disregard for consequences. In such a state, we can, without karmic effect, do any deed which for the unenlightened would produce merit or demerit perpetuating the cycle of rebirths. Since the enlightened have internalized a perspective from which deeds motivated by personal concerns are no longer possible, they are "beyond good and evil" only in the sense of not having the factual beliefs permitting an evil (selfish) option to be elected. They may be moral or may be "non-moral" (i.e., operating by a value system in which actions are chosen without regard to motives of selfishness and other-regardingness). The Theravāda factual framework, like any world-view, would also limit what the enlightened see as possible options. But because the *motivation* has been transformed, the *acts* themselves may remain the same as before enlightenment. That is, the enlightened's behavior may not change—the basic precepts of *sīla* are so internalized that the enlightened are incapable of violating them (cf. D 3.133). The enlightened would then follow the precepts but without consideration of whether an action is good (productive) or bad (harmful). The only difference would be the spontaneity acquired from enlightenment, that is, from fully internalizing a point of view and set of action-guides.

The alternative is that behavior will change after enlightenment. A Buddhist version of Augustine's precept, "Love God and do what you will," would then operate. The Theravāda code of conduct in such circumstances would no longer be absolute, but merely a "raft" designed for the path leading to enlightenment and to be abandoned once enlightened (M 1.134–35). No act per se is bad, only the motivations for doing it are good or bad. The enlightened could not kill for self-gain because such a consideration could not enter their minds. Yet, as mentioned previously, there is a justification for killing for the victim's own sake. No action-guides would then govern the enlightened's actions, unless the enlightened decided to choose one.

In addition, rigidly holding to a set of action-guides designed for those still in the realm of nescience might be taken as absolutizing the realm of nescience. In support of the latter position, it can be noted that in the *Jātaka Tales,* the Buddha-to-be is portrayed as breaking all the five precepts except lying, as he used his "skillful means" to lead the unenlightened to enlightenment. The Buddha also upon occasion told people something he knew to be wrong in order to help the listeners' spiritual advancement. For example, he told beginners that there is no mental development while he told more advanced followers the correct doctrine that there is (A 1.10).

Regardless of which of these alternatives applies, enlightenment does not entail any one course of action. Buddhist values and beliefs collectively do not uniquely determine one reaction or set of action-guides. A specific course of action must be elected—none is obligated. No enlightened "ought" (one set of action-guides) can be deduced from an enlightened "is" (the set of factual beliefs). Accepting the "no self" doctrine does not even eliminate either a positive or negative response to other people, since we can react in different ways to the impermanent configurations of elements constituting what the unenlightened take to be a "self."

This can be seen by looking at the actions of the enlightened Buddhists. There are three categories of enlightened beings: "fully and completely enlightened Buddhas" (*sammāsambuddhā*), who enlighten themselves without teachers of the complete path and who show others the path; solitary Buddhas (*paccekabuddhā*), who also enlighten themselves without teachers but who do not show others the path; and Arahants ("worthies"), both lay (A 3.451; M 1.490; Mlp 368) and within the Order, who enlighten themselves by following the Doctrine taught by the Buddhas. Each has escaped the cycle of rebirths, as the basic formula for Arahants states:

> Destroyed is birth; lived is the highest life (*brahmacariyaṃ*); done is what ought to be done (*kataṃ karanīyaṃ*); and there is no future existence (M 1.184).

And because each has done what ought to be done, they now do not have to do anything. They are free to choose their course of action, be it moral or nonmoral. Each has the same world-view internalized, but this does not compel only one way of acting. None can be motivated selfishly, but they need not be other-regarding either. This can be seen by contrasting the moral actions of fully and completely enlightened Buddhas and some Arahants with the nonmoral actions of solitary Buddhas and other Arahants.

Fully and Completely Enlightened Buddhas

In the Pāli versions of his enlightenment, Gotama the Buddha is portrayed as having doubts about the value of teaching the Doctrine that leads to the radical end of suffering because he did not think any people would understand. But, after being entreated by the *deva* Brahma to lead others to enlightenment, he finally decided to take up the life of a teacher out of compassion for the unenlightened (D 2.36–39; M 1.13, 1.21, 1.168–169; S 1.136–138; VP 1.5 et seq.). The Buddha's course of action was freely chosen—he was beyond the sanction of *kamma* and therefore could have elected not to help others without suffering in any manner. He had "done what ought to be done" in attaining enlightenment, and therefore there is nothing he had to do. He voluntarily undertook a restriction on his actions for the sake of others, a restriction which he could have renounced at any time since he was free. This led, according to the

Theravāda tradition, to forty-five years of totally selfless activity helping others.

The important point of these accounts, regardless of their authenticity, for the issue of morality is that the Buddha's enlightenment did not spontaneously produce a life of other-regarding action. The Buddha had *to choose* to be actively concerned with others' welfare. Thus, at the end of the Buddhist path, there remains a choice—neither the path of the unenlightened way of life nor the enlightenment-experience compels the enlightened to adopt a moral way of life.

The decision of Gotama to teach and his subsequent actions were moral. His course of action was freely chosen; and the action-guides involved were intelligible, supreme, generalizable, and other-regarding. In fact, his instructing others in religious matters appears to be totally altruistic since, from his point of view, he had absolutely nothing to gain by doing it or to lose by refraining from doing it. In contrast to followers on the path, the Buddha was genuinely compassionate, not someone who used compassion as no more than a means to further his own ends.[60] Such actions also showed a much more active concern for others than just remaining an example for others to follow. He acted exclusively for other people's sake (or, more accurately from his point of view, for the sake of other streams of consciousness). Ironically, he was being moral in teaching a nonmoral way of life, because this way of life was in the best interests of his listeners.

Moral Arahants

Enlightening themselves is the principal task of the monks on the path. However, once they are enlightened, the Buddha recommended that they lead others to deliverance by teaching the Doctrine out of compassion for the world (D 2.119; M 1.45, 1.167–168; S 1.38, 1.131–132, 1.206; VP 1.21; Dhp 158). But the Arahants have to opt for this way of life, and those who do so are moral. Their teaching, as with the Buddha's, would be done solely for the benefit of the world.

The enlightened monks and laity have the opportunity to opt for a moral course of action. The Order has constant contact with society at large. The monks on the path are to be "islands to themselves, their own resort" (D 2.100) for their own development. But the Order, along with the Buddha and the Doctrine, is a refuge (*saraṇa*) for the lay community. Indeed, the purpose of the Order is often said to be to advance the happiness of all beings. Thus, those enlightened monks who choose to re-direct streams of consciousness toward enlightenment by teaching fulfill the criteria of morality by engaging in other-regarding actions.

In practice, unenlightened monks also teach, since monks in general are commended to restrain the laity from doing demeritorious courses of actions, to exhort them to do the propitious, to cultivate the sublime attitudes, to instruct the Doctrine, to deal with the laity's misunderstandings, and to show the laity the way to the *deva*-worlds (D 3.183). But only the enlightened Buddhists have the proper world-view and disposition which enable them to help others without attachment. If persons along the path have the desire to teach or to be compassionate (to gain merit or to weaken a sense of self), their concern is misguided at least insofar as it is directed toward an inappropriate (unreal) object. Teaching could therefore be detriment karmically to themselves and be misleading to others in the guidance given. Only the enlightened have totally replaced mistaken views and selfish ends with benevolence and compassion, enabling them to help without any negative consequences for themselves or others. Gaining enlightenment first is thus of supreme benefit to others (*if* a moral way of life is opted for) within this religion. It also enhances the monks' merit-value for the giving by others.

In fact, teaching and preaching, being a spiritual friend (*kalyāṇamitta*) and preserving the Doctrine are the most fundamental aid monks can offer, since ultimately each person must accomplish for himself or herself the end of suffering. Within this framework of factual beliefs, instructing others is the highest manifestation of other-regardingness. Thus, the karmically worst actions (along with killing one's parents) are any actions which hurt the propagation of the Doctrine, that is, killing the enlightened, even hurting a Buddha, and causing a schism in the Order.

Passively, the Arahants function as exemplars for the laity (A 1.211): the monks who have traveled the path prescribed by the Doctrine, not the Buddhas, are the paradigms of Theravāda Buddhist practice. The Order is also the best merit-field (*puññākkhetta*) for acts of giving (A 1.208); thereby, according to this tradition, it provides a valuable service to the laity. Since the merit that the laity receive for giving compensates them for the material they give the monks, this practice is as moral as any fair exchange is. But enlightened monks are acting morally by making themselves available for the laity in this regard.

Throughout the Order's history, monks have also performed nonreligious services for the laity (i.e., services not directly related to advancing the laity to *nibbāna*), often in direct conflict with the full set of precepts (the *Vinaya*) governing their actions. It is not recommended that they engage in this-worldly good works—even an occupation as morally commendable (from our point of view) as being a doctor (D 1.12)—because such deeds may become objects of attachment (S 2.3). These actions may karmically damage the impinged-upon parties by making them more comfortable in the realm of nescience, thereby rendering them less inclined to take up the religious quest, or otherwise harming them. And since the actions are done by the unenlightened, that is, by those who do not see things "as they really are," they may not be effective and only hurt the actor. At best, these acts do no harm and no (real) good.

Becoming enlightened provides the opportunity to be other-regarding. Again, this is not the objective (ending the practitioner's own suffering is). But the actions of the enlightened Buddhists who opt to teach and to be available for merit-making are in principle clear instances of wholly altruistic actions. Having overcome any self-centeredness, they can react solely to the needs of others. Their welfare is secure, not varying with the reactions of the persons upon whom their actions impinge. These could even be called acts of love, not in the sense of desiring a personal emotional profit from another's happiness or being attached to another's happiness in any way, but in the sense of giving oneself to others without regard to possible personal consequences.

Non-Moral Enlightened Buddhists

Commentators often attempt to justify the unenlightened Theravāda way of life as a selfish means to a moral way of life (i.e., after enlightenment, one can lead others to the end of suffering).[61] But while enlightened Buddhists may opt for a moral way of life, they need not. All enlightened Buddhists have the option to do nothing for others. This can be seen in the lives of the solitary Buddhas (*paccekabuddhā*) and certain Arahants.

Solitary Buddhas (*Paccekabuddhā*)

Solitary Buddhas epitomize the "self-interested ascetic."[62] The epithet of the Arahants—"wandering lonely as a rhinoceros"—is really only applicable to the solitary Buddhas who live separately from society. These enlightened ones may restrict their actions by the rules governing Buddhist conduct, but nothing about them requires them to perform other-regarding action.

Commentaries centuries after the Buddha expanded the doctrine of the solitary Buddhas and did ascribe certain minimal moral practices to them. In order to remove suffering, some solitary Buddhas may beg for alms, thereby permitting the exchange arrangement involving merit. Some also teach elementary aspects of the Doctrine (sometimes by gesture only, not by word), although they do not teach the entire path to enlightenment. Others may engage in the sublime attitudes (although whether this meditative practice is moral was questioned earlier).

However, the option remains for these enlightened Buddhists not to engage in any other-regarding action. They may remain wandering ascetics who do nothing to aid others or look out for others' interests. Since according to the tradition, these solitary Buddhas exist only when there are no fully and completely enlightened Buddhas in the world, they would be opting for a course of action that is not other-regarding when their teaching would be especially valuable.

Nonmoral Arahants

While the Buddha recommended that the Arahants teach, they did not have to—this was merely the Buddha's recommendation. One example of an alternative course of action will suffice: the suicide of certain Arahants.

There is an incident of a mass suicide of monks during the Buddha's life.[63] The Buddha criticized the unenlightened who committed suicide, for it revealed disgust with the present body and an attachment to another body (M 3.266; S 4.59). Such an act produces negative karmic consequences. Thus, there is a precept against the unenlightened committing suicide (VP 3.82; Mlp 195–196).

The situation, however, is different in the case of enlightened monks who commit suicide. Thus, Godhika committed suicide when, due to a painful disease, he was not able to maintain the enlightened state outside of meditative concentration (*samādhi*). But he had no attachments to his life or to future life. Thus, his suicide was approved by the Buddha, although it took the life of a sentient being, because it was done with no craving and so was karmically neutral (S 1.21). Two other monks who also suffered from painful diseases, Chaṇṇa (M 3.262; S 4.55) and Vakkali (S 3.119), became Arahants at their death from suicide. (The last solitary Buddha before Gotama, Matanga, also is said to have committed suicide.)

These acts of suicide cannot be taken to be other-regarding actions in any manner. The suffering monks could have been exemplars for other monks of enduring pain on the path to enlightenment; thus, enduring the suffering would have been other-regarding. Only the monk's own welfare figures in the decision-making, even if selfish options are eliminated.

The incidents of enlightened Buddhists who opt for nonmoral actions may or may not be rare. But they show that enlightenment does not necessitate other-regarding attitudes and actions. The enlightened have to elect a moral way of life. If the training compelled otherwise, there would be no solitary Buddhas who did not teach and the Pāli accounts of Gotama's enlightenment would be simpler, emphasizing the moral flowering of the enlightenment-experience.

Conclusion

The conclusions from the above are that (1) the Theravāda Buddhist path is pursued for selfish reasons unjustified by a concern about the effect of one's actions upon others, and (2) the enlightened Buddhists may or may not choose a moral way of life.[64] Thus, because all enlightened Theravāda Buddhists have the option not to be concerned with the welfare of others, the enlightened state cannot be deemed necessarily moral. And consequently the path of the unenlightened way of life cannot be indirectly justified as moral by arguing that it leads to a necessarily moral way of life; therefore, the path commended by the Theravāda remains essentially selfish and in this way is not moral. The vast majority of the enlightened Buddhists may opt for a moral way of life, but the logical significance of the opportunity not to do so cannot be denied. The final verdict has to be that the ideal Theravāda way of life is nonmoral, with being moral as one option available in the enlightened state.

The procedure for this study was to ask questions reflecting a modern Western concern (about what constitutes moral choices and ways of life) of an ancient South Asian tradition. Since the questions asked are not theirs, we must look for answers entailed by their doctrines and practices. Buddhists may dismiss these questions as of theoretical interest only, not aiding in the central concern of a radical end to suffering. Nevertheless, this approach can lead to understanding the tradition in its own terms. That is, the answers advanced here are the answers which the Theravāda doctrines and practices require. Modern scholars too often facilely translate "*sīla*" as "morality" and thereafter view the Theravāda way of life through that perspective rather than on its own terms.

A negative normative judgment will be inferred by many readers from the conclusions reached here. But no argument has been presented on why the moral point of view is superior or necessary to a way of life. Nor is the superiority of any other Buddhist or other religious tradition suggested. Merely differences in a world-view and values from modern Western commitments are revealed. Thereby, we can see our own factual and value commitments more clearly. But concluding that the value system underlying the Theravāda-commended way of life is not moral may offend the sensibilities of some Westerners who feel that all religions have the same values. Perhaps, then, another conclusion of this study should be a greater willingness on the part of modern Westerners to understand ways of life on their own terms rather than by imposing our answers to questions upon them.

Notes

Introduction

1. No terminology currently in use in the comparative study of mysticism captures the distinctions between types of experiences that are most important for philosophical purposes. The dichotomy Walter Stace advanced between extrovertive and introvertive experiences fails to capture the important dichotomy—that between awareness still having content (whether introvertive or extrovertive) and awareness free of all content. The term "nature-mystical experience" derives from the English mystical tradition and is misleading to the extent that it suggests that the only content of such experiences can be sensory, since a nature-mystical experience may also involve awareness with interior, rather than sensory, imagery. The term "depth-mystical experience" also may not be ideal. It may appear judgmental to the extent that it suggests that the depth-mystical experience is simply a more thorough application of the processes leading to the nature-mystical experiences when in fact it represents a distinct type of experience related to different meditative techniques.

2. Robert K. C. Forman, ed., *The Problem of Pure Consciousness* (New York: Oxford University Press, 1990), p. 8 et passim.

3. Other alleged features of the experience—ecstasy, energy, and so forth—are not as important to the philosophical examination of mysticism.

4. Not all mystics claim that the mystical reality is ineffable. For example, in the *Yoga Sūtras* the self (*puruṣa*) is not called ineffable, even though it cannot be "grasped" by our subject-object consciousness. In chapter 5, it will be argued that mystics claim language is inadequate to describe the mystical reality because the use of language introduces a mode of consciousness foreign to the mystical experiences.

5. The arguments for these beliefs and values vary between mystics and nonmystics because of the role of mystical experiences in the former's way of life. (See chapter 1.) Because of the role of mystical experiences in

mystical knowledge, one may ask whether terms with nonmystical denotations really refer to the same concepts when used by mystics. For example, does the concept "God" when used by nonmystics mean the same, or refer to the same reality, as when Meister Eckhart uses the term? Or do all religious terms evolve with mystical and nonmystical contributions?

6. The term "mysticism" may be a convenient modern concept introduced by nonmystics to isolate a phenomenon for study, but this does not mean that the phenomenon so isolated does not exist. As with any anthropological term, a term may be useful for understanding even if it is an outsider's term, just as the term "gravity" would apply to phenomena in cultures that do not have that concept. But we should not reify the term "mysticism" and hold that there is only one abstract mysticism to which all mystics belong. Instead, there are many mystical traditions and each mystic must be studied within the context of his or her individual life. Whether various mystics have common features (beyond having the features that place them within a broad category which we have created) will be found by the result of study, not by the use of a word.

7. To understand mystics may require a certain sympathy on our part in two senses. First, just to understand any other culture or era may require a certain sympathy. (This is an issue often addressed in anthropology.) Second, to understand mystical utterances the unenlightened may have to follow metaphors; but the unenlightened will always remain in a subject-object dualistic mode of awareness when attempting this. This presents a problem discussed in chapter 5.

8. Steven Katz, ed., *Mysticism and Philosophical Analysis* (New York: Oxford University Press, 1978); and *Mysticism and Religious Traditions* (New York: Oxford University Press, 1983). See also R. Gale, "Language and the Interpretation of Mystical Experience," *International Journal for the Philosophy of Religion* 3 (1972): 93–102; Jerry H. Gill, "Mysticism and Mediation," *Faith and Philosophy* 1 (1984): 111–121; John Hick, "Mystical Experience as Cognition," in Richard Woods, O.P., ed., *Understanding Mysticism* (Garden City: Doubleday, 1980), pp. 415–421; Wayne Proudfoot, *Religious Experience* (Los Angeles: University of California Press, 1985), chapter 4.

9. Mary Hesse, "Socializing Epistemology," in Ernan McMullin, ed., *Construction and Constraint: The Shaping of Scientific Rationality* (Notre Dame, Indiana: University of Notre Dame Press, 1988), p. 111.

10. Forman, note 2. See also Donald Evans, "Can Philosophers Limit What Mystics Can Do? A Critique of Steven Katz," *Religious Studies* 25 (1989): 53–60; Anthony Perovich, Jr., "Mysticism and the Philosophy of Science," *Journal of Religion* 65 (1985): 63–82; Huston Smith, "Is There a Perennial Philosophy?" *Journal of the American Academy of Religion* 55 (1987): 533–566.

11. See chapter 1, pp. 27–28.

12. Thus, nonconstructivists as well as constructivists can accept genuine differences between mystics and a genuine plurality of mystical systems. For nonconstructivists these differences arise from differences in the conceptual elements that contribute to mystical knowledge-claims but do not affect the depth-mystical experience itself. (For constructivists, such conceptual elements are alleged to be present in the depth-mystical experience itself.) This means that, contrary to what constructivists assert, nonconstructivists are not committed to accepting the position that all mysticism is the same—different mystical knowledge-claims contain different conceptual elements that genuinely distinguish the claims even if the depth-mystical experiences do not. The nonconstructivist interpretation is consistent with any of a variety of different positions on the relation between mystical traditions: nonconstructivists can construct their own mystical system (e.g., as perennial philosophers appear to do), accept one traditional mystical system as the best, accept a relativism of mystical traditions, or still reject all mystical knowledge-claims.

13. Pragmatists such as Richard Rorty, perhaps following Donald Davidson's attack against the very possibility of a distinction between a conceptual scheme and something alleged to be beyond all conceptions, may see no real difference between constructivism and nonconstructivism. But those who follow a realist intuition see a major difference between the two positions.

14. Most mystics see themselves as foundationalists. But the diversity of belief-claims among mystical traditions most naturally leads to the conclusion that neither depth-mystical nor nature-mystical experiences can produce an unshakeable foundation for knowledge—all mystical claims are interpretations open to revision, culturally contingent, and lacking ultimate certainty. Perennial philosophers disagree, claiming that all apparent diversity among mystical traditions is illusory. This leads to the issue of whether perennial philosophy is itself merely a theory constructed for religious or other reasons in light of the modern encounter between religious traditions.

Chapter 1.

1. Ninian Smart, "Interpretation and Mystical Experience," *Religious Studies* 1 (1965): 75.

2. Terminology from Claudio Naranjo and Robert E. Ornstein, *On the Psychology of Meditation* (New York: Viking Press, 1971).

3. See Smart, pp. 75–87; Walter T. Stace, *Mysticism and Philosophy* (Philadelphia: J. B. Lippincott, 1960), chap. 2; R. C. Zaehner, *Mysticism*

Sacred and Profane (New York: Oxford University Press, 1961); and William J. Wainwright, *Mysticism* (Madison: University of Wisconsin Press, 1981), chap. 1.

4. See, e.g., Carl R. Kordig, "The Theory-Ladenness of Observation," *Review of Metaphysics* 24 (1971): 448–84. For a discussion of some of the problems involved in comparing mystical and sense experiences, see Wainwright, chap. 3, and William Alston, "Perceiving God," *Journal of Philosophy* 83 (1986): 655–665.

5. *Bhagavad-gītā* III.27–28.

6. *Enneads* 3.8.9, 6.9.2.

7. Ray C. Petry, ed., *Late Medieval Mysticism* (Philadelphia: Westminster, 1957), p. 210.

8. Charles T. Tart, *States of Consciousness* (New York: Dutton, 1975), pp. 84–85.

9. See, e.g., Norwood Russell Hanson, *Observation and Explanation* (New York: Harper & Row, 1971), pp. 1–8; Frederick Suppe, ed., *The Structure of Scientific Theories,* 2nd ed. (Chicago: University of Illinois, 1977), pp. 192–99; and Thomas S. Kuhn, "Reflections on My Critics," in Imre Lakatos and Alan Musgrave, eds., *Criticism and the Growth of Knowledge* (Cambridge: Cambridge University Press, 1970), pp. 276–77.

10. Steven T. Katz, ed., *Mysticism and Philosophical Analysis* (New York: Oxford University Press, 1978), p. 26. For further discussions of this issue, see the Introduction and the works cited there.

11. See J. F. Staal's account of this process, *Exploring Mysticism* (Los Angeles: University of California Press, 1975), pp. 170–73. He does not distinguish types of mystical experiences and so does not deal with whether this is true of only one type.

12. Raymond B. Blakney, ed. and trans., *Meister Eckhart* (New York: Harper & Row, 1941), p. 97.

13. For more on the problems of mystics' use of language, see chapter 5.

14. Cited in Stace (n. 3 above), p. 112. Porphyry mentions that Plotinus was "oned" with the One four times while he knew him (*Life of Plotinus,* chap. 23).

15. Jan Vanneste, "Is the Mysticism of Pseudo-Dionysius Genuine?" *International Philosophical Quarterly* 3 (1963): 304.

16. For a depth-mystical experience to occur, all knowledge must be eliminated from the mind. Also, new knowledge-claims may not be revealed. See R. J. Zwi Werblowsky, "On the Mystical Rejection of Mystical Illuminations," *Religious Studies* 1 (1966): 177–84. But a new inward wis-

dom is usually felt to be obtained that is cognitive (an insight into the nature of reality).

17. Petry (n. 7 above), p. 47.

18. Cited in Mircea Eliade, *Patanjali and Yoga* (New York: Schocken, 1975), p. 171.

19. Cited in William James, *The Varieties of Religious Experiences* (New York: New American Library, 1958), pp. 313–14.

20. E.g., K. N. Jayatilleke, *Early Buddhist Theory of Knowledge* (London: George Allen & Unwin, 1963), with the qualification that the Theravādins accept paranormal experiences as veridical.

21. Ninian Smart, *Doctrine and Argument in Indian Philosophy* (London: George Allen & Unwin, 1964), p. 50.

22. Ibid., p. 78; cf. Stace (n. 3 above), p. 125.

23. J. F. Staal, *Advaita and Neo-Platonism: A Critical Study in Comparative Philosophy* (Madras: University of Madras, 1961), pp. 88–89, 158–60.

24. *Brahma-sūtra-bhāsya* 1.1.1, 1.1.4.

25. Ibid., 1.1.1.

26. Ibid., 2.1.1.

27. Ibid., 2.1.17; e.g., 2.3.1–3.

28. Blakney (n. 12 above), p. 156; Mark 11: 15–17 and parallels.

29. John Hick, ed., *Truth and Dialogue in World Religions: Conflicting Truth-Claims* (Philadelphia: Westminister, 1974), p. 149.

30. Matthew Fox, *Breakthrough: Meister Eckhart's Creation Spirituality in New Translation* (Garden City, N.Y.: Doubleday, 1980), p. 23. Ecclesiastical authorities were hostile to some Christian and Muslim mystics. Some mystical utterances seem intentionally provocative, although the mystics usually said that if properly understood the claims were orthodox.

31. E.g., Thomas S. Kuhn, *The Structure of Scientific Revolutions*, 2nd ed. (Chicago: University of Chicago Press, 1970), pp. 205–7.

32. John Blofield, *The Tantric Mysticism of Tibet* (New York: Dutton, 1970), pp. 45–46.

33. Staal (n. 11 above), p. 25.

34. Ibid., p. 147.

35. See chapter 9.

36. Even the idea that mystical teachings are rafts to be jettisoned once we become enlightened is misleading since enlightenment involves the internalization of a conceptual system: we come to see reality by means of the raft even if we are not consciously trying to employ it (which would involve a dualistic stance toward the concepts present).

37. Frithjof Schuon, *The Transcendent Unity of Religions* (New York: Harper & Row, 1975), p. xxviii. This position holds not only that all mysticism is ultimately one but also the questionable claim that mysticism is the essence of all religiosity and hence that all religions are one.

38. Gleaned from Aldous Huxley, *The Perennial Philosophy* (New York: Harper & Row, 1944).

39. Schuon, p. 82.

40. D. T. Suzuki, *Mysticism, Christian and Buddhist* (New York: Harper & Row, 1957), p. 44.

41. Ibid., p. 9.

42. Evelyn Underhill, *Practical Mysticism* (New York: Dutton, 1915), p. 3.

43. Gilbert Ryle, *Dilemmas* (Cambridge: Cambridge University Press, 1954), p. 90. For a discussion in philosophy of science on this point, see Kordig (n. 4 above).

44. Agehananda Bharati, *The Light at the Center* (Santa Barbara, Calif.: Ross-Erikson, 1976), pp. 69, 109.

45. Harold I. Brown, *Perception, Theory and Commitment* (Chicago: University of Chicago Press, 1979), p. 120.

46. Cited in C. F. Kelley, *Meister Eckhart on Divine Knowledge* (New Haven, Conn.: Yale University Press, 1977), pp. 49, 143, and 143 respectively.

47. Cited in Frederick H. Holck, ed., *Death and Eastern Thought* (New York: Abingdon, 1974), p. 111.

48. Cited in William A. Christian, *Oppositions of Religious Doctrines* (New York: Macmillan, 1972), pp. 115–16.

49. Mystics are never critical realists since ultimate reality is directly experienceable. The mystical is not known by inference or speculation, but understanding and interpreting its status are required.

50. W. M. Watt, *The Faith and Practice of al-Ghazālī* (London: Allen & Unwin, 1963), pp. 21, 19, 55–56.

51. Martin Buber, *Between Man and Man* (London: Routledge & Kegan Paul, 1947), pp. 24–25.

52. E.g., can any post mortem experience—even those lasting a great length of time—decide between a cycle of rebirths and one eternal life?

Would even impressions of past lives assure that these lives were ours? For a discussion of philosophical problems in this area, see John Hick, *Death and Eternal Life* (New York: Harper & Row, 1976).

53. Ernest Nagel, *Logic Without Metaphysics* (Glencoe, Ill.: Free Press, 1956), p. 390.

54. See Paul Feyerabend, *Against Method* (London: NLB, 1975) and Imre Lakatos, "Falsification and the Methodology of Scientific Research Programmes," in Lakatos and Musgrave (n. 9 above).

55. Joachim Wach, *Understanding and Believing* (New York: Harper & Row, 1968), p. 148.

56. Clifford Geertz, *Islam Observed* (Chicago: University of Chicago Press, 1968), pp. 17, 97.

57. Feyerabend, p. 44.

58. Smart (n. 1 above), p. 86.

59. Staal (n. 23 above), pp. 88–89, 158–60.

60. Paul W. Taylor, *Normative Discourse* (Englewood Cliffs, N.J.: Prentice-Hall, 1961), p. 132.

61. See Lakatos (n. 54 above), pp. 91–195. Since mystical ways of life involve normative values and goals for one's life, it is difficult to view them as "research programs" in Lakatos's sense of the phrase. But even if mystical systems could be viewed as research programs (i.e., series of complex theories whose core theory remains the same and whose auxiliary hypotheses are successfully modified or replaced), the absence of new experiential data renders impossible any increase in the program's testable content and therefore no novel, unexpected facts can be predicted. This precludes the possibility of a progressive problem shift. Therefore mystical ways of life would have to be considered degenerating research programs.

62. According to Reinhold Niebuhr mysticism is at total variance with the Christian faith (*The Nature and Destiny of Man* [New York: Scribner, 1941], 1: 135–36). For certain Protestants (such as Karl Barth), mysticism is sinful because it is an attempt to become God.

63. Antimystical positions in this situation are just other positions of the same fundamental level of decision: they are no less metaphysical than the acceptance of a mystical alternative.

Chapter 2.

1. S. N. Dasgupta says *avidyā* in the *Upaniṣads* is ignorance of the *ātman*-doctrine and contrasts with knowledge (*A History of Indian Philosophy* [Cambridge: Cambridge University Press, 1922], vol. 1, p. 111). See

Alex Wayman, "The Meaning of Unwisdom (*Avidyā*)," *Philosophy East and West* 7 (1957): 21–25, for distinctions concerning "*avidyā*."

2. Deeds or rituals may enable one to cross over death, and knowledge completes the process. But actually finding an Upaniṣadic warrant for equating *avidyā* and *karman* is difficult to do. *Bṛhadāraṇyaka Up.* IV.4.2 states that knowledge and deeds (*karmāṇi*) both play roles in determining one's future rebirth; and *Bṛhadāraṇyaka Up.* I.5.16 comes close to contrasting *karman* and *vidyā*. *Muṇḍaka Up.* I.2.9 also connects *avidyā* and *karman*. But this cannot justify *equating* the two. And in the case of the *Muṇḍaka* passage, both are considered quite negatively (and thus could not play a role in the attainment of immortality). Further complications also arise: (1) *Īśa Up.* 2 discusses deeds (*karmāṇi*) without any indication that a connection with *avidyā* is intended; neither *vidyā* nor *avidyā* is mentioned until verse 9. (2) It may be that deeds or rituals aid in reaching immortality (if they do at all) only when the acts are informed by *vidyā*—*Chāndogya Upaniṣad* I.1.10 (after contrasting *vidyā* and *avidyā*) and IV.14.1, 3 reveal that *vidyā* can be connected to such acts (confer Śaṁkara's *Brahmasūtrabhāṣya* III.1.7 on joining knowledge to works).

3. P. Thieme, "*Īśopaniṣad* 1-14," *Journal of the American Oriental Society* 85 (1965): 97. I shall not question Thieme's total interpretation of the *Īśa* here. But how the first half of the *Upaniṣad* is to be understood and how the two halves fit together seem more difficult than understanding verses 9–14 treated separately.

4. Robert E. Hume, *The Thirteen Principal Upanishads* (New York: Oxford University Press, 1971), pp. 363–364.

5. Sarvepalli Radhakrishnan and Charles A. Moore, ed., *A Sourcebook in Indian Philosophy* (Princeton, New Jersey: Princeton University Press, 1957), pp. 40–41. Throughout his own translation, Radhakrishnan uses "ignorance" (*The Principal Upaniṣads* [London: George Allen and Unwin Ltd., 1953], pp. 573–575).

6. Faulty "knowledge" is an error, not even lower knowledge (*aparā vidyā*), the sciences connected to the *Vedas* (*Muṇḍaka Upaniṣad* I.1.4).

7. Verse 10 (and 13) will not be discussed much. The contrast of *vidyā* and *avidyā* is also present in *Kaṭha Up.* I.2.4. It could mean (1) that Brahman/*ātman* contains and controls both knowledge and nescience (following *Śvetāśvatara Up.* V.1), and thus is other than either—neither alone will accomplish immortality. Or (2) that the *results* of knowledge and nescience are distinct. Either interpretation amounts to the same point: knowledge and nescience are both required to gain immortality.

8. This idea was later picked up by the medieval English contemplative who authored *The Cloud of Unknowing*, by Meister Eckhart, and by a few others. Nicholas of Cusa's *De docta ignorantia* speaks of "learned igno-

rance" more in a Socratic than Dionysian sense: learned ignorance is knowing that we are ignorant.

9. The *Īśa Upaniṣad* may have used *"avidyā"* rather than *"ajñāna"* to contrast with *"vidyā"* because there was no fixed vocabulary at the time or to maintain the contrasts between pairs of *x*'s and non-*x*'s occurring throughout the text (*"vidyā"* is more common than *"jñāna"* in these texts).

10. Śaṁkara understood these terms as meaning "the manifest" and "the unmanifest (*avyakṛta*)," respectively. This enabled him to maintain his nondualism. But he still had difficulties: he amended the text (changing *"sambhūti"* to *"asambhūti"*), and altered his understanding of immortality from what he had given in his commentary upon verse 11.

11. If "worship destruction" means simply "deny the existence of rebirth" (compare *Kaṭha Up*. I.2.6), then "delight in rebirth" must mean "accept the existence of rebirth." This latter does not lead to darkness, nor do these definitions explain why both knowledge and nescience are necessary. Mixing *denial* of rebirth and *craving* for rebirth would destroy the parallel structure.

12. For a discussion of *jñāna, vijñāna,* and *vidyā* based primarily upon Buddhist texts, see Alex Wayman, "Notes on the Sanskrit Term *Jñāna,*" *Journal of the American Oriental Society* 75 (1955): 253–268.

13. There is a problematic passage in the *Bṛhadāraṇyaka Up*. II.4.5 where it is said that the self should be sensed and thought about, and that by understanding and sensing the self, all this is known (*idaṃ sarvaṃ viditam*). Perhaps this is merely the first step in a graduated teaching that Yājñavalkya is giving to his wife Maitreyī. Or perhaps this means that to one who even understands the self all more mundane matters become known. The *Bṛhadāraṇyaka Up*. II.3 may have been added as a preface to explain this. There are two forms (*rūpas*) of Brahman: the fixed (*mūrta*) and the nonfixed (*amūrta*), the mortal and immortal, the unmoving and the moving, the phenomenal reality (*sat*) and that beyond (*tyat*) (compare *Īśa Up*. 4–5). With regard to the world, the nonfixed Brahman is the air and the sky, and the fixed the rest. With regard to the person, the nonfixed Brahman is the breath and the inner space, and the fixed the rest. It is not clear where the inner controller, the one who understands, is to fit into this scheme. In Śaṁkara's commentary upon II.3.1, he said the two forms of Brahman are superimposed images of the formless (*arūpa*) Brahman, that is, the self or inner controller. The alternative interpretation is that the nonfixed Brahman is the inner self. Usually the inner self is said to lie *within* the space of the heart, indicating that the rest is set in opposition to this. The picture is further complicated by the fact that each form here is just as real as the other, while elsewhere it is said that the self within everything is Brahman or is everything (II.5.1; compare *Īśa Up*. 6, 8); this led to considering only the nonfixed form as real, the fixed being unreal

(*asatya*), as in the *Maitrī Up*. VI.3 and Śaṁkara's nondualism. Under this interpretation, the fixed Brahman can be understood as objects are, and with this understanding, all phenomena are known (*viditam*): one becomes what one knows. (*Īśa Up*. 7 affirms that all beings become the self of one who understands.) The nonfixed self, however, cannot be understood (II.4.14), because it cannot be presented as an object: when we are one with understanding, there is nothing to understand. This self is "not this, not this" (*na iti na iti*), that is, no object that can be designated, but is the reality of the real (*satyasya satyam*) (II.3.6). One can thus know/become the inner self only through this knowledge and an unknowing of the objects of understanding.

Chapter 3.

1. For suggestions of appropriate distinctions concerning mystical experiences, see Ninian Smart, "Interpretation and Mystical Experience," *Religious Studies* 1 (1965), 75–87, and chapter 1.

2. See Thomas S. Kuhn, "Commensurability, Comparability, Communicability," in P. Asquith and T. Nickles (eds.), *PSA 1982,* Vol. 2 (East Lansing: Philosophy of Science Association, 1983), pp. 669–688. If terms are incommensurable, no equivalents within another system could be found for them in principle. Philosophical systems have survived translation (e.g., Greek thought into Arabic, a non-Indo-European language, and later translated a second time into Latin) with the basic ideas remaining intact. So, too, bilingual speakers accept European language translations of Islamic and Chinese philosophical works. There may be, however, core theoretical terms for which English placeholders are merely being substituted.

3. Benjamin L. Whorf, *Language, Thought and Reality,* John B. Carroll, ed. (Cambridge: MIT Press, 1956), pp. 212–213. Whorf believes perception differs between speakers of uncalibratable languages (since observation is theory-laden), but certain obvious difficulties arise: just because the Hopi classify all flying objects together by one term does not mean that they cannot visually differentiate airplane pilots from flies. It is doubtful that concepts from all levels of a belief-system enter into the process of structuring experiences. In addition, there is the danger of attributing too much literalness to expressions; e.g., while English speakers refer to "a flash of lightning" instead of the Hopi expression of the event "flash" (*Reh-pi*), this does not mean that the English speakers think that lightning exists apart from the flash or that lightning could do something else. How much of the language's structure or the origins of a term's meaning can be attributed to modern speakers, as language and knowledge evolve, is not clear; nor is it clear how an etymological history affects our perception.

4. Whorf, *Language, Thought and Reality,* p. 147. Whether there is a "standard average" Indo-European language is questionable. For example,

a translation of the English phrase "The pot is blue" into Sanskrit would produce an expression containing an abstraction without a verb, more literally reading "(There is) blueness of the pot." Furthermore, what exactly is meant by an "implicit metaphysics" in language is not clear. Whorf concedes that there is no "correlation" between culture and language but that there are only "affinities" (pp. 138–139) and that science is not caused by grammar but merely "colored" by it (p. 221). But very different metaphysical systems are statable in the same language (e.g., Platonic and Aristotelian thought); and even if Newtonian space-time is implicit in Standard Average European, still scientists were able to develop relativistic theories of space and time. Thus, speakers of the same language may have very different frameworks. How different explicit metaphysical and other highly theoretical frameworks could be possible if there were an inherent implicit metaphysical system (controlling beliefs to some extent) within any language is not clear.

5. The effect of classic Chinese ideograms on Chinese thought and on the adoption of Buddhism is a major theme in Hajime Nakamura's *Ways of Thinking of Eastern Peoples*, Philip P. Weiner, ed. (Honolulu: University Press of Hawaii, 1964), pp. 177–195. But see Joseph S. Wu, "Chinese Language and Chinese Thought," *Philosophy East and West* 19 (1969), 423–434, and Henry Rosemont, Jr., "On Representing Abstractions in Archaic Chinese," *Philosophy East and West* 24 (1974), 71–88.

6. For an explication of this view, see chapter 5.

7. Practical problems in translation remain. Any translation may lose the particular connotations of a given language, although of interest here is only whether the cognitive content is lost in the process of translating. In addition to the incommensurability of terms discussed above, the symbolic use of language, which mystics employ to point beyond the original references of words to the mystical referent, presents difficulties of its own. Most broadly, this presents a problem to speakers of the same language—that of the unenlightened trying to understand the enlightened's words. Whether the enlightened are addressing the listeners in their native languages or not, the enigmatic sayings of such texts as the Indian *sūtras* are still enigmatic, requiring extensive commentary. Thus, texts such as the *Tao te ching* have produced so many translations, not because of any possible indeterminancy of translation, but because the texts themselves are open to very different interpretations by classical and modern thinkers. Some texts also may be deemed untranslatable for normative reasons unconnected to this problem, as with the *Qu'rān* being considered by Muslims to be untranslatable because Arabic is the language in which the book in heaven is written.

8. Attention here will be focused primarily upon the first three principles because deduction is more problematic. For example, the justifica-

tion of deduction itself involves a deduction. See Susan Haack, "The Justification of Deduction" *Mind* 85 (1976), 112–119.

9. Whorf, *Language, Thought and Reality* (n. 3 above), p. 211. If this is correct, it should not be surprising that J. F. Staal has found that the law of contradiction is formulated and adhered to in Sanskrit grammar and Indian logic (and in some but not all Indian philosophical schools). See his "Correlations Between Language and Logic in Indian Thought," *Bulletin of the School of Oriental and African Studies* 23 (1960), 109–122, and "Negation and the Law of Non-Contradiction in Indian Thought: A Comparative Study," *ibid.*, 25 (1962), 52–71. In particular, Staal notes the operation of Sanskrit's negating particle which he claims has correlates in all Indo-European languages.

10. J. F. Staal, "Negation and the Law of Non-Contradiction in Indian Thought: A Comparative Study," *ibid.*, p. 71. It should be noted that Whorf showed no new "logic" in the strict sense discussed here in any American Indian language or gave any evidence of incommensurable natural logics. Similarly, classical Chinese, a non-Indo-European language, can handle the classical Aristotelian propositional forms (contra Nakamura). See Y. R. Chao, "Notes on Chinese Grammar and Logic," *Philosophy East and West* 5 (1955), 31–41; and Chad Hansen, *Language and Logic in Ancient China* (Ann Arbor: University of Michigan Press, 1983), pp. 10–23.

11. See chapter 5, p. 114. The fact that systems of logic can be artificially created which explicitly deny one or more of the principles of logic is trivial and is not relevant to the issue of whether natural languages can operate without implicit adherence to these principles. And on the other hand, Zeno's paradoxes are evidence that we can conceptualize situations in such a way that everyday experiences appear incomprehensible.

12. Martin Hollis, *Models of Man: Philosophical Thoughts on Social Action* (Cambridge: Cambridge University Press, 1977). Also see his "The Limits of Irrationality" and Steven Lukes, "Some Problems about Rationality," in Bryan R. Wilson (ed.), *Rationality* (New York: Harper & Row, Publishers, 1970), pp. 194–220. Anthropologists usually persist until they can make sense of such claims as the Bororo's assertion, "We are red macaws." See Dan Sperber, "Apparently Irrational Beliefs," in Martin Hollis and Steven Lukes (eds.), *Rationality and Relativism* (Cambridge: MIT Press, 1982), pp. 152–153.

13. See A. C. Graham (trans.), *Chuang-tzu: The Inner Chapters* (London: George Allen & Unwin, 1982), pp 9–14.

14. Two recent entries in the series in which authors survey the literature and propose their own views are F. J. Hoffman, "Rationality in Early Buddhist Fourfold Logic," *Journal of Indian Philosophy* 10 (1982), 309–337, and V. K. Bharadwaja, "Rationality, Argumentation and Embarrassment:

A Study of Four Logical Alternatives (*Catuṣkoṭi*) in Buddhist Logic," *Philosophy East and West* 34 (1984), 303–319.

15. Of course, this may be just another instance of forcing other belief-systems to be rational. But see Bharadwaja, *ibid.;* and chapter 4, pp. 89–91. Only if the Buddha elsewhere were concerned with theoretical issues of logic would one be led to think that this was his concern here; however, the Buddha only exhibited a concern with ending suffering.

16. For a different assessment of Nāgārjuna's program, see chapter 4. For an exposition of the logical structure of one of his arguments, see that chapter, pp. 260–261, note 6. Far from denying that Nāgārjuna's arguments are logical, their logical nature is always central in recent evaluations of his thought. See, e.g., Guy Bugault, "Logic and Dialetics in the *Madhyamakakārikās," Journal of Indian Philosophy* 11 (1983), 7–76.

17. J. F. Staal, *Exploring Mysticism* (Berkeley/Los Angeles: University of California Press, 1975), pp. 49, 54. Elsewhere, he concludes that the principle of non-contradiction is explicitly formulated and strictly adhered to in another Indian mystical tradition, Advaita Vedānta. ("Negation and the Law of Non-Contradiction in Indian Thought: A Comparative Study" [n. 9 above], p. 68.) Staal also concludes that all Asian "mystical doctrines in general are rational." (*Exploring Mysticism,* p. 40.)

18. See chapters 2 and 5, pp. 113–119.

19. Morris Kline, *Mathematics: The Loss of Certainty* (New York: Oxford University Press, 1980), p. 318. On mathematical proof, see pp. 313–320.

20. For an overview of post-empiricist theories of the nature of science, see Frederick Suppe (ed.), *The Structure of Scientific Theories*, 2nd ed. (Urbana: University of Illinois Press, 1977), Introduction.

21. See Thomas Kuhn, "Objectivity, Value Judgment, and Theory Choice," in his *The Essential Tension: Selected Studies in Scientific Tradition and Change* (Chicago: University of Chicago Press, 1977), pp. 320–339.

22. See Richard J. Bernstein, *Beyond Objectivism and Relativism: Science, Hermeneutics and Praxis* (Philadelphia: University of Pennsylvania Press, 1983).

23. See Paul Feyerabend, *Against Method: Outline of an Anarchistic Theory of Knowledge* (London: New Left Books, 1975).

24. E. E. Evans-Pritchard, *Witchcraft, Oracles, and Magic Among the Azande* (Oxford: Oxford University Press, 1976), p. 139.

25. Ernest Nagel, *Logic Without Metaphysics* (Glencoe, Ill.: Free Press, 1956), p. 390.

26. Edmund Colledge, O.S.A., and Bernard McGinn (trans. and eds.), *Meister Eckhart: The Essential Sermons, Commentaries, Treatises, and Defense* (New York: Paulist Press, 1981), pp. 26–29.

27. Chapter 1, pp. 27–32.

28. Feyerabend, *Against Method* (n. 23 above), p. 44.

29. Cifford Geertz, *Islam Observed* (Chicago: University of Chicago Press, 1968), pp. 17, 97.

30. See, e.g., Karl R. Popper, "Towards a Rational Theory of Tradition," in his *Conjectures and Refutations* (London: Routledge & Kegan Paul, 1963), pp. 120–135.

31. Not only are there competing positions on whether relativism is reasonable or not, there is no one universally accepted definition of exactly what "cognitive relativism" is. See, e.g., the various essays in Hollis and Lukes (eds.), *Rationality and Relativism* (n. 12 above); Jack W. Meiland and Michael Krausz (eds.), *Relativism: Cognitive and Moral* (South Bend: Notre Dame University Press, 1982); I. C. Jarvie, "Rationality and Relativism," *The British Journal of Sociology* 34 (1983), 44–60; and *The Monist* 67 (July, 1984).

32. See Robin Horton, "Tradition and Modernity Revisited," in Hollis and Lukes (eds.), *Rationality and Relativism* (n. 12 above), pp. 201–60.

33. For a reply to the charge that relativism is self-refuting (i.e., that it cannot be stated consistently without becoming a form of absolutism), see Jack W. Meiland and Michael Krausz (eds.), *Relativism: Cognitive and Moral* (n. 31 above), pp. 31–32. Absolutism and relativism are in the same class—each is a second-order, philosophical judgment about the truth-giving power of first-order claims about reality given within belief-systems.

34. In Roger Trigg's characterization, relativism concerns the denial of any objective reality rather than the relation between conceptual systems and the lack of objective standards to determine truth. See his *Reason and Commitment* (Cambridge: Cambridge University Press, 1973), *Reality at Risk: A Defense of Realism in Philosophy and the Sciences* (Totowa, N.J.: Barnes & Noble Books, 1980), and "Religion and the Threat of Relativism," *Religious Studies* 19 (1983), 297–310. For criticism of his characterization, see J. Kellenberger, "The Slippery Slope of Religious Relativism," *Religious Studies* 21 (1985), 39–52.

35. Thomas S. Kuhn, *The Structure of Scientific Revolutions* (Chicago: University of Chicago, 1970, second edition), p. 206. For criticism of the distinction between reality and reality as conceived, see Donald Davidson, "On the Very Idea of a Conceptual System," in Meiland and Krausz (eds.), *Relativism: Cognitive and Moral* (n. 31 above), pp. 66–80.

36. Nelson Goodman, "The Way The World Is," *The Review of Metaphysics* 14 (1960), 55.

37. See chapters 1 and 9 for examples of differences in beliefs, values, and goals.

38. Those non-mystical systems of thought which deny the significance of mystical experiences compete with mystical systems on a fundamental metaphysical level, thereby raising the issue of whether there is a common standard by which to evaluate this class of systems against the class of mystical belief-systems.

Chapter 4.

1. When no text is indicated, chapter and verse numbers refer to this text. Translations from the *Kārikās* are my own. The other two primary texts (and their abbreviations) are:

VV = *Vigrahavyāvartanī.* Translation from K. Bhattacharya, "The Dialectical Method of Nāgārjuna," *Journal of Indian Philosophy* 1 (1971): 217–261.

R = *Ratnāvalī.* Translation from G. Tucci, "The *Ratnāvali* of Nāgārjuna," *Journal of the Royal Asiatic Society* (1934): 307–325; (1936): 237–252, 423–435.

Only occasional reference will be made to later Mādhyamika thinkers. The focus will be Nāgārjuna's works, not those hundreds of years later.

2. Perhaps it should be added that although Nāgārjuna is concerned with stilling conceptual proliferation (*prapañca*), he does not intend to destroy concepts per se. (For a discussion of *prapañca* in the Theravāda and the Mādhyamika traditions, see Bhikkhu Ñananda, *Concept and Reality in Early Buddhist Thought* [Kandy, Ceylon, 1971]). Getting caught up in conceptualizations is condemned (22.15), but not the proper use of concepts. Dependent arising, after all, is a concept; and the qualification "from the absolute point of view" (*tattvatas*) occurs frequently in the *Ratnāvali* with no suggestion that anything can invalidate the claims so advanced. As long as linguistic distinctions are not projected ontologically, language is deemed very useful and even essential for enlightenment (see the discussion of the two types of truth below).

3. T. Stcherbatsky, *The Conception of Buddhist Nirvāṇa* (The Hague: Mouton, 1965), p. 209.

4. Āryadeva's *Śataśāstra* in G. Tucci, *Pre-Diṅnāga Buddhist Texts on Logic from Chinese Sources* (Baroda: Oriental Institute, 1929), p. 82.

5. Perhaps his opponent is speaking here since seeing an *anyathābhāva* is seeing a *bhāva,* but perhaps only change is indicated as in the other two instances cited. Verses 7.21, 7.24 and 21.8 stress that no entity is found without arising and falling—obviously an empirical observation. Verse 21.11 says that seeing arising and falling is the result of delusion (*moha*), but this could just as easily mean that seeing *real* entities

is a misapprehension. Thus, "The Hymn to the Incomparable One" (G. Tucci, "Two Hymns of the *Catuḥstava* by Nāgārjuna," *Journal of the Royal Asiatic Society* [1932]: 309–325) says that the Buddha saw no beings (without losing compassion for all beings) and the *Kārikās* speak of the cessation of the seeable (that is, the real, 5.8). Observing change is definitely appealed to—it is only that no real entities are involved that is being emphasized. He is making an empirical claim here and not recommending a metaphysical prescription (that is, that all entities should be viewed as void of self-existence).

6. The logical form is: (1) $p \supset q$; (2) $\bar{q} \supset \bar{p}$; (3) $\bar{q}$; therefore, (4) $\bar{p}$. This is not making an independent argument in support of his thesis; Candrakīrti occasionally reconstructs arguments into Indian syllogisms (for example, Stcherbatsky, *Conception of Buddhist Nirvāṇa,* pp. 139, 192). Quine raises the prospect that logic is such a deep-rooted belief that we would not allow a translation to be illogical—we would impute or impose our "orthodox logic" upon the text. See W. V. Quine, *Philosophy of Logic* (Englewood Cliffs, N.J.: Prentice-Hall, 1970), p. 83. But the structures of English and Sanskrit are similar enough that this problem should not arise here. Although we cannot step back from the Sanskrit and the translation to see if a logical translation is distortive, at least an almost literal, word for word, translation can be shown to be logical. Consider 15.1–5:

> (1) The rising of self-existence from causes and conditions is not justifiable. For self-existence arisen through causes and conditions would be something produced.
>
> (2) How then can there be produced self-existence? Indeed, self-existence is not produced and is independent of anything else.
>
> (3) If there is no self-existence (*svabhāvasyābhāve*), how can there be other-existence (*parabhāva*)? For self-existence of another entity is called other-existence.
>
> (4) Without self-existence and other-existence, how again can there be an entity? Indeed, when there is self-existence and other-existence, an entity is proved.
>
> (5) If there is no proof of an entity, then the absence of an entity (*abhāva*) is not proved. Indeed, people call the absence of an entity an entity in another manner (*anyathābhāva*).

Verses 1 and 2 do not establish that there is no self-existence, since the possibility of self-existence not arising from causes and conditions is not dealt with. In VV 21 (considered elsewhere), Nāgārjura presents his argument for maintaining that all entities are void. Assuming then at least that with respect to entities "there is no self-existence," the argument from verse 3 on proceeds as follows:

(i) Everything is void of self-existence.

(ii) If self-existence is absent, there is no other-existence.

(iii) Without self-existence and other-existence, no entity exists.

(iv) If there is no entity, there is no absence of a real entity (*abhāva*).

(v) Thus, there are neither real entities nor their absences.

The peculiarity of this claim is dealt with elsewhere. All that is claimed here is that it is logical. Although not necessary, its logicality can be illustrated with some elementary symbolic terminology:

Let o = existence *via* self-existence

p = existence *via* other-existence

b = "There is a real entity"

a = "There is the absence of a real entity"

(1)	$\bar{o}$	("There is no self-existence" with regard to entities)
(2)	$\bar{o} \supset \bar{p}$	(from verse 3)
(3)	$\bar{p}$	(from 1, 2)
(4)	$(\bar{o} \cdot \bar{p}) \supset \bar{b}$	(from verse 4, line 1)
(5)	$-(o \vee p) \supset \bar{b}$	(De Morgan's Law)
(6)	$b \supset (o \vee p)$	(from 5)
(7)	$(o \vee p) \supset b$	(from verse 4, line 2)
(8)	$(o \vee p) \equiv b$	(from 6, 7. Note that the two lines of verse 4 are not equivalent and together they form a biconditional.)
(9)	$\bar{b}$	(from 1, 3, 4)
(10)	$\bar{b} \supset \bar{a}$	(from verse 5)
(11)	$\bar{a}$	(from 9, 10)

7. Richard Robinson, "Some Logical Aspects of Nāgārjuna's System," *Philosophy East and West* 6 (1957): 303.

8. Verses with the same form occur at 4.4, 13.4, 15.9, 20.1–2, 20.21, 21.9, 25.1–2, and 27.21, 23–24.

9. Even if Nāgārjuna's opponent is speaking in the first statement (which is doubtful), still in the second claim Nāgārjuna does not deny the former but states only that, if the antecedent of the conditional is wrong, there is still no real entity involved—the denial of the antecedent does not entail the negation of the consequent. Taking causation for an example: if there are real entities, the process of causation cannot occur; but if there are no real entities, then the terms "cause" and "effect" are without referents, and there is nothing to enter into the process of causation—so again the process does not occur.

10. Stcherbatsky, *Conception of Buddhist Nirvāṇa,* p. 195.

11. In 22.14, the words *"bhavati"* and *"na bhavati"* carry the same intent as *"asti"* and *"nāsti."* Some verses contrast *"sat"* and *"asat"* (for example, 1.6, 7 and 7.20) or *"sadbhūta"* and *"asadbhūta"* (8.9).

12. As cited in Alex Wayman, "Who Understands the Four Alternatives of the Buddhist Texts?" *Philosophy East and West* 27 (1977): 13–14, 18, Candrakīrti affirms that there is self-existence and denies merely that entities *arise* by means of it. This would be a significant departure from Nāgārjuna's thought: for Nāgārjuna, if an entity had self-existence, it would be real (from the absolute point of view). Elsewhere (cited by Wayman, "Who Understands," p. 8) Candrakīrti's understanding of the fourth alternative is not based upon the third—a shift from Nāgārjuna's explicit position.

13. Āryadeva's *Śataśastra, Pre-Diṅnāga Buddhist Texts,* p. 10.

14. Perhaps the reason Nāgārjuna does not bother to state that *nirvāṇa* and *saṃsāra* are not identical is because in their ordinary context they are contrasted (as in 25.9)—that they are not different, not that they are not identical, is all that is of interest. This contrasts with the *Heart Sūtra,* where what is normally opposed is equated: the aggregates (*skandhas*) are said to be voidness.

15. From 20.20, if the producer and the product were the same, the cause would be the same as that which is not a cause—in other words, if cause and effect are identical, there is no reason to speak of a cause or effect.

16. Example adapted from Āryadeva's example in the *Śataśāstra, Pre-Diṅnāga Buddhist Texts,* p. 39. Confer also Śāntideva's *Bodhicaryāvatāra* 9.113–114.

17. There is nothing primitive or archaic in Nāgārjuna's exploitation of the relationships between a property and its entity. Today there are similar arguments (although not involving self-existence). For instance, philosophers debate such alleged paradoxes as someone both knowing and not knowing how to get to Philadelphia based upon the fact that the person does not know one property of that city—that it is called "The City of Brotherly Love." (Thus, the person knows how to get to Philadelphia but not to the City of Brotherly Love, that is, Philadelphia—or so it is argued.)

18. The first three alternatives alone occur often (1.7, 2.24–25, 7.20, 12.9, 21.13). All four occur at 1.1, 12.1, 22.11, chapter 25, and at 18.8 where the alternatives are not denied. Candrakīrti feels that different alternatives were taught at different stages of meditative development (J. W. de Jong, *Cinq Chapitres de la Prasannapadā* [Paris: P. Geuthner, 1949], p. 28). Perhaps such gradation of teaching would explain 18.6,8 and Candrakīrti's remark that under some circumstances it may be expedient to teach

that there *is* a self (Edward Conze, *Buddhist Thought in India* [Ann Arbor, Michigan: University of Michigan Press, 1962], p. 130). *Aṅguttara Nikāya* 1.10 presents the Buddha teaching opposed doctrines to different groups too.

19. Stcherbatsky, *Conception of Buddhist Nirvāṇa,* pp. 172–173, 200.

20. In 27.25, Nāgārjuna deals with the possibility that the world is partly infinite and partly finite; but again he rejects this for the logical reason that then the world would be *both.*

21. Stcherbatsky, *Conception of Buddhist Nirvāṇa,* p. 204. Elsewhere (5.6, 12.9) the third alternative is said to be established only if the first two are. Verse 27.20 goes so far as to maintain that if the first alternative cannot be established, then *none* of the remaining ones can be either.

22. *Saṃyutta Nikāya* 4.400–401; *Majjhima Nikāya* 1.482–488.

23. *evaṃ dṛṣṭir atīte yā nābhūm / aham abhūm aham/ubhayaṃ nobhayaṃ ceti naiṣā samupapadvate//*

24. *śūnyam iti na vaktavyam aśūnyam iti vā bhavet / ubhayaṃ nobhayaṃ ceti . . .*

25. In the *Aṣṭasāhasrikā Prajñāpāramitā*, each of the four alternatives is denied because they are predicated to subjects explicitly denied to exist (confer Edward Conze, *The Perfection of Wisdom in Eight Thousand Lines and its Verse Summary* [Bolinas, California: Four Seasons Foundation, 1973], p. 85), or in the case of the Buddha because they refer only to the aggregates (*skandhas*), which arise dependently (ibid., p. 176). In the Pāli canon, each alternative is said not "to fit the case" (*upeti*) (*Saṃyutta Nikāya* 4.373–402) and not to be conducive to enlightenment.

26. Again, "is" and "is not" are not exhaustive alternatives but are interdependent terms denoting only what involves self-existence. Since they are not logically exhaustive, the law of the excluded middle is not violated when both "is" and "is not" are denied. No multivalued logic is necessary to understand that there are no unicorns white in color nor not white in color since there are no unicorns. The same applies to what exists by self-existence.

27. My own translation from J. W. de Jong, *Cinq Chapitres,* p. 83.

28. *"Paramārthatas"* is equivalent to *"tattvatas."* Thus, the Prāsaṅgika made *"paramārtha"* equivalent to *"tattva."* But if for them *paramārthasatya* became "beyond words" and the negation of *saṃvṛtisatya,* their position contrasts with Nāgārjuna's in *Ratnāvali* 1.47 where the two truths do not conflict.

29. Williard van Orman Quine, *The Ways of Paradox and Other Essays* (New York: Random House, 1966), p. 19.

30. Cited in Paul Henle (editor), *Language, Thought and Culture* (Ann Arbor, Michigan: University of Michigan Press, 1966). Confer also Arthur Danto on "Grammatical Realism" in his "Language and the Tao: Some Reflections on Ineffability," *Journal of Chinese Philosophy* 1 (1973): 45–55.

31. This is what he says of his opponents. The Buddha's use of language, he feels, is free of this error because of the two types of truth. For the enlightened there is a change in how the nature of language is seen, not how it is used—words are seen as directing attention to aspects of the flux of experience without establishing concrete objects. The problem with Nāgārjuna's method for pointing this out is still there, though.

32. Tucci, "The *Ratnāvalī* of Nāgārjuna," op. cit., p. 319.

33. Ben-Ami Scharfstein, *Mystical Experience* (Baltimore, Maryland: Bobbs-Merrill, 1974), p. 58.

34. Richard Robinson, "Did Nāgārjuna Really Refute All Philosophical Views?" *Philosphy East and West* 22 (1972): 325–331.

35. I would like to thank Professors Alex Wayman and Frederic B. Underwood for a number of valuable discussions.

Chapter 5.

1. C. de B. Evans, trans., *Meister Eckhart* (London: John M. Watkins, 1924), volume 1, p. 143.

2. *Taittirīya Upaniṣad Bhāṣya* II.7.1

3. Ninian Smart, "Interpretation and Mystical Experience," *Religious Studies* 1 (1965): 75.

4. *Enneads* III.8.9, VI.9.2.

5. Raymond B. Blakney, trans., *Meister Eckhart* (New York: Harper and Row, 1941), p. 226.

6. *Brahmasūtra Bhāṣya* II.1.27.

7. *Bṛhadāraṇyaka Upaniṣad Bhāṣya II.3.6.*

8. Arthur C. Danto, "Language and the Tao: Some Reflections on Ineffability," *Journal of Chinese Philosophy* 1 (1973): 53.

9. *Maitrī Upaniṣad* VI.7 (Radhakrishnan's translation). Confer *Bṛhadāraṇyaka Upaniṣad* II.4.14.

10. Confer Dorothy D. Lee, *Freedom and Culture* (Englewood Cliffs, N.J.: Prentice-Hall, 1959). Most philosophers who study the issue do not believe there are universal or neutral categories of language. However, Saul Kripke disagrees: concepts carve up the world into "natural kinds" (and

also separate essential from accidental features of those kinds and particulars). His position makes a correspondence of language with reality possible.

11. Edwin A. Burtt, *The Metaphysical Foundations of Modern Physical Science* (Garden City, N.J.: Doubleday, 1954), p. 85.

12. Bertrand Russell, *History of Western Philosophy* (New York: Simon and Schuster, 1945), p. 202.

13. Danto, "Language and the Tao," p. 50.

14. Verse 9 and his commentary.

15. *Mūla-madhyamaka-kārikās* I.10; XIII.3; XXIV.18–19.

16. Ibid., XXII.1.

17. Ibid., XVIII.9; XXV.24.

18. For a more detailed discussion of Nāgārjuna on this point see chapter 4.

19. *Majjhima Nikāya* I.500; *Digha Nikāya* I.195. Also see the discussion of the term "chariot" in *Saṃyutta Nikāya* I.135. This also explains an unusual remark from the *Prajñā-pāramitā* literature. Subhūti in the *Vajracchedikā-prajñāpāramitā* says: "I am, O Lord, an Arhat free from greed. And yet, O Lord, it does not occur to me, 'an Arhat am I and free from greed.' " Edward Conze, trans., *Buddhist Wisdom Books* (New York: Harper and Row, 1972), p. 44. Subhūti can say this because he uses language conventionally without projecting grammatical distinctions ontologically into separate objects—and therefore he does not think he is an Arhat in the sense of a separately existing entity.

20. Cited in Rudolf Otto, *Religious Essays* (London: Oxford University Press, 1931), p. 84 (italics mine).

21. *Enneads* VI.9.5.

22. *Brahmasūtra Bhāṣya* III.3.9.

23. *Tao Te Ching* XXV.

24. William Johnston, *The Still Point* (New York: Harper and Row, 1970), p. 93.

25. K. S. Murty, *Revelation and Reason in Advaita Vedānta* (New York: Columbia University Press, 1959), p. 56 (italics mine).

26. *Enneads* VI.9.11.

27. Ibid., V.5.6.

28. Cited in Ronald W. Hepburn, "Nature and Assessment of Mysticism," *The Encyclopedia of Philosophy* (New York: Macmillan, 1967), volume 5, p. 433.

29. Blakney, *Meister Eckhart,* p. 80.

30. Cited in F. C. Happold, *Mysticism: A Study and an Anthology* (Baltimore, Maryland: Penguin Books, 1963), p. 142.

31. Blakney, *Meister Eckhart,* p. 96.

32. *Brahmasūtra Bhāṣya* III.2.17.

33. Introduction to the *Brahmasūtra Bhāṣya; Bṛhadāraṇyaka Upaniṣad Bhāṣya* II.3.6.

34. *Bṛhadāraṇyaka Upaniṣad Bhāṣya* II.3.6.

35. *Brahmasūtra Bhāṣya* III.2.22.

36. Ibid., I.1.11; I.2.21.

37. *Saṃyutta Nikāya* III.251; II.117.

38. *Sutta Nīpata* 1075, 1076.

39. *Saṃyutta Nikāya* IV.373–402.

40. *Enneads* VI.9.3.

41. Blakney, *Meister Eckhart,* p. 289.

42. *The Mystical Theology,* chapter 5.

43. *Kena Upaniṣad* II.3.

44. Paul Henle, "Mysticism and Semantics," *Philosophy and Phenomenological Research* 9 (1949): 416–422; confer Galen K. Pletcher, "Mysticism, Contradiction, and Ineffability," *American Philosophical Quarterly* 10 (1973): 201–211.

45. John A. Wilson, "Egypt," in H. Frankfort and H. A. Frankfort, eds., *Before Philosophy* (Baltimore, Maryland: Penguin Books, 1972), pp. 45–46.

46. Cited in Rudolf Otto, *Mysticism East and West* (New York: The Macmillan Company, 1932), p. 43.

47. *Brahmasūtra Bhāṣya* III.3.9.

48. *Enneads* V.2.1–2.

49. Edward Conze, *The Perfection of Wisdom in Eight Thousand Lines and its Verse Summary* (Bolinas, California: Four Seasons Foundation, 1973), p. 90.

50. Edward Conze, *Buddhist Thought in India* (Ann Arbor, Michigan: The University of Michigan Press, 1967), p. 225.

51. *Tao Te Ching* XXXXV.

52. Blakney, *Meister Eckhart,* p. 85.

53. Cited in Otto, *Mysticism East and West,* p. 80.

54. William J. Wainwright, "State and Mysticism," *Journal of Religion* 50 (1970): 153.

55. *Enneads* VI.9.4.

56. *Taittirīya Upaniṣad Bhāṣya* II.1.1.

57. Ibid., II.4.1; *Brahmasūtra Bhāṣya* III.2.21.

58. Murty, *Revelation and Reason,* pp. 66–67. Confer Śaṁkara's *Brahmasūtra Bhāṣya* I.2.11 and II.1.17.

59. Mircea Eliade, *Patterns in Comparative Religion* (New York: The World Publishing Company, 1963), p. 445.

60. William Johnston, ed., *The Cloud of Unknowing* (Garden City, N.Y.: Image Books, 1973), p. 128.

61. Plotinus: *Enneads* VI.8.13. Śaṁkara: *Bṛhadāraṇyaka Upaniṣad Bhāṣya* I.4.7.

62. Mary B. Hesse, *Models and Analogies in Science* (Notre Dame, Indiana: University of Notre Dame Press, 1966), pp. 130–156.

63. *Enneads* III.8.10.

64. Introduction to the *Brahmasūtra Bhāṣya.*

65. This is a rewritten version of the main section of my Master of Arts thesis of the same title (Columbia University, 1975) done under the supervision of Professors J. A. Martin, Jr., and Frederic Underwood.

Chapter 6.

1. *TTC* = *Tao te ching.* Arthur Waley's and W. T. Chan's translations are being relied upon here.

CT = *Chuang tzu.* Any direct quotation is from Burton Watson, *Chuang tzu: Basic Writings* (New York, Columbia University Press, 1964). Understanding and translation are intimately connected. Thus, when Needham's understanding is misdirected, his translations are also misleading.

2. Max Black, "The Definition of Scientific Method" in Robert C. Stauffer (ed.), *Science and Civilization* (Madison: University of Wisconsin Press, 1949), pp. 80–81.

3. Page numbers without further explanations refer to: Joseph Needham, *Science and Civilisation in China.* Volume II: History of Scientific Thought (Cambridge: Cambridge University Press, 1956).

4. List from Wing-Tsit Chan, *A Source Book in Chinese Philosophy* (Princeton: Princeton University Press, 1969), p. 244; also see p. 246.

5. See Ninian Smart, "Interpretation and Mystical Experience," *Religious Studies* 1 (1962): 75–87, and chapter 1.

6. In other words, science deals with an explanatory layer of theoretical entities and process "beneath" appearances in order to explain the structure of "surface" differences, not the "depth" factors relating to sources of being of existents. In discussing the relation of non-being to the undifferentiate one and this to the differentiated (*TTC* 42), Taoism differs from natural science. Also see note 11.

7. Although a cosmogony could be an exception to the uniformity of the post-cosmogonic period, there is little in Taoist thought on the origin of the universe. *TTC* 42 contains a cosmogony interpretable as ontologically, not temporally, prior.

8. Norwood Russell Hanson, *Observation and Explanation* (New York: Harper and Row, Publishers, 1971), p. 22.

9. Cited in Ian G. Barbour (ed.), *Science and Religion* (New York: Harper and Row, Publishers, 1968), p. 66.

10. Ian G. Barbour, *Issues in Science and Religion* (New York: Harper and Row, Publishers, 1966), pp. 139–140. The ideas and most of the wording of the next two sentences are from here also.

11. This is often stated as a reality "behind" or "beneath" phenomena. But this should be distinguished from the "depth" cause of the Way: a scientific explanation gives reasons for believing that the empirical phenomena under study should have occurred—and not some other phenomena—while the Way operates evenly for all phenomena. Thus the Way cannot figure in a scientific explanation. Because of its uniform operation for everything, the Way is the ultimate nature of everything in its aspect as the mysterious depth (*hsüan*). The Way could not provide information for any "horizontal" causal question of science; it is not a *deus ex machina.* When Needham says *"cognoscere causas"* is the motto of Taoists (p.53), he is correct, but not in the sense he intends: to know the Mother (the Way), the ultimate nature, is to know the sons (phenomena) (*TTC* 52).

12. W. V. O. Quine, "Two Dogmas of Empiricism," in his *From a Logical Point of View* (New York: Harper and Row, Publishers, 1952), pp. 20–46.

13. Mysticism for Needham appears to be anything standing over against rationalism; thus, magic and mysticism are not distinguished even

for heuristic purposes (pp. 90–95). Mysticism in the sense discussed here is involved in philosophical Taoism, not magic.

14. Hans Reichenbach, *The Rise of Scientific Philosophy* (Berkeley: University of California Press, 1951), pp. 32–33.

15. Arthur C. Danto, *Mysticism and Morality* (New York, Harper and Row, Publishers, 1972), pp. 101–120.

16. F. S. C. Northrop, *The Meeting of East and West* (New York: The MacMillan Company, 1946), pp. 300 ff. Both components of nature (the immmediately sensed and the theoretically unseen) are real, equally primary, and absolutely distinct for Northrop, but not for Taoists.

17. Moss Roberts, "The Metaphysical Polemics of the *Tao Te Ching:* An Attempt to Integrate the Ethics and the Metaphysics of Lao Tzu," *Journal of the American Oriental Society* 95 (1975): 36–42.

18. Barbour (n. 10 above), p. 130.

19. Hanson (n. 8 above), p. 5.

20. Roberts (n. 17 above).

21. Herrlee G. Creel, *What is Taoism?* (Chicago: University of Chicago Press 1970), p. 5.

22. Ibid., p. 45.

23. Ibid., p. 11.

24. See Ellen Marie Chen, "Is there a Doctrine of Physical Immortality in the *Tao Te Ching*?" *History of Religions* 12 (1973): 231–249.

25. Joseph Needham, *Science and Civilisation in China,* Vol. 5 (Cambridge: Cambridge University Press, 1965), Part II, p. 332.

26. Cited in Arthur Waley, *Three Ways of Thought in Ancient China* (Garden City: Doubleday and Company, Inc., n.d.), pp. 69–70.

27. Ibid., p. 70.

28. See "Pure Science and the Idea of the Holy" in his *Time: The Refreshing River* (New York: The MacMillan Company, 1943).

29. That Needham wrote Volume II at a time when a currently out of fashion philosophy of science reigned (i.e., logical empiricism) does not bear on the issues raised here. Even the contemplation which might appear to fulfill the empirical ideal of observation does not do so since it does not direct attention to particulars (as discussed above).

Chinese Glossary

a 道家
b 道德經
c 莊子
d 陰陽
e 道
f 無
g 自然
h 電，施
i 玄
j 常
k 五行
l 虛
m 樸
n 心齋
o 坐忘
p 觀
q 德
r 混沌
s 無爲
t 列子
u 道教
v 仙道
w 爲

Chapter 7.

1. Cyril C. Richardson, "The Strange Fascination of the Ontological Argument," *Union Seminary Quarterly Review* 18 (1962), 1–21.

2. For two discussions, see Steven M. Cahn, "The Irrelevance to Religion of Philosophic Proofs for the Existence of God," *American Philosophical Quarterly* 6 (1969), 170–72, and Philip E. Devine, "The Religious Significance of the Ontological Argument," *Religious Studies* 11 (1975), 97–116.

3. Alvin Plantinga, *God, Freedom, and Evil* (New York: Harper and Row, 1974), p. 2.

4. Paul Tillich, *Systematic Theology* (Chicago: University of Chicago Press, 1951), I, p. 237.

5. Plantinga, *God, Freedom, and Evil,* p. 1; Charles Hartshorne, "The Theistic Proofs," *Union Seminary Quarterly Review* 20 (1965), 117–18.

6. *Brahma-sūtra bhāṣya* I.1.11.

7. J. N. Chubb, "Commitment and Justification: A New Look at the Ontological Argument," *International Philosophical Quarterly* 13 (1973), p. 340.

8. Charles Hartshorne, *The Logic of Perfection* (LaSalle, Illinois: Open Court, 1962), pp. 40–41.

9. J. N. Findlay, "Can God's Existence be Disproved?" in Anthony Flew and Alasdair MacIntyre, eds., *New Essays in Philosophical Theology* (New York: Macmillan, 1955), pp. 47–56.

10. Richardson, "Strange Fascination," p. 11.

11. Paul Henle, "Uses of the Ontological Argument" in Alvin Plantinga, ed., *The Ontological Argument* (Garden City: Doubleday, 1965), pp. 171–80.

12. Hartshorne, *Logic of Perfection,* pp. 50–51.

13. Plantinga, *God, Freedom, and Evil,* p. 91.

14. *Chuang tzu,* chapter II. As just stated, the Way is non-personal, but it holds a similar role within the Taoist way of life to the god of theism—that is, as the fundamental reality—and so the remark is applicable.

15. For example, the *Tao te ching*, against the Confucians on right and wrong, says that heaven and earth are not humane (*jên*) (chapter V). Also see chapters 9 and 10 herein.

16. Cf. Robert J. Richman, "Ontological Proof of the Devil," *Philosophical Studies* 9 (1958), 63–64. Richman does not treat evil as a perfection.

17. Plantinga, *God, Freedom, and Evil,* p. 68.

18. See R. Palingandla, "What Do the Arguments for the Existence of God Really Prove?" *Indian Philosophical Quarterly* 3 (1975), 127–37.

19. Charles Hartshorne, Comments upon Richardson's article, *Union Seminary Quarterly Review* 18 (1963), 245.

20. See Paul Henle, "Mysticism and Semantics," *Philosophy and Phenomenological Research* 9 (1949), 416–22, for an example. Zeno's parodoxes also show that we can conceptualize ordinary situations in such ways that they appear paradoxical.

21. Hartshorne, "The Theistic Proofs," p. 118.

22. *Reply to Gaunilon,* chapter II.

23. For problems with this position, see chapter 5.

24. *Charles S. Peirce: Selected Writings,* Philip P. Weiner, ed. (New York: Dover, 1958), p. 92.

25. *Chuang tzu,* chapter XXV.

26. John Hick, *Arguments for the Existence of God* (New York: Macmillan, 1970), p. 104.

27. Norman Malcolm, "Anselm's Ontological Arguments," in John Hick, ed., *The Existence of God* (New York: Macmillan, 1964), p. 67.

28. James F. Ross, *Introduction to the Philosophy of Religion* (New York: Macmillan, 1969), pp. 19–20.

29. Frank B. Dilley, "Fool-Proof Proofs of God?" *International Journal for Philosophy of Religion* 8 (1977), 34. This is said of all proofs of God; he dismisses the ontological argument as "plainly fallacious," p. 28.

30. Charles Hartshorne, "Can There Be Proofs for the Existence of God?" in Robert H. Ayers and William T. Blackstone, eds., *Religious Language and Knowledge* (Athens, Georgia: University of Georgia Press, 1972), p. 67.

31. Ross, *Philosophy of Religion,* pp. 12–14.

32. For example, see Thomas S. Kuhn, "Reflections on My Critics" in Imre Lakatos and Alan Musgrave, eds., *Criticism and the Growth of Knowledge* (Cambridge: Cambridge University Press, 1970), pp. 260–61.

33. Malcolm, "Anselm's Ontological Arguments," p. 67.

34. Charles Hartshorne, "What the Ontological Proof Does Not Do," *Review of Metaphysics* 17 (1963–1964), 608–09.

35. Findlay, "God's Existence Disproved," p. 71.

36. Ibid., p. 72.

37. Ibid., p. 73.

38. J. N. Findlay, *Ascent to the Absolute* (New York: Humanities Press, 1970), p. 13.

39. Hartshorne, "The Theistic Proofs," p. 112.

40. Plantinga, *God, Freedom, and Evil,* p. 2; Hick, *Existence of God,* p. 109; Hartshorne, "The Theistic Proofs," p. 109.

41. Plantinga, *God, Freedom, and Evil,* p. 112.

42. Ibid. Being "sound" means being formally valid and having true premises.

43. Charles Hartshorne, *Anselm's Discovery* (LaSalle, Illinois: Open Court, 1965), p. 98.

44. Richardson, *"Strange Fascination,"* p. 21.

Chapter 8.

1. Evans-Wentz's translation of the line upon which this is based actually reads "To the Divine Ones, the *Tri-Kāya,* Who are the Embodiment of the All-Enlightened Mind Itself, obeisance."

2. To facilitate reference, most citations of Jung's works will be incorporated into the text; the numbers in parentheses refer to the volume and

page(s) of Jung's *Collected Works* as published by the Bollingen Foundation and Princeton University Press. Works cited: Volume 9, Part 1: "Conscious, Unconscious and Individuation," pp. 275–89; "A Study in the Process of Individuation," pp. 290–354; "Concerning Mandala Symbolism," pp. 355–84. Volume 10: "What India Can Teach Us," pp. 525–30. Volume 11: "Psychology and Religion," pp. 3–105; "Psychological Commentary on the Tibetan Book of the Great Liberation," pp. 475–508; "Psychological Commentary on the Tibetan Book of the Dead," pp. 509–26; "Yoga and the West," pp. 529–37; "Foreword to Suzuki's *Introduction* to *Zen Buddhism,*" pp. 538–57; "The Psychology of Eastern Meditation," pp. 558–75; "The Holy Men of India," pp. 576–86; "Foreword to the *I Ching,*" pp. 589–609. Volume 12: "The Symbolism of the Mandala," pp. 95–223. Volume 13: "Commentary on 'The Secret of the Golden Flower'," pp. 1–56. Most of these are reprinted, with other essays, in C. Jung, *Psychology and the East,* trans., R. F. Hull (Princeton: Princeton University Press, 1978).

3. The selectivity of psychological concerns is revealed in, say, Jung's treatment of mandalas. Within Indo-Tibetan religiosity, mandalas are usually square, two-dimensional projections of three-dimensional square palaces enclosed by a circular border. Alex Wayman, *The Buddhist Tantras* (New York: Samuel Weiser, 1973), p. 82. They are used as meditational devices. Jung's concern is with the squareness, the circle, and the center of the drawings in order to show, not that the psychological mechanism underlying all circle drawing is the same, but more specifically that all circles are used in a meditational sense and therefore are entitled to be called mandalas in the strict sense (9.1: 355–84). More problems may appear if his conclusion that all circles are meditational tools is mistaken, but at a minimum only certain aspects of the complex drawings come through his conceptual filter as relevant.

4. As an historical note, it may be pointed out that when Buddhist texts were first translated into Chinese a method of correlation called "*ko-i*" between Indian Buddhist concepts and Taoist concepts was employed. It soon became apparent, however, that this was inadequate. If problems arose in correlating two Eastern traditions, surely even greater problems would arise between Jungian psychology and each Asian religious tradition.

5. Why he should use *"buddhi"* for covering the various types of "enlightened mind" is not clear. *Buddhi* ("intellect") within Sāṁkhya-Yoga, for example, is part of the matter (*prakṛti*) from which the self (*puruṣa*) is to be freed. Elsewhere Jung refers to *buddhi* as "personal consciousness" ("Psychological Commentary on Kundalini Yoga," *Spring* 1975, p. 22) thereby indicating that he sees a sense of "I" as necessary to the "enlightened mind."

6. Either characterization differs from classical Indian descriptions of nescience. For Śaṁkara, nescience is the superimposition of what is not the self (*ātman*) upon the self and vice versa (*Brahmā-sutra-bhāṣya,*

Introduction). For the Theravāda Buddhists, nescience is taking what is by nature impermanent as permanent, what can only bring suffering as pleasurable, what is repulsive as fair, and what is without self as having a self (*Aṅguttara-Nikāya* 4.52).

7. Jung recognizes four conscious functions: sensation (sense-experience), thinking, feeling, and intuition. Presumably, he feels "mystical" experiences do not fall within any of these categories.

8. C. G. Jung, *Psyche and Symbol,* ed. Violet S. de Laszlo, (Garden City N.Y.: Doubleday, 1958), p. 249.

9. Also the archetypes cannot be the contaminated content since they are never directly experienced. The theoretical substratum remains present.

10. Jolande Jacobi, ed., *Psychological Reflections: An Anthology of the Writings of C. G. Jung* (New York: Pantheon Books, Bollingen Series, 1953), p. 258.

11. *Kleśas* are in some sense "instinctual forces of the psyche" (11: 560), but not the "instinct toward individuation" or the "germ of personality," "Psychological Commentary on Kundalini Yoga," *Spring* 1975, pp. 2–3. Even if they were this instinct, still they are, according to Indian thought, to be eliminated.

12. He is inconsistent in his use of "the East." But it is very difficult to be consistent with such a generalization.

13. See Erich Fromm, "Psychoanalysis and Zen Buddhism," in Erich Fromm, D. T. Suzuki, and Richard De Martino, *Zen Buddhism and Psychoanalysis* (New York: Harper and Row, 1960), pp. 77–141.

14. W. Y. Evans-Wentz, *The Tibetan Book of the Great Liberation* (New York: Oxford University Press, 1968), p. viii.

15. D. T. Suzuki, *The Essentials of Zen Buddhism,* Bernard Phillips, ed. (New York: E. P. Dutton, 1962), pp. 62, 215.

16. Cited in H. Saddhatissa, *The Buddha's Way* (New York: George Braziller, 1971), p. 87.

17. Abraham H. Maslow, *Religions, Values, and Peak-Experiences* (New York: Viking Press, 1970), p. 67.

18. Edward Conze, *Buddhist Meditation* (New York: Harper and Row, 1969), p. 38; see pp. 37–40. For similar positions see Rune E. A. Johansson, *Psychology of Nirvana* (London: George Allen and Unwin, 1969), pp. 135–7; Mircea Eliade, *Patanjali and Yoga* (New York: Schocken, 1975), pp. 51–9; Jacob Needleman and Dennis Lewis, eds, *On the Way to Self Knowledge* (New York: Alfred A. Knopf, 1976), especially the articles by Jacob Needle-

man and A. C. Robin Skynner; even Alan Watts, *Psychotherapy East and West* (New York: Ballantine, 1969), pp. 117, 120–7; and Joseph Campbell, *Myths to Live By* (New York: The Viking Press, 1972), pp. 71–2.

19. Edward Conze, *Buddhist Meditation,* pp. 38–9.

20. Peter L. Berger and Thomas Luckmann, *The Social Construction of Reality* (Garden City, N.Y.: Doubleday, 1967), pp. 112–14.

21. Robert E. Ornstein, *The Mind Field* (New York: Pocket Books, 1978), p. 68.

22. Ibid., pp. 73–4. The self incorporating the unconscious is still ordinary in contrast to other modes of awareness.

23. See Jacob Needleman, "Psychiatry and the Sacred," in Jacob Needleman and Dennis Lewis, eds., *On the Way to Self-Knowledge* (New York: Knopf, 1976), pp. 3–23.

24. Thus, psychotherapy in Japan reflects Japanese values. Both psychotherapy and the spiritual disciplines are present in these countries. See A. Roland, *In Search of Self in India and Japan* (Princeton: Princeton University Press, 1988).

Chapter 9.

1. David Little and Sumner B. Twiss, Jr., *Comparative Religious Ethics* (New York: Harper & Row, 1978). The first condition is usually unproblematic. The third and fourth are intimately connected (see pp. 223–225).

2. Karl H. Potter, *Presuppositions of India's Philosophies* (Englewood Cliffs, New Jersey: Prentice-Hall, 1963), chapter 1.

3. Ninian Smart, "Interpretation and Mystical Experience," *Religious Studies* 1 (1965): 75.

4. For example, the Theravādin Buddhist norm "do not kill other sentient beings" falls into the same class as "do not stick your hand in a fire"—it is advice having only the repercussions upon the *actor* as its concern. See chapter 10 for a fuller discussion.

5. An image applied both to Francis of Assisi and the Japanese Zen poet Bashō contrasts the ease and steadiness with which they walk in the exact footsteps of their respective masters—precisely because of their lack of effort to accomplish that—with the faulty and clumsy efforts of the learned who try to do the same but with thought and hesitation.

6. Peter L. Berger, "Identity As a Problem in the Sociology of Knowledge," in James E. Curtis and John W. Petras, eds., *The Sociology of Knowledge: A Reader* (New York: Praeger, 1970), p. 375.

7. Burton Watson, trans., *Chuang tzu: Basic Writings* (New York: Columbia University Press, 1964), pp. 46–47.

8. Har Dayal, *The Bodhisattva Doctrine in Buddhist Sanskrit Literature* (Delhi: Motilal Banarsidass, 1932), pp. 153–154 (hereafter cited as *Bodhisattva Doctrine*).

9. See chapter 10, pp. 238–239.

10. The moral issue here is whether someone motivated exclusively by love for others can make the judgments necessary for morality: does being moral require us to be rationally self-interested?

11. The possibility of killing for the victim's own sake will be mentioned later. Such actions may appear immoral, but the motivation is other-regarding, and, if the factual beliefs of rebirth and compensation in the future for acts committed in the present are true, they may indeed be beneficial.

12. Matt. 22: 37–40; Mk. 12: 29–31; Lk. 10: 27–28. Salvation related to these matters is their ultimate concern, and so their mystically enlightened state is still restricted by the basic religious commands.

13. On the Free Spirits, see Norman Cohn, *The Pursuit of the Millenium: Revolutionary Millenarians and Mystical Anarchists of the Middle Ages* (New York: Oxford University Press, 1970, revised and expanded ed.), pp. 148–186.

14. Cited in Raymond B. Blakney, *Meister Eckhart* (New York: Harper & Row, 1941), pp. 14, 238, and 37, respectively.

15. Ibid., p. 82.

16. Ibid., p. 193.

17. C. de B. Evans, trans., *Meister Eckhart* (London: John M. Watkins, 1924), volume 1, p. 391.

18. C. F. Kelley, *Meister Eckhart on Divine Knowledge* (New Haven: Connecticut: Yale University Press, 1973), p. 217.

19. Blakney, *Meister Eckhart,* p. 127.

20. Edward Conze, trans., *The Perfection of Wisdom in Eight Thousand Lines and Its Verse Summary* (Bolinas, California: Four Seasons Foundation, 1973), p. 109 (hereafter cited as *Perfection*).

21. Dayal, *Bodhisattva Doctrine,* p. 181.

22. Conze, *Perfection,* p. 90.

23. Contra William J. Wainwright, "Mysticism and Morality," *Journal of Religious Ethics* 4 (1976): 31; cf. his *Mysticism* (Madison, Wisconsin: Uni-

versity of Wisconsin Press, 1981), pp. 198–231. Terms such as "they," "others," and "persons" become mere conveniences that can be described more accurately if necessary in terms of the factors of the experienced world (the *dharmas*). Nothing more mysterious is involved here then when scientists treat the solar system as a point-mass for convenience in constructing certain theories: the correct description of what is real in both cases is merely more cumbersome.

24. Dayal, *Bodhisattva Doctrine,* p. 208.

25. Franklin Edgerton, "Dominant Ideas in the Formation of Indian Culture," *Journal of the American Oriental Society* 62 (1942): 155.

26. Surama Dasgupta, *Development of Moral Philosophy in India* (New York: Frederick Ungar, 1965), pp. 14–15.

27. The presupposition is that any act other than the duties determined by one's nature cannot be performed disinterestedly (cf. II.3, III.35).

28. There is a problem of consistency here: if the true self (*puruṣa*) has no material "personality," how does one act according to one's true nature? Does "matter" rather than the "self" choose to fulfill a *dharma*-role? What is reborn? So, too, why does Kṛṣṇa work so that the people do not perish if the true selves cannot in principle perish?

29. Herrlee G. Creel, *What is Taoism? And Other Studies in Chinese Cultural History* (Chicago: University of Chicago Press, 1970), pp. 3–4. A. C. Graham would agree concerning Chuang Tzu; see his *Chuang tzu* (London: Allen and Unwin, 1981), pp. 4, 13.

30. Antonio S. Cua, "Forgetting Morality: Reflections on a Theme in *Chuang tzu,*" *Journal of Chinese Philosophy* 4 (1977): 305–328.

31. Watson, *Chuang tzu,* p. 113.

32. Antonio S. Cua, "Chinese Moral Vision, Responsive Agency, and Factual Beliefs," *Journal of Chinese Philosophy* 7 (1980): 13.

33. This distinction is from Herrlee G. Creel, *What Is Taoism?* pp. 4–5.

34. Watson, *Chuang tzu,* pp. 90–91; Creel, *What Is Taoism?* p. 74. Chuang Tzu would say that those sages "who cannot avoid governing the world" should do so through non-striving (Creel, p. 55). Chuang Tzu neither conforms to nor deserts the world. His is an even-mindedness of indifference. Even the simplicity of the ideal purposive Taoist society (*TTC* 81) is not necessary for the contemplative Taoist—simplicity may be more congenial and may result from detachment, but this detachment is applicable in any society.

35. Tantrism should not be seen as libertine, considering the amount of work usually required before the rituals can be entered into and the

mindfulness that in principle is employed during the rituals. Tantric texts are encoded in a "twilight language" (*saṁdha-bhāsā*) to protect the mystical knowledge.

36. Later Tantrics adopted moral codes conventional by Buddhist and orthodox Indian standards. The rituals were given symbolic and innocuous interpretations.

37. Problems arise also for any theory of "ideal observers" who know all the facts and all the consequences of a deed: even if such disinterested observers all adopt a moral point of view, they will differ according to the world-view they adopt as to what the "facts" and "consequences" of a deed actually are.

38. Conze, *Perfection,* p. 218. On the relatively soft and passive attitude of Buddhist traditions, see Winston L. King, "Buddhist Self-World Theory and Buddhist Ethics," *The Eastern Buddhist* 22 (1989): 22–26.

39. See chapter 10, p. 235.

40. In this context, laws differ from the precepts of mysticism in that the latter govern personal development within a freely opted-for way of life.

41. There is also tension between long-range perspectives on goals and any response to the immediate situation of mystical action.

42. Steven E. Ozment, *Mysticism and Dissent: Religious Ideology and Social Protest in the Sixteenth Century* (New Haven, Connecticut: Yale University Press, 1973), p. 9.

43. Ibid., pp. 12, 247.

44. Raymond B. Blakney, *Meister Eckhart,* pp. 156–160; Matthew Fox, trans., *Breakthrough: Meister Eckhart's Creation Spirituality in New Translation* (Garden City, New York: Doubleday, 1980), pp. 450–455 (hereafter cited as *Breakthrough*).

45. Blakney, ibid., pp. 129–132.

46. Ibid., pp. 179, 182.

47. Ibid., p. 71.

48. Fox, *Breakthrough,* pp. 209, 418.

49. See, e.g., Rufus M. Jones, *Mysticism and Democracy in the English Commonwealth* (Cambridge, Massachusetts: Harvard University Press, 1932).

50. Matthew Fox, "Meister Eckhart and Karl Marx: The Mystic as Political Theologian," in Richard Woods, O.P., ed., *Understanding Mysticism* (Garden City, New York: Doubleday, 1980), p. 557.

51. Blakney, *Meister Eckhart,* p. 231; Fox, *Breakthrough,* pp. 217–218.

52. Fox, "Meister Eckhart and Karl Marx," p. 550; *Breakthrough,* pp. 510–518.

53. Fox, *Breakthrough,* p. 199.

54. Ibid., pp. 463, 464, 472, 495.

55. Agehananda Bharati, *The Light at the Center* (Santa Barbara, California: Ross-Erickson, 1976), pp. 74–75.

56. Ibid., p. 53. That some mystical training need not limit the way of life one chooses is illustrated by the fact that the author of *Zen in the Art of Archery* became a Nazi.

57. See, for example, Huiren Li, "Some Notes on the Ethics of Mystical Militancy," *Insight: A Journal of World Religions* 2 (1977): 37–46; R. C. Zaehner, "Mysticism Without Love," *Religious Studies* 10 (1974): 257–64; R. C. Zaehner, "Mason, Murder, and Mysticism," *Encounter* 42 (April, 1974): 50–58.

58. For a discussion of the complex interaction of experience and doctrine, see chapter 1.

59. Clifford Geertz, *Islam Observed* (Chicago: University of Chicago Press, 1971), pp. 17, 39, 97.

60. Problems arise in speaking of the world-view *justifying* the values insofar as there is no one-to-one correlation between specific world-views and values—there may be different justifications of the same values (e.g., Mo Tzu's nonmystical justification of universal love) or different values and practices attached to the same world-view (e.g., Mahāyāna and Buddhist Tantric practices). Value systems must be justified by more than merely citing factual beliefs.

61. A common error in this regard is that the Buddhist ontological "no-self" doctrine requires moral concern for others as a consequence. That is, immorality results from a sense of self. But if in reality there is no self for the actor to be selfish about, so, too, there are no other selves to be concerned about—immoral selfishness and moral other-regarding are in this way both tied to a sense of individuality if either is. Their opposite (amorality) would result from a lack of selves to help. But ontology does not determine values so simplisticly. Instead selfishness, amorality, and morality are all compatible with a sense of self, and morality and amorality are both consistent with the no-self doctrine.

62. Walter Stace, *Mysticism and Philosophy* (Philadelphia, Pennsylvania: J. B. Lippincott, 1960), pp. 323–333.

63. Arthur C. Danto, *Mysticism and Morality* (New York: Harper & Row, 1972); "Role and Rule in Oriental Thought: Some Metareflections on

Dharma and *Li*," *Philosophy East and West* 22 (1972): 213–220; "Ethical Theory and Mystical Experience: A Response to Professors Proudfoot and Wainwright," *Journal of Religious Ethics* 4 (1976): 37–46.

64. This is not the position that factual claims are more primary than moral action-guides or that the latter are derived from the former—how we see the world may depend as much upon how we act as vice versa—but only that logically the latter cannot operate without a commitment to the former.

65. Wayne Proudfoot, "Mysticism, the Numinous, and the Moral," *Journal of Religious Ethics* 4 (1976): 22.

Chapter 10.

1. All the Indian words are Pāli unless otherwise noted. Plurals are indicated by an "-ā." The abbreviations used for the Theravāda texts are as follows:

D = *Digha-nikāya*
M = *Majjhima-nikāya*
A = *Aṅguttara-nikāya*
S = *Saṃyutta-nikāya*
VP = *Vinaya Piṭaka*
Dhp = *Dhammapada*
Mlp = *Milinda-pañha*

All numbers refer to the Pāli Texts Society editions.

2. See, for example, Roy W. Perrett, "Egoism, Altruism and Intentionalism in Buddhist Ethics," *Journal of Indian Philosophy* 15 (1987): 71–85; Steven T. Katz, "Ethics and Mysticism," in Leroy S. Rouner, ed., *Foundation of Ethics* (South Bend, Indiana: University of Notre Dame Press, 1983), pp. 184–202.

3. David Little and Sumner B. Twiss, Jr., *Comparative Religious Ethics* (New York: Harper & Row, 1978), pp. 231–236.

4. Melford E. Spiro, *Buddhism and Society* (New York: Harper & Row, 1970), pp. 10–11. Spiro also notes that *despite* their beliefs, Burmese Buddhists are friendly and humane. This raises the problems of ideal ways of life and of a coherent world-view within a way of life.

5. David Little and Sumner B. Twiss, Jr., "Basic Terms in the Study of Religous Ethics," in Gene Outka and John P. Reeder, Jr., eds., *Religion and Morality* (Garden City: Anchor Press/Doubleday, 1973), pp. 35–77.

6. "Enlightened self-interest" in ethics means one's own good is advanced by being moral because everyone's good is advanced if everyone is

moral. At least one component of this approach involves a concern for the welfare of others.

7. How actions can be the same whether the motive is moral or nonmoral is illustrated by the social activity of Gandhi, an orthodox Indian. When asked why he was helping certain people, he is said to have answered "I am here to serve no one else but myself, to find my own self-realization through the service of these village folks." His actions were no less helpful for this motivation.

8. Clifford Geertz, *Islam Observed* (Chicago: University of Chicago Press, 1971), pp. 97–117 (on the relation of *ethos* to world-view in a religion); Arthur Danto, *Mysticism and Morality* (New York: Harper & Row, 1972), pp. 3–21 (on the relation of moral rules to factual beliefs in a "form of life").

9. Thus, the simplistic solutions to the problem of whether Theravāda Buddhism is moral (because there are no "selves") are inaccurate. There is a reality to what we conventionally call a "person" whose interests and feelings can be taken into account when "we" decide how to act.

10. If the simplistic approach to the issue of morality prevails, then there is no reality which can be *killed,* and so we could not but follow the precept not to kill no matter what we did. (See the discussion of the *Bhagavad-gītā* in chapter 9.) Nothing we could do would in principle violate any moral precept. But there would be no "selves" to help either, and so we could not be other-regarding either.

11. For all the necessary conditions for an act to be considered a "killing" in the karmic sense, see Winston King, *In Hope of Nibbana* (LaSalle, Illinois: Open Court, 1964), p. 120.

12. One can be "nibbanized" (*parinibbuto*) in this life or at death (D 3.55; S 4.204).

13. Enlightenment is only possible from a human rebirth—the heavenly realms present too much pleasure for the urge of ending rebirth to develop. Thus, the "devil" for Buddhism is not the ruler of a place of suffering but the god of the highest pleasure heaven, Māra.

14. See Melford E. Spiro, above n. 4.

15. Edward Conze (trans.), *Buddhist Scriptures* (Baltimore: Penguin Books, 1959), pp. 70–73; H. Saddhatissa, *Buddhist Ethics* (London: George Allen & Unwin, 1970), pp. 87–112.

16. Winston L. King, above n. 11, pp. 72 and 127 respectively. Elsewhere (p. 159) he says:

> . . . if one can remain perfectly neutral in feeling toward the drowning man, neither rejoicing nor sorrowing in the slightest over

that man's death agonies, there is nothing *kammically* evil in letting him drown. That is, no evil rebirth will result from refusing to save his life.

17. The "transfer of merit" discussed below is the one possible exception to the law of *kamma.*

18. Winston King, above n. 11, p. 181.

19. Certain contemporary commentators have attempted to discover a "socially-engaged Buddhism" in these peripheral remarks. See Fred Eppesteiner, ed., *The Path of Compassion* (Berkeley: Parallax Press, 1985). This phenomenon has not been manifested in over 2000 years in numerous historical and cultural milieus. But supposedly this socially-engaged Buddhism is "latent" in the Buddhist tradition but has been "inhibited in premodern Asian settings." (P. xiii.) In short, after two millenia, Westerns have discovered in these peripheral passages of the Pāli canon the "essence" of the Theravāda Buddhist tradition free of all cultural accretions. Such an absurd position requires no further comment.

20. Melford E. Spiro, above n. 4, pp. 289–290.

21. Trevor Ling, *The Buddha* (Baltimore: Penguin Books, 1976), p. 20.

22. Richard Gombrich, *Theravāda Buddhism: A Social History from Ancient Benares to Modern Colombo* (London: Routledge & Kegan Paul, 1988), p. 81. He concedes that some scholars disagree with him.

23. Winston L. King. "Buddhist Self-World Theory and Buddhist Ethics," *The Eastern Buddhist* 22 (1989): 25. King notes this Buddhist "passive accommodative acceptance" of the traditional cultural patterns and dominant forms of social organization in the countries it has penetrated, and notes that "concern for individual and depressed-groups freedoms and rights has been almost totally missing from the Buddhist message." Pp. 24–25.

24. Richard Gombrich, above n. 22, p. 30. At best, the transformation of society comes about "only as a by-product of the religious transformation of individual beings." Joseph M. Kitagawa, "Buddhism and Social Change: An Historical Perspective," in S. Balasooriya et al., eds., *Buddhist Studies in Honour of Walpola Rahula* (London: Gordon Fraser, 1980), p. 87. "[C]ontrary to the popular notion that the Buddha was a crusading social reformer, fighting for the common man against the establishment of his time, there is no evidence that he attempted, directly at any rate, to change society. He seems to have accepted the various forms of socio-political order known to him." Ibid.

25. Winston L. King, above n. 23, p. 26. What the Buddhists require is "an inner awakening" that can be done "without lifting a finger to change historical-social conditions." P. 25.

26. Edward Conze, *Buddhist Thought in India* (Ann Arbor: University of Michigan, 1967), p. 110; cf. H. Saddhatissa, above n. 15, p. 149.

27. In Theravāda texts, the giving and the practice of *sīla* of the Buddha-to-be (*bodhisatta*) in his lives before his enlightenment are discussed, but the texts carefully avoid saying that he was accumulating merit. See Roy Amore, "The Concept and Practice of Doing Merit in Early Theravāda Buddhism," Ph.D. diss., Columbia University, 1970, p. 92.

28. The Pāli *Jātaka Tales* portray the Buddha-to-be in various lives as giving up everything, including all his possessions, his limbs, his body, and his wife and children, out of compassion for the well-being of all beings and for the attainment of enlightenment. These tales may reflect genuine other-regardingness. (Reasons are given for why even giving his wife and children to an ogre helped *them*.) But these moralizing folk tales are more in keeping with the enlightened activity of the Buddha than with the ultimate goal of the unenlightened of the Theravāda tradition (where the goal is to become an enlightened disciple (i.e., an Arahant), not a Buddha). They conform more with the *ethos* of Mahāyāna Buddhism where the *bodhisattva* emerged as an ideal for practitioners and where these tales have remained more popular.

29. E.g., Melford E. Spiro, above n. 4, p. 106.

30. The Theravāda texts also have similar passages concerning the basic code of conduct (*sīla*). For example, Buddhaghosa in the *Visuddhimagga* (I.34) discusses the different foci of attention that a practitioner of the precepts may have—for example, focusing upon oneself, others, or the Buddhist doctrine. But these foci are not the motives for the practice—one does not practice the action-guides for the sake of others any more than for the sake of the Buddhist Doctrine. Concern for one's own welfare remains central.

31. Melford E. Spiro, above n. 4, p. 111.

32. Ibid., p. 410.

33. Ibid., pp. 413–414.

34. Ibid., p. 414.

35. Ibid., p. 106.

36. G. P. Malalasekera, "Transfer of Merit in Ceylonese Buddhism," *Philosophy East and West* 17 (1967): 86.

37. Melford E. Spiro, above n. 4, p. 127.

38. See comments of Richard Gombrich, above n. 22, pp. 125–26.

39. Melford E. Spiro, above n. 4, p. 127. The "more sophisticated" monks realize that such a transfer is impossible, and the "very sophisticated"

monks practice the ritual for accomplishing the transfer only as means of spiritual discipline for themselves. (P. 125.)

40. Cf. Richard Gombrich, " 'Merit Transfer' in Sinhalese Buddhism: A Case Study in the Interaction of Doctrine and Practice," *History of Religions* 11 (1971): 217.

41. Melford E. Spiro, above n. 4, p. 106.

42. Ibid., p. 105.

43. Winston L. King, above n. 11, p. 154.

44. Harvey B. Aronson, *Love and Sympathy in Theravāda Buddhism* (Delhi: Motilal Barnarsidass, 1980), p. 64.

45. Ibid., p. 64. Book reviewers have criticized Aronson's book for being uncritical on the issue of morality. Aronson must admit that the texts never *explicitly* speak of moral action in connection with these practices and that he *assumes* they are connected to moral action. (P. 54.) However, nothing in the texts would support such an assumption about these attitudes even indirectly.

46. Ibid., p. 65. Similarly, benevolence is merely wishing "May all beings be happy." (P. 64.) And "[s]ympathetic joy means to take joy in others' success." (P. 65.) Elsewhere, Aronson states that benevolence and compassion are never described or prescribed as the motive for social activity but are limited to meditative cultivation. (He does give great weight to a few passages on simple compassion (*kāruñña*) and simple sympathy (*anukampā*) as justification for social action.) "Motivations to Social Action in Theravāda Buddhism: Uses and Abuses of Traditional Doctrines," in A. K. Narain, ed., *Studies in History of Buddhism* (Delhi: B. R. Publishing Corp., 1980), pp. 3–4.

47. Ibid., p. 65.

48. Edward Conze, above n. 26, p. 90.

49. Winston King, *Theravāda Meditation: The Buddhist Transformation of Yoga* (University Park: Pennsylvania State University Press, 1980), p. 60.

50. Ibid., p. 64.

51. Harvey B. Aronson, above n. 44, p. 54.

52. Arthur Danto, above n. 8.

53. Trevor Ling, above n. 21, p. 155.

54. David Little and Sumner B. Twiss, Jr., above n. 5, p. 50.

55. Ibid., pp. 73–74.

56. Ibid., p. 74. Little and Twiss realize that they are open to the charge of arbitrariness here.

57. Alex Wayman, "Buddhism," in C. J. Bleeker and Geo Widengren, eds., *Historia Religionum,* vol. 2 (Leiden: E. J. Brill, 1971), p. 412.

58. Roy Amore, above n. 27, pp. 135–137.

59. Karl Potter, *Presuppositions of India's Philosophies* (Englewood Cliffs: Prentice-Hall, 1963), p. 39.

60. The enlightened could also practice the sublime attitudes free from any karmic merit. The attitudes of the enlightened who so practice are other-regarding, either if these particular actions are not.

61. P. D. Premasiri, "Ethics of the Theravāda Buddhist Tradition," in S. Cromwell Crawford, ed., *World Religions and Global Ethics* (New York: Paragon House, 1989), p. 47.

62. Martin Wiltshire, "The 'Suicide' Problem in the Pāli Canon," *Journal of the International Association of Buddhist Studies* 6 (1983): 124–140.

63. Ibid., p. 124.

64. In their study of the Theravāda tradition, Little and Twiss (above n. 3, pp. 210–250) come to the opposite conclusions: the unenlightened Buddhists are moral to a limited extent in accepting the other-impinging attitudes and acts prescribed by the first four precepts of the *sīla* (p. 215). But this morality is only provisional since the enlightened cannot be moral because (1) material welfare is subordinated to spiritual ends, and (2) ultimately there are no discrete, independent "selves" and consequently no "actors" to consider the welfare of "others" (pp. 231–236; cf. pp. 108–109). Both of these two points concerning enlightened Buddhists were discussed earlier. As for the point concerning the unenlightened, Little and Twiss emphasize the other-impingingness of Buddhist action-guides, but whether these action-guides are other-*regarding*—the necessary moral requirements—is not so much discussed. Whether the precepts are in fact other-regarding has been disputed above. As for the other elements of the Theravāda tradition which Little and Twiss discuss, even their own discussion of the sublime attitudes concludes these are meditative techniques for the ultimate benefit of the meditators, with benefits to others being only a side effect (pp. 231–233). They consider giving (*dāna*) moral because (1) it impinges on the welfare of the recipient; and (2) it is conceived in such a way as to require some positive consideration on the part of the giver of the welfare of the recipient (p. 228). Spiro's examples cited earlier of giving by the Burmese to the monks counter this claim for the actual practice of Buddhists and thereby raise doubts as to whether it ever was the ideal. Other issues could also be discussed—for example, whether the realization of *nibbāna* is only temporary (p. 233) or whether no enlightened Theravāda Buddhist could ever violate the basic precepts of the system (p. 235)—but major problems with their conclusions are all that need to be highlighted.

Selected Bibliography

1. *Philosophical and Comparative Studies of Mysticism.*

Alston, William. "Ineffability." *Philosophical Review* 65 (1956): 506–22.

———. "Perceiving God." *Journal of Philosophy* 83 (November, 1986): 655–665.

Bharati, Agehananda. *The Light at the Center.* Santa Barbara: Ross-Erickson, 1976.

Coward, Harold, and Terence Penelhum, eds. *Mystics and Scholars.* Waterloo: Wilfrid Laurier University Press, 1977.

Danto, Arthur. "Language and the Tao: Some Reflections on Ineffability." *Journal of Chinese Philosophy* 1 (1973): 45–55.

Eliade, Mircea. *Shamanism.* Princeton: Princeton University Press, 1964.

Ellwood, Jr., Robert S. *Mysticism and Religion.* Englewood Cliffs: Prentice-Hall, 1980.

Evans, Donald. "Can Philosophers Limit What Mystics Can Do? A Critique of Steven Katz." *Religious Studies* 25 (1989): 53–60.

Findlay, John N. *Ascent to the Absolute.* London: George Allen and Unwin, 1970.

———. "The Logic of Mysticism." *Religious Studies* 2 (1966): 145–162.

Forman, Robert. "The Construction of Mystical Experience." *Faith and Philosophy* 5 (1988): 254–267.

———, ed. *The Problem of Pure Consciousness: Mysticism and Philosophy.* New York: Oxford University Press, 1990.

Gale, R. "Mysticism and Philosophy." *Journal of Philosophy* 57 (1960): 471–481.

Garside, Bruce. "Language and the Interpretation of Mystical Experience." *International Journal for the Philosophy of Religion* 3 (1972): 93–102.

Gilbert, J. "Mystical Experience and Public Testability." *Sophia* 9 (1970): 13–20.

Gill, Jerry. "Mysticism and Mediation." *Faith and Philosophy* 1 (1984): 111–121.

———. "Response to Perovich." *Faith and Philosophy* 2 (1985): 189–190.

Henle, Paul. "Mysticism and Semantics." *Philosophy and Phenomenological Research* 9 (1949): 416–422.

Hepburn, Ronald. "Nature and Assessment of Mysticism." *The Encyclopedia of Philosophy,* Paul Edwards, ed., vol. 5, pp. 429–434 (1967).

Hick, John. *An Interpretation of Religion: Human Responses to the Transcendent.* New Haven: Yale University Press, 1989.

———, ed. *Truth and Dialogue in World Religions: Conflicting Truth-Claims.* Philadelphia: Westminster, 1974.

Horne, James R. "Which Mystic Has the Revelation?" *Religious Studies* 11 (1974): 283–291.

Huxley, Aldous. *The Perennial Philosophy.* New York: Harper and Row, 1944.

Inge, William Ralph. *Mysticism in Religion.* Chicago: University of Chicago Press, 1948.

James, William. *The Varieties of Religious Experiences.* New York: New American Library, 1958.

Johnston, William. *The Inner Eye of Love: Mysticism and Religion.* New York: Harper and Row, 1978.

———. *The Still Point.* New York: Harper and Row, 1970.

Jones, Richard H. *Science and Mysticism.* Lewisburg: Bucknell University Press, 1986.

Jones, Rufus M. *The Inner Life.* New York: MacMillan, 1916.

———. *Studies in Mysticism.* New York: MacMillan, 1936.

Katz, Steven T., ed. *Mysticism and Philosophical Analysis.* New York: Oxford Press, 1978.

———, ed. *Mysticism and Religious Traditions.* New York: Oxford University Press, 1983.

King, Sallie B. "Two Epistemological Models for the Interpretation of Mysticism." *Journal of the American Academy of Religion* 56 (1988): 257–279.

Kvastad, Nils Bjorn. *Problems of Mysticism.* Oslo: Scintilla Press, 1980.

Larson, Gerald and Eliot Deutsch, eds. *Interpreting Across Boundaries: New Essays in Comparative Philosophy.* Princeton: Princeton University Press, 1988.

Matilal, B. "Mysticism and Reality: Ineffability." *Journal of Indian Philosophy* 3 (1975): 217–252.

McGuinness, B. F. "The Mysticism of the *Tractatus.*" *Philosophical Review* 75 (1966): 305–328.

Moore, Peter G. "Recent Studies of Mysticism: A Critical Survey." *Religion* 4 (1974): 146–156.

Nasr, Seyyed Hossein. *Knowledge and the Sacred.* New York: Crossroad, 1981.

Needleman, Jacob. *A Sense of Cosmos.* Garden City: Doubleday, 1975.

Otto, Rudolf. *Mysticism East and West: A Comparative Analysis of the Nature of Mysticism,* Bertha L. Bracey and Richenda C. Payne, trans. New York: MacMillan, 1932.

Perovich, Jr., Anthony N. "Mysticism and Mediation." *Faith and Philosophy* 2 (1985): 179–188.

———. "Mysticism and the Philosophy of Science." *Journal of Religion* 65 (1985): 63–82.

Phillips, Stephen H. "Mysticism and Metaphor." *International Journal for the Philosophy of Religion* 23 (1988): 17–41.

Pletcher, Galen K. "Agreement Among the Mystics." *Sophia* 11 (1972): 5–15.

———. "Mysticism, Contradiction, and Ineffability." *American Philosophical Quarterly* 10 (1973): 201–211.

Proudfoot, Wayne. *Religious Experience.* Los Angeles/Berkeley: University of California Press, 1985.

Russell, Bertrand. "Mysticism and Logic." In his *Mysticism and Logic and Other Essays.* New York: Longmans, Green and Co., 1918.

Scharfstein, Ben-Ami. *Mystical Experience.* Baltimore: Bobbs-Merrill, 1974.

Schuon, Frithjof. *The Transcendental Unity of Religions.* New York: Harper and Row, 1975.

Smart, Ninian. "Interpretation and Mystical Experience." *Religious Studies* 1 (1965): 75–87.

Smith, Huston. *Forgotten Truth.* New York: Harper and Row, 1976.

———. "Is There a Perennial Philosophy?" *Journal of American Academy of Religion* 55 (1987): 553–566.

Staal, J. Frits. *Exploring Mysticism.* Berkeley/Los Angeles: University of California Press, 1975.

Stace, Walter. *Mysticism and Philosophy.* Philadelphia: J. B. Lippincott, 1960.

———. *The Teachings of the Mystics.* New York: New American Library, 1960.

Tillich, Paul. *Dynamics of Faith.* New York: Harper and Row, 1957.

———. "The Nature of Religious Language." In his *Theology of Culture,* edited by Robert C. Kimball. New York: Oxford University Press, 1959.

Underhill, Evelyn. *Mysticism.* New York: E. P. Dutton, 1911.

———. *Practical Mysticism.* New York: E. P. Dutton, 1915.

Vanneste, Jan. "Is the Mysticism of Pseudo-Dionysius Genuine?" *International Philosophical Quarterly* 3 (1963): 286–306.

Wainwright, William J. "Interpretation, Description and Mystical Consciousness." *Journal of American Academy of Religion* 45 (1977): 989–1010.

———. *Mysticism.* Madison: University of Wisconsin Press, 1981.

———. "Mysticism and Sense Perception." *Religious Studies* 9 (1973): 257–278.

———. "Stace and Mysticism." *Journal of Religion* 50 (1970): 139–154.

Werblowsky, R. J. Zwi. "On the Mystical Rejection of Mystical Illumination." *Religious Studies* 1 (1966): 177–184.

Woods, Richard, O. P., ed. *Understanding Mysticism.* Garden City: Doubleday, 1980.

Zaehner, R. C. *Mysticism: Sacred and Profane.* New York: Oxford University Press, 1961.

2. *Mysticism and Ethics.*

Amore, Roy. *The Concept and Practice of Doing Merit in Early Theravāda Buddhism.* Ph.D. diss., Columbia University, 1960.

Aronson, Harvey B. *Love and Sympathy in Theravāda Buddhism.* Delhi: Motilal Banarsidass, 1980.

———. "Motivations to Social Action in Theravāda Buddhism: Uses and Abuses of Traditional Doctrines." In A. K. Narain, ed., *Studies in History of Buddhism.* Delhi: B. R. Publishing Corp., 1980.

Bastow, David. "Buddhist Ethics." *Religious Studies* 5 (1969): 195–206.

Bhargava, Dayanand. *Jaina Ethics.* Delhi: Motilal Banarsidass, 1968.

Chatterjee, D. "Karma and Liberation in Śaṅkara's Advaita Vedānta." In S. S. Rama Rao Pappu, ed., *Perspectives on Vedanta: Essays in Honor of Professor P. T. Raju.* Boston: E. J. Brill, 1988.

Cohn, Norman. *The Pursuit of the Millenium: Revolutionary Millenarians and Mystical Anarchists of the Middle Ages,* rev. ed. New York: Oxford University Press, 1970.

Crawford, S. Cromwell. *The Evolution of Hindu Ethical Ideals.* Honolulu: University Press of Hawaii, 1982.

Creel, Austin B. *Dharma in Hindu Ethics.* Calcutta: Firma KLM Private Ltd., 1977.

———. "The Reexamination of *Dharma* in Hindu Ethics." *Philosophy East and West* 25 (1975): 161–173.

Cua, Antonio S. "Chinese Moral Vision, Responsive Agency, and Factual Beliefs." *Journal of Chinese Philosophy* 7 (1980): 3–26.

———. "Forgetting Morality: Reflections on a Theme in *Chuang tzu.*" *Journal of Chinese Philosophy* 4 (1977): 305–328.

Danto, Arthur C. "Ethical Theory and Mystical Experience: A Response to Professors Proudfoot and Wainwright." *Journal of Religious Ethics* 4 (1976): 37–46.

———. *Mysticism and Morality* (2nd ed.). New York: Columbia University Press, 1987.

———. "Role and Rule in Oriental Thought: Some Metareflections on *Dharma* and *Li.*" *Philosophy East and West* 22 (1972): 213–220.

Dasgupta, Surama. *Development of Moral Philosophy in India.* New York: Frederick Ungar, 1965.

Dayal, Har. *The Bodhisattva Doctrine in Buddhist Sanskrit Literature.* Delhi: Motilal Banarsidass, 1932.

Edgerton, Franklin. "Dominant Ideas in the Formation of Indian Culture." *Journal of the American Oriental Society* 62 (1942): 151–156.

Fox, Douglas A. "Zen and Ethics: Dōgen's Synthesis." *Philosophy East and West* 21 (1971): 33–41.

Gombrich, Richard F. *Precept and Practice: Traditional Buddhism in the Rural Highlands of Ceylon.* Oxford: Oxford University Press, 1971.

Goodwin, William F. "Ethics and Value in Indian Philosophy." *Philosophy East and West* 4 (1955): 321–344.

———. "Mysticism and Ethics: An Examination of Radhakrishnan's Reply to Schweitzer's Critique of Indian Thought." *Ethics* 67 (1956): 25–41.

Hindery, Roderick. *Comparative Ethics in Hindu and Buddhist Traditions.* Delhi: Motilal Banarsidass, 1978.

Hopkins, Edward W. *Ethics of India.* New Haven: Yale University Press, 1924.

Horne, James R. *The Moral Mystic.* Waterloo: Wilfrid Laurier University Press, 1983.

Jantzen, Grace M. "Ethics and Mysticism: Friends or Foes?" *Netherlands Theologisch Tijdschrift* 39 (1985): 314—325.

Jones, Rufus M. *Mysticism and Democracy in the English Commonwealth.* Cambridge: Harvard University Press, 1932.

Kattackal, Jacob. *Religion and Ethics in Advaita.* Kerala, India: C.M.S. Press Kottayam, 1982.

King, Winston L. *In Hope of Nibbana.* LaSalle: Open Court, 1964.

———. "Buddhist Self-World Theory and Buddhist Ethics." *The Eastern Buddhist* 22 (1989): 14–26.

———. "Motivated Goodness and Unmotivated Perfection in Buddhist Ethics." *Anglican Theological Review* 71 (1989): 143–152.

Kitagawa, Joseph M. "Buddhism and Social Change: An Historical Perspective." In S. Balasooriya et al., eds., *Buddhist Studies in Honour of Walpola Rahula.* London: Gordon Fraser, 1980.

Kupperman, Joel J. "The Supra-Moral in Chinese Ethics." *Journal of Chinese Philosophy* 1 (1974): 153–160.

Li, Huiren. "Some Notes on the Ethics of Mystical Militancy." *Insight: A Journal of World Religions* 2 (1977): 37–46.

Masson, J. "Positions et Problemes d'une 'Morale' Theravada." *Studia Missionalia* 27 (1978): 135–158.

Mathur, D. C. "The Concept of Action in the *Bhagavad Gītā.*" *Philosophy and Phenomenological Research* 35 (1974): 34–43.

McKenzie, John. *Hindu Ethics: A Historical and Critical Essay.* London: Oxford University Press, 1922.

Misra, G. S. P. *Development of Buddhist Ethics.* New Delhi: Munshiram Manoharlala Publishers Pvt. Ltd., 1984.

Ozment, Steven E. *Mysticism and Dissent: Religious Ideology and Social Protest in the Sixteenth Century.* New Haven: Yale University Press, 1973.

Pappu, S. S. Rama Rao. "Detachment and Moral Agency in the *Bhagavad Gītā*." In S. S. Rama Rao Pappu, ed., *Perspectives on Vedanta: Essays in Honor of Professor P. T. Raju*. Boston: E. J. Brill. 1988.

Peacock, J. L. "Mystics and Merchants in Fourteenth Century Germany." *Journal for the Scientific Study of Religion* 8 (1969): 47–59.

Perrett, Roy W. "Egoism, Altruism and Intentionalism in Buddhist Ethics." *Journal of Indian Philosophy* 15 (1987): 71–85.

Premasiri, P. D. "Ethics of the Theravāda Buddhist Tradition." In S. Cromwell Crawford, ed., *World Religions and Global Ethics*. New York: Paragon House, 1989.

Proudfoot, Wayne. "Mysticism, the Numinous, and the Moral." *Journal of Religious Ethics* 4 (1976): 3–28.

Radhakrishnan, Sarvepalli. "Mysticism and Ethics in Hindu Thought." In his *Eastern Religions and Western Thought*. London: Oxford University Press, 1959, pp. 58–114.

Reynolds, Frank. "Contrasting Modes of Action: A Comparative Study of Buddhist and Christian Ethics." *History of Religions* 20 (1980): 128–146.

Saddhatissa, H. *Buddhist Ethics*. New York: George Braziller, 1970.

Sangharakshita, Maha Sthavira. "Aspects of Buddhist Morality." *Studia Missionalia* 27 (1978): 159–180.

Smurl, James F. "Cross-Cultural Comparisons in Ethics: A Critical Response to Sally Wang." *Journal of Religious Ethics* 4 (1976): 47–56.

Spiro, Melford E. *Buddhism and Society,* 2nd ed. Los Angeles/San Francisco: University of California Press, 1982.

Suzuki, Daisetz T. "Ethics and Zen Buddhism." In Ruth N. Ashen, ed., *Moral Principles of Action*. New York: Harper and Row, 1952.

Tachibana, S. *Ethics of Buddhism*. London: Oxford University Press, 1926.

Upadhyayaya, K. N. *Early Buddhism and the Bhagavad Gītā*. Delhi: Motilal Banarsidass, 1971.

Van Loon, Louis H. "Some Buddhist Reflections on Suicide." *Religion in Southern Africa* 4 (1983): 3–12.

Wainwright, William J. "Mysticism and Morality." *Journal of Religious Ethics* 4 (1976): 29–36.

Wang, Sally. "Can Man Go Beyond Ethics? The System of Padmasambhava." *Journal of Religious Ethics* 3 (1975): 141–155.

Whitehill, James. "Is There a Zen Ethic?" *Eastern Buddhist* 20 (1987): 9–33.

Wiltshire, Martin. "The 'Suicide' Problem in the Pāli Canon." *Journal of the International Association of Buddhist Studies* 6 (1983): 124–140.

Zaehner, R. C. "Mason, Murder, and Mysticism." *Encounter* 42 (April, 1974): 50–58.

———. "Mysticism Without Love." *Religious Studies* 10 (1974): 257–264.

3. Mysticism and Psychology.

Bucke, Richard Maurice. *Cosmic Consciousness.* New York: Dutton, 1923.

Coward, Harold. *Jung and Eastern Thought.* Albany: State University of New York, 1985.

Deikman, Arthur. "De-Automatization and the Mystic Experience." *Psychiatry* 29 (1966): 324–338.

Hardy, A. *The Spiritual Nature of Man.* New York: Oxford University Press, 1979.

Hood, Ralph W., Jr., "Conceptual Criticisms of Regressive Explanations of Mysticism." *Review of Religious Research* 16 (1976): 179–188.

———. "Mysticism." In Phillip E. Hammond, ed., *The Sacred in a Secular Age.* Berkeley/Los Angeles: University of California Press, 1985.

Hood, Ralph W., Jr., and Ronald J. Morris, "Knowledge and Experience Criteria in the Report of Mystical Experience." *Review of Religious Research* 23 (1981): 76–84.

Huxley, Aldous. *The Doors of Perception.* New York: Harper and Row, 1954.

———. *Heaven and Hell.* New York: Harper and Row, 1954.

Johansson, Rune. *The Psychology of Nirvana.* London: George Allen and Unwin, 1969.

Jung, Carl. *Psychology and the East,* R. F. Hull, trans. Princeton: Princeton University Press, 1978.

Naranjo, Claudio and Robert E. Ornstein. *On the Psychology of Meditation.* New York: Viking Press, 1971.

Needleman, Jacob and Dennis Lewis, eds. *On the Way to Self-Knowledge.* New York: Knopf, 1976.

Ornstein, Robert E. *The Mind Field.* New York: Pocket Books, 1978.

———, ed. *The Nature of Human Consciousness.* San Francisco: W. H. Freeman, 1973.

——— . *The Psychology of Consciousness.* Baltimore: Penguin, 1975.

Pahnke, Walter N. "Drugs and Mysticism." *International Journal of Parapsychology* 8 (1966): 295–314.

Schneiderman, L. "Psychological Notes on the Nature of Mystical Experience." *Journal for the Scientific Study of Religion* 6 (1967): 91–100.

Smith, Huston. "Do Drugs Have Religious Import?" *Journal of Philosophy* 61 (1964): 517–530.

Tart, Charles T., ed. *Altered States of Consciousness.* New York: J. Wiley, 1969.

——— . *States of Consciousness.* New York: Dutton, 1975.

———, ed. *Transpersonal Psychologies.* New York: Harper and Row, 1975.

Watts, Alan W. *Psychotherapy East and West.* New York: Ballantine, 1961.

4. Western Mysticism.

Arberry, A. J. *Sufism: An Account of the Mystics of Islam.* London: George Allen and Unwin, 1950.

Blakney, Raymond B., ed. and trans. *Meister Eckhart.* New York: Harper and Row, 1941.

Boehme, Jacob. *Six Theosophic Points.* Ann Arbor: University of Michigan Press, 1958.

Buber, Martin. *Tales of the Hasidim,* 2 vols. New York: Schocken Books, 1947–48.

Capps, Walter H. and Wendy M. Wright, eds. *Silent Fire: An Invitation to Western Mysticism.* New York: Harper and Row, 1978.

Caputo, John D. "Fundamental Themes in Meister Eckhart's Mysticism." *The Thomist* 42 (1978): 197–225.

Clark, James. *Meister Eckhart: An Introduction.* Edinburgh: Thomas Nelson and Sons, 1957.

Colledge, Edmund, O.S.A., and Bernard McGinn, trans. and eds. *Meister Eckhart: The Essential Sermons, Commentaries, Treatises, and Defense.* New York: Paulist Press, 1981.

Colledge, Eric, ed. *The Medieval Mystics of England.* New York: Charles Scribner's Sons, 1961.

Dionysius the Areopagite. *The Divine Names and the Mystical Theology,* C. E. Rolt, trans. London: S.P.C.K., 1920.

Evans, C. de B., trans. *Meister Eckhart,* 2 vols. London: John M. Watkins, 1924.

Fox, Matthew. *Breakthrough: Meister Eckhart's Creation Spirituality in New Translation.* Garden City: Doubleday, 1980.

Fremantle, Anne, ed. *The Protestant Mystics.* London: Weidenfels & Nicholson, 1964.

Green, Deidre. "Saint John of the Cross and Mystical 'Unknowing.'" *Religious Studies* 22 (1986): 29–40.

Happold, F. C. *Mysticism: A Study and an Anthology.* Baltimore: Penguin Books, 1971.

Inge, William Ralph. *Christian Mysticism.* London: Methuen & Co., 1921.

———. *Philosophy of Plotinus* (3d ed.). New York: Longmans, Green & Co., 1929.

John of the Cross. *Dark Night of the Soul,* E. Allison Peers, trans. Garden City: Image Books, 1959.

Johnston, William, ed. *The Cloud of Unknowing.* Garden City: Image Books, 1973.

Jones, Rufus M. *The Flowering of Mysticism.* New York: MacMillan, 1939.

Kelley, Carl F. *Meister Eckhart on Divine Knowledge.* New Haven: Yale University Press, 1977.

Linge, David E. "Mysticism, Poverty, and Reason in the Thought of Meister Eckhart." *Journal of the American Academy of Religion* 46 (1978): 465–488.

MacKenna, Stephen, trans. *The Enneads.* London: Faber and Faber, 1962.

McGinn, Bernard, ed. *Meister Eckhart: Teacher and Preacher.* New York: Paulist Press, 1986.

Nicholson, Reynold A. *The Mystics of Islam.* New York: Schocken Books, 1975.

O'Brien, Elmer, trans. *The Essential Plotinus.* New York: New American Library, 1964.

Owen, H. P. "Christian Mysticism: A Study in Walter Hilton's *The Ladder of Perfection.*" *Religious Studies* 7 (1971): 31–42.

Petry, Ray C. *Late Medieval Mysticism.* Philadelphia: Westminster, 1957.

Rist, J. M. *Plotinus: The Road to Reality.* Cambridge: Cambridge University Press, 1967.

———. "Back to the Mysticism of Plotinus: Some More Specifics." *Journal of the History of Philosophy* 27 (1989): 183–197.

Schimmel, Annemarie. *Mystical Dimensions of Islam.* Chappel Hill: The University of North Caroline Press, 1975.

Scholem, Gershom G. *Major Trends in Jewish Mysticism.* New York: Schocken Books, 1961.

———. *On the Kabbalah and Its Symbolism.* New York: Schocken, 1965.

———, trans. by R. J. Zwi Werblowsky. *Sabbatai Sevi: The Mystical Messiah.* Princeton: Princeton University Press, 1973.

Schurman, Reiner. *Meister Eckhart: Mystic and Philosopher.* Bloomington: University of Indiana Press, 1978.

Shah, Idries. *The Sufis.* Garden City: Doubleday, 1964.

Stoudt, John Joseph. *Jacob Boehme: His Life and Thought.* New York: Seabury Press, 1968.

Teresa of Ávila. *The Complete Works of St. Teresa.* 3 vols., E. Allison Peers, trans. New York: Sheed and Ward, 1957.

Underhill, Evelyn. *The Mystics of the Church.* New York: Schocken Books, 1964.

Watt, W. M. *The Faith and Practice of al-Ghazālī.* London: George Allen & Unwin, 1963.

5. Asian Mysticism.

Bastow, David. "Metaphysical Knowledge in the Yoga-Sutras." *Scottish Journal of Religious Studies* 1 (1980): 101–118.

Blofield, John. *The Tantric Mysticism of Tibet.* New York: Dutton, 1970.

Bugault, Guy. "Logic and Dialetics in the *Madhyamakakārikās.*" *Journal of Indian Philosophy* 11 (1983): 7–76.

Chan, Wing-Tsit, ed. and trans. *A Source Book in Chinese Philosophy.* Princeton: Princeton University Press, 1969.

———, trans. *The Way of Lao Tzu.* New York: Bobbs-Merrill Co., 1963.

Chen, Ellen Marie. "Is There a Doctrine of Physical Immorality in the *Tao Te Ching?*" *History of Religions* 12 (1973): 231–249.

———, trans. *The Tao Te Ching.* New York: Paragon House, 1989.

Conze, Edward. *Buddhist Thought in India.* London: George Allen and Unwin, 1962.

Creel, Herrlee G. *What is Taoism?* Chicago: University of Chicago Press, 1970.

Dasgupta, Surendranath. *A History of Indian Philosophy.* 5 vols. Cambridge: Cambridge University Press, 1922–1955.

Deutsch, Eliot. *Advaita Vedānta: A Philosophical Reconstruction.* Honolulu: The University Press of Hawaii, 1969.

Edgerton, Franklin. "The Upaniṣads: What Do They Seek and Why?" *Journal of the American Oriental Society* 49 (1929): 97–121.

———. "Did the Buddha Have A System of Metaphysics?" *Journal of the American Oriental Society* 79 (1959): 81–85.

Eliade, Mircea. *Yoga: Immortality and Freedom.* Princeton: Princeton University Press, 1969.

———. *Patanjali and Yoga.* New York: Schocken, 1975.

Gombrich, Richard F. *Theravada Buddhism: A Social History from Ancient Benares to Modern Colombo.* New York: Routledge & Kegan Paul, 1988.

Graham, A. C., trans. *Chuang-tzu: The Inner Chapters.* London: George Allen & Unwin, 1981.

Hoffman, Frank J. "Rationality in Early Buddhist Fourfold Logic." *Journal of Indian Philosophy* 10 (1982): 309–337.

Hume, Robert, trans. *The Principal Upanishads.* New York: Oxford University Press, 1921.

Ingalls, Daniel H. H. "Śaṁkara on the Question: Whose is Avidyā?" *Philosophy East and West* 3 (1953): 291–306.

———. "Śaṁkara's Arguments Against the Buddhists." *Philosophy East and West* 3 (1954): 291–306.

Jayatilleke, K. N. *Early Buddhist Theory of Knowledge.* London: George Allen and Unwin, 1963.

Kaltenmark, Max. *Lao Tzu and Taoism.* Stanford: Stanford University Press, 1969.

Kalupahana, David J. *Causality: The Central Philosophy of Buddhism.* Honolulu: The University Press of Hawaii, 1976.

———. *Buddhist Philosophy: A Historical Analysis.* Honolulu: The University Press of Hawaii, 1976.

Kapleau, Philip. *The Three Pillars of Zen.* Boston: Beacon Press, 1967.

King, Winston L. *Theravāda Meditation: The Buddhist Transformation of Yoga*. University Park: The Pennsylvania State University Press, 1980.

Loy, David. *Nonduality: A Study in Comparative Philosophy*. New Haven: Yale University Press, 1988.

Mitchell, Donald W. "Analysis in Theravāda Buddhism." *Philosophy East and West* 21 (1971): 23–31.

Nakamura, Hajime. *Ways of Thinking of Eastern People*. Honolulu: East-West Center Press, 1964.

Ñāṇananda, Bhikkhu. *Concept and Reality in Early Buddhist Thought*. Kandy: Buddhist Publication Society, 1971.

Nyanaponika, Bhikkhu. *The Heart of Buddhist Meditation*. New York: Samuel Weiser, 1973.

Potter, Karl. *Presuppositions of India's Philosophies*. Englewood Cliffs: Prentice-Hall, 1963.

———, ed. *Advaita Vedānta up to Śaṁkara and His Pupils*. Princeton: Princeton University Press, 1981.

Pye, Michael. *Skillful Means*. London: Duckworth & Co., Ltd., 1978.

Rahula, Walpola. *What the Buddha Taught*. New York: Grove Press, 1959.

Robinson, Richard. "Did Nāgārjuna Really Refute All Philosophical Views?" *Philosophy East and West* 22 (1972): 325–331.

Saso, Michael. *The Teachings of Master Chuang*. New Haven: Yale University Press, 1978.

Schwartz, Benjamin I. *The World of Thought in Ancient China*. Cambridge, Mass.: Belknap Press, 1985.

Smart, Ninian. *Doctrine and Argument in Indian Philosophy*. London: George Allen and Unwin, 1964.

Staal, J. F. *Advaita and Neo-Platonism: A Critical Study in Comparative Philosophy*. Madras: University of Madras, 1961.

———. "Correlations Between Language and Logic in Indian Thought." *Bulletin of the School of Oriental and African Studies* 23 (1960): 109–122.

———. "Negation and the Law of Contradiction in Indian Thought: A Comparative Study." *Bulletin of the School of Oriental and African Studies* 25 (1962): 52–71.

Streng, Frederick. *Emptiness: A Study in Religious Meaning*. Nashville: Abington Press, 1967.

Suzuki, Daisetz T. *Mysticism, Christian and Buddhist*. New York: Harper and Row, 1957.

Swearer, Donald K. "Two Types of Saving Knowledge in the Pali Suttas." *Philosophy East and West* 22 (1972): 355–71.

Underwood, Frederic B. "Buddhist Insight: The Nature and Function of *Paññā* in the Pāli Nikāyas." Ph.D. diss., Columbia University, 1973.

———. "Notes on Conscience in Indian Tradition." *Journal of Chinese Philosophy* 2 (1974): 59–65.

Waley, Arthur. *The Way and its Power.* London: George Allen and Unwin, 1934.

———. *Three Ways of Thought in Ancient China*. Garden City: Doubleday, n.d.

Watson, Burton, trans. *Chuang tzu: Basic Writings*. New York: Columbia University Press, 1964.

Wayman, Alex. *The Buddhist Tantras.* New York: Samuel Weiser, 1973.

———. "The Meaning of Unwisdom (*Avidyā*)." *Philosophy East and West* 7 (1957): 21–25.

Zaehner, R. C. *Hinduism*. New York: Oxford University Press, 1962.

———. *Hindu and Muslim Mysticism*. New York: Schocken, 1969.

Index